Riding in the Wind
A Bikers View on the Road

J. T. Thomas

To Mike
Without your Wisdom
I would be lost
#64 of 200

Thunder

Riding in the Wind
A Bikers View on the Road

Story By J.T. Thomas

IUNIVERSE, INC.
New York Lincoln Shanghai

Riding in the Wind A Bikers View on the Road

iUniverse, Inc.

For information address:
iUniverse, Inc.
2021 Pine Lake Road, Suite 100
Lincoln, NE 68512
www.iuniverse.com

ISBN: 0-595-26933-8

Printed in the United States of America

Contents

The Book of a Biker

"Biker" definition: Websters Dictionary: (motorcyclist)
(one who is a member of a organized gang). "OK?".
"Biker" definition: Britannica Dictionary: (none).
"Biker" definition: Gollier Dictionary: (none).
"Biker" definition: Little Old Lady standing on the street corner
(Hooligans).

When I say the words Book and Biker in the same sentence somehow it does not sound right in my mind. In this particular case I believe they do go together. I know most of you have a book that you carry around in your head. For me I hope my book will bring your memories from the past back to the front of your thoughts and hopefully as I write this we will learn something along the way. So there are two things that I question in my mind in the beginning. First, what is a Book? The second question is what my book is all about. What is a Biker and Riding In The Wind mean? Humm, the first question is, what is a Book. Lets go to the dictionary. Webster "Book": definition: A written or printed work consisting of pages blank for writing in or other wise written on for reading or pictures in for looking at, that are glued or sewn together along one side and bound in covers. This seems pretty wide open and very simple. "R-I-G-H-T". So, can a book be written or does it have to pass a English test at Harvard College, "I hope not". Can a book be interesting to read or does it have to be prefect in every way, "all I can do is try". Are you reading this book so you can take it apart, every thought, every phrase or can it be an adventure for you to live and enjoy as you read it. I would hope as you read my book you hear me with a kind voice because this is how I wrote it. I also hope you see me as your friend and we are having a conversation about Riding In The Wind: A Bikers View On The Road. I will try to ad a few pictures along the way so you can see what I am seeing. The pictures in this book will be in black and white and only 25 because of the format. The second question, what does it take to wear the name Biker. What is the make up or mold of a Biker, what makes a Biker a Biker. Humm, is it the guy or girl or lets say a rider that rides back and forth to work everyday except for when it rains or its to cold out. Maybe the wind is blowing to hard to get on the bike that day. There might be a few to many clouds in the sky and they just do not feel like getting the bike out. "I don't think so". Is it the rider who rides up and down the main drag on the weekends and takes a short trip down the highway and back so they can say, Yeah man, I went for a ride it was awesome. Can it be a Biker is someone who rides a Harley or maybe a particular Harley, Yamaha, BMW, Honda or dozens of other motorcycles. "That might be it". Is it possible that it is the size of the bike 750, 1200, 1500, or a massive 110 cubic. inch engine of shire ground pounding power and torque. "I don't think so". Is it the rider who has a $5000.00 set of leathers with there bike logo pasted all over it and emblems of power and strength that tells there story, riding a $40,000.00 motorcycle looking as good as any in there eyes. "How cute". How about the rider wearing a sweatshirt, jeans, a pair of old dingo boots and a second hand helmet that just loves having something to Ride In The Wind and cant wait to go somewhere. "close but maybe not". Consider the rider who has the noisiest certain sounding pipes roaring down the road, "how cool". Bringing more attention to themselfs than is necessary. Would you think you need to belong to a group or a motorcycle club of some kind. Ride around town looking like you belong to something important. Is that what a Biker is? I don't know yet. It is possible, maybe it is all of those people above, the love for the machine that flies thru the air between your legs. The power and to control it as you wish. The feel of the wind in your face. The search for the prefect road and the day where the wind is at you back. That one day the sky is blue and all the people you meet are the best people in the world. Everywhere you go is more beautiful than the last and the most beautiful places on earth. To me a

Biker is the rider who has just done 1500 miles, 4 days 3 nights on the road in the wind. He is beat down, butt hurts, soar, tired, hungry, hot, dried out, thirsty or wet, cold, stiff, freezing and has been sleeping on the ground all this time. He has not had any sleep for 3 nights and coming to the end of his trip. Going home and all he can think about is when and where his next trip is going to take him. What dose it take to wear the name Biker. A old Biker once told me, J.T., the wind always blows when you ride a motorcycle, some days it just blows harder, then it starts to rain and you get cold. If you don't like the wind or the rain or the cold, then you cant be a Biker. That is the difference between a want to bee biker and a Biker. I mentioned this question to my lady and she tells me she is a Biker. Wow, wait a minute here. She has 4 months total time on a bike, two rally's and two short trips in the wind with about 4,000 miles all together. I tell her that she is close to being a Biker and give me 6 years and about 30,000 miles in the wind on the road and lets talk about you being a Biker. So my lady, what is a Biker. She said, someone who lives on a bike. Humm, I said, you mean someone who would rather ride there motorcycle as to do anything else and has been for many years. Always looking to ride there bike no matter what the conditions, where they are going or what they are doing. Yes she said. I said do you know anyone like that, her answer, you. Thing is I have been all those people above in my bike life and I still am, except one. It is not to hard to figure out which one I am not. There is a certain kind of feeling I have when I get on my bike. It is the same feeling I had the first time I got on a motorcycle 30 yrs. ago. It just feels right. It has not changed. I love riding, every day, every where, every condition, every time, but that is just me. I am J.T.. Today I ride a plain 2002' Harley 88 Super Glide silver in color with a line of red on the gas tank. I call it the Silver Ghost returned. More on that later. I wear a old traditional leather jacket with no emblems or symbols on it, steel toed motorcycle boots I got at Walmart. An old half bucket helmet sits atop my head when I wear one. I guess I like to think that I am a Biker. But maybe I am not. It seems that we are still not sure if we know what a Biker is yet. I have an old saying, there are three ways to see things, 1. With your eyes, 2. With my eyes and 3. With the eyes of the way it really is. Most of the time I try to see things with all our eyes.

This is where my story begins. Riding In The Wind: A Bikers View On The Road. Hopefully at the end of my story we will know just what a Biker is. Also in days past we did not think much about taking pictures. For the most part I took pictures of everyone else. A few were taken of me and that is about it. Today I am somewhat of a photographer and I guess you will have to be the judge of that. The Ghost and I travel the streets and hwys, city to city, place to place, looking for that one prefect picture that says it all. Most all the pictures you see in my book are taken form my bike as I am riding down the road. Some are taken as I am stopped and shot thru or over the windshield, others are just off the bike hand held or on a tripod. All the pictures are of the place that I am seeing and the bike is there because it is. The Ghost and I are looking for that one prefect day on the road in the wind. Not sure if we have found it yet, been pretty damned close a few times. The Ghost and I will be traveling and looking on the roads and hwys because that is what we do best, we ride looking for the wonders that are out there for us to find. You may wonder how I am able to write this story and why I am not riding. It is the winter of 2002, I pace the floor and stare out the window like a wild animal in a cage, all the time trying to maintain and write this story. Then remembering all the great trips and the adventures I have had. Seeing the most beautiful things that I have been a part of. I still ride but I can only do short trips 20 miles or so before my face becomes num and I fear frost bit. I stop for a while to thaw and then continue on. I am waiting on the spring, the Laughlin River Run 2003 and the next Dream which will come in mid May 2003. It is the dream of Hwy One down the coast of California, known as the Light House Run. More on that later, I have not had this Dream yet and cant wait. Yes I know you can wear a full face electric heated helmet, electric heated vest, electric heated pants with electric heated gloves, so you feel nothing, smelling your own bad breath and hearing no sounds, feeling no wind, what is the point, you might as well be in a car. The biggest fear for me is snow and ice hiding in corners and shaded places, no since hurting the Ghost we have so much to do. Before I get started, I would like to tell you a true story about how I saw it growing up and how I got to this point in time.

Eyes Of A Biker

Growing up in the 50's and 60's. It seemed all the wars were over and all was as it should be. So we thought. Motorcycles where not yet a common sight. I really don't remember seeing any around or on the streets. In those days I think that 1 in 20,000 people had some kind of motorcycle as compared to today probably 1 in 50 have a motorcycle of some type. At that time it was flat top hair cuts with duck tails, White t-shirts, bobby socks, penny loafers and blue jeans. Rock N Roll hit the radio waves and music has never been the same since. We were still playing cowboys and indians trying to hide from Russia, Castro and the atomic bomb. But this is not a story about Wars, Russia, Castro or the atomic bomb. Motorcycles were something you saw in the movies. James Dean, Elvis Presley and Marlon Brando are a few that come to mind. They were in all cases loners with egos, misunderstood rebels of some kind, much like the Bikers of today. Always trying to stay out of trouble and always managing to get into trouble and then out. At that time even having a bicycle was something only a few kids had in my neighborhood. My one and only bicycle as a kid was a used one. I was riding it one night down my street and looked back to check traffic, there was none. There were no street lights in those days, well not on my street anyway. When I turned back I ran right into the back of a black parked car. Me and the bicycle went head over heals across the top of the car on to the street in front of it. As I laid there bleeding and crying and wondering what had happen. A lady came out of her house and said "are you all right". At the time this seemed like a strange question and I could not believe she ask that. I looked at her and said "no I don't think so, I just ran into the back of a car and I am lying here bleeding and it hurts". She seemed concerned and to be a nice lady. I got up and with some cuts and bruises I manage to get the bicycle up and back home. The bicycle in itself was relatively unharmed. Did not say much to anyone cause I did not want get a beating, just went to bed. My dad came home from Korea in 1952 dead but still alive. In 1951 he was wounded in action somewhere in Korea up by the DMZ, lying in a field of muddy snow, the cold and after two days frost bitten they found him and to the rear he went and then home. Alcohol became a major part of his life and with out choice mine as well. Short time after hitting the rear of that car with my bicycle. I came home from school and left the bicycle laying in the driveway. My dad came home that night from work and ran over it mangling it to pieces. The bad thing was, not only was I out a bicycle I also got a beating for leaving it in the driveway and that was my one and only bicycle as a kid. I was in the 4th grade 1963 Dallas Tex. The place and year President Kennedy was assassinated. But this is not a story about the Kennedy assassination, the Korean war, alcohol or my Dad.

Early to mid 60's there were a few motorcycle shops around and Harley was trying to get into the main stream of the general public but was not having much success. Most of the Harley riders back then where lets say a little rough around the edges and I guess that has not changed. Indian motorcycles where around as well, along with the jap bikes being very popular. Europe had been a major motorcycle area for a long time with lots of enthusiast. They made some great European bikes back then. BSA, Norton and Triumph were a few that you saw here in the USA. It seemed at the time that people where riding equally all of the bikes being manufactured from all over the world. In most cases had to be kick started as compared to today were everything is electric start and most of them you can not even get a kick starter on them. It was funny in the late 60's, there was always that one guy in high school that rode a motorcycle. Always parked in the same place and seemed to see things a little different from the rest of us. The other thing that seemed to be, there where little or no woman riders to speak of in those days. It seemed that the Ladies where content to watch and ride on the backs of motorcycles. One other thing that was happening at that time. Between Rock N Roll

Mt. Sopris, Co.. It is not where you have been but where you are going

and motorcycles there was a major generation gap happening between the ages. There where other factories of course that came into play to create this generation gap. But this is not a story about Rock N Roll or generation gaps.

The first time I really had anything to do with a motorcycle I was 13 yrs. old. The Vietnam war was unfolding but they where being very quite about it. We did not understand and I had my own problems to deal with living in east Dallas. It was a tough place then and now. You had to be careful, Dallas is a very easy place to die in. In a small back parking lot of my apartment complex, must have been 66'. A friend Ricky of a friend Danny, you might say, came up on a 60's Honda 50. At the time it was unbelievably cool. It was white and black with a touch of chrome. As we talked. Danny suggested that I ride it. Of course I was reluctant but it was a very short time till I was crawling onto the bike. Never ridden one before or anything as far as that goes. He kinda explained what had to happen to make it go. Well, I gave it some throttle and let the clutch out, it took of like a bat out of hell across the small parking lot. As I went out of control something came across my mind. He had failed to mention to me on how to stop the thing. I looked up and ran right into a telephone pole. Did not do any damage to the bike but broke my left thumb and dislocated it. Needless to say I did not want anything to do with motorcycles from that point on and the end of 1966 was just around the corner.

Early in 1967 my older brother Darrell and his friend Fred went to Vietnam. They were about to be drafted. In those days you had to go or be arrested. My bother could have been drafted and spent two years in the Army like Fred did. Instead he went down to volunteer because he wanted to pick a certain goal for his life and would have to do 4 years. While he was down at the recruiting station, they came up to him and said you're a Marine and off he went. This was not what he wanted. Sad thing was he came home with tears in his eyes because he knew the road in the Marine Corp in those days was tougher than you can imagine. During his boot camp three men tried to commit suicide because of pressure they were under to become Marines, two fail and one did not. His stories of boot camp and this ordeal are unbelievable and don't seem real In his four year stay in the Marines, he spent two years in Vietnam. Third Division C company I believe. As far as I remember he spent most of the time up or near the DMZ. The rest in Saigon. (DMZ) is the line drawn between North and South Vietnam. Just deep jungle mostly. He did his share of Ops in the jungle and did his share of fighting as well. At this time they were spraying a defoliant called Asian Orange on the DMZ to kill the thick jungle off so they could see some kind of line between where they were and where they had been. He spent some time other places in Vietnam as well. Then to the rear and home in 1971. He was not the same brother that I new and loved before he left. But after what he had seen and done I don't think you would every be the same as well. Stayed around for a year and moved to a small city Marshall, Texas. Met his wife to be and got married. Then had a child, seemed a real short time went by, She must have been pregnant when they got married. One year had gone by and he was not feeling to well all this time. His second child was on the way. He began to feel very sick at this time in 1973. Like me and most of you, you cant make me go to the doctor. There was something really wrong and he had no choice but to go see the doctor. He was told along with the rest of us that he had terminal cancer. They tried everything. The cure was more painful than the cancer. This was a Marine. He was 5" 9" of harden steel 200 lbs of shear power and strength. His second son was born at this time and was not as he should be. One year went by as the cancer ate him up from the inside. My 75 lb. Brother died late 1974. The horror. The horror of it all. I loved him dearly. The government denied all when it came to Asian Orange and with some help from others and a few battles. The government decided to help his wife and two kids. They still live in Marshall TX. today. Fred came home after one tour in Vietnam with no problems. My brother was never a Biker or cared anything about them but his Vietnam buddies did. I guess this is not a story about my brother, cancer, the draft but it does have something to do with Vietnam.

Late in 1967 somehow my family ended up in California. Up near San Francisco. Job transfers I think. One night while I was at a 7-11 store getting a coke to drink. Up pulled five or six men on motorcycles. One of them went into the store for something. The men where dressed in leather vest, motorcycle boots and looking a little rough but that did not keep me from going over and looking at there bikes. I was just a kid at that time and no threat to them. I had not been this close to real bikes so I was quite curious. They said hello and allowed me to look. As I looked at the bikes a man about 30 yrs. old pulled up in his car next to us and got out saying something negative to the men on the motorcycles. They did not take kindly to what he said and were on him in a flash backing him into a corner and begging him to step up or shut up. The man apologized and was allowed to go on his way. Out of the store came the one and they talked for a second. One of them came over to me and said, "don't take nothing off anyone boy". Got on their bikes and rode off. Funny thing was on the backs of there vest were some angle wings and the words Hells Angels. This did not mean anything to me at the time. I did not know about these things or what Bikers were. I have never forgotten what happened or what he told me that night.

I think this is where the bike generation began 1968. There were a lot of military Harley's to be seen over seas along with the military men being over seas during the Vietnam War. As they took there leaves in Europe, Japan, and other places where bikes were already very popular and had been for many years. Combined with the music and movies about them helped fuel the desire for motorcycle's. They would go to the Px's and order there motorcycles and have them waiting for them when they got home or sent to there homes. The men in Nam had to be different mentally and physically in order to survive. Bikes were also a way to separate themselves from the main stream of the population, which fits right in with the Bikers of today. If you would just for a second here. Freedom, Freedom is what biking and Bikers are all about. It is a simple word that so many have given there lives for. To me Freedom is not just for me but for everyone, everywhere, every country. Of corse I know there is a certain reality but I still feel this way. Freedom is what our flag stands for. Freedom is for everyone not just you. If would for me someday? Go to a Veterans Memorial graveyard or park and just say thanks to all those who have made the effort to see that you have the right to say this one simple word, Freedom. I have the upmost respect for all who have served and are serving in our military. I have a saying that is true to my heart. I may not always agree with what you have to say but I will fight to the death your right to say it. O' by the way in 1969 someone landed on the moon and that seemed like a odd thing to do at the time as our boys died over seas.

There was another major factor why bikes suddenly were in the main stream of society. His name was Evel Knievel. He rode a customized 750 Harley Sportrster and other bikes as well. He hit the airwaves with the most daredevil stunts ever seen on a motorcycle. The news madia, T.V. and Radio could not get enough of the on the edge things that he did. When he jumped the fountains at Caesars Palace Las Vegas in 1968, it was the craziest thing I had ever seen. He crashed hard, broke a lot of bones and yet in a sense he walked away. What really set him apart from the rest was his willingness to take another step towards death each time him jumped. The idea of jumping over the Grand Canyon in 1973 was unbelievable. It was awesome. Everyone it seemed tried to stop him from doing this jump across the Grand Canyon and they succeeded. So he went to the Snake River Canyon and everyone involved gave him there permission to do the jump in 1974. It was a long drawn out process, building the rocket bike and the ramp to meet his objective of making the jump. With T.V. and newspaper coverage almost daily. Finally the day came and he made his jump right off the cliff into the canyon below. No matter what you think about that day, crawl into a bomb and then launch it off a cliff and see how you feel as you fall towards the bottom of the canyon and the rocks below. I believe the fraise is, making a mess in your pants. He was a hero to anyone who loved motorcycles and as far as I know he is the only man to ever do anything like this. Just a thought, if given the chance I would do it, but that's just me. Funny thing is, right after my son was born in 1981. I took him to see my wife's dad who lived in western Idaho. I said, being that we were so close to Oregon, we should drive over to the border, so I could say that I had been to Oregon. While driving down the Hwy along the Snake River, there was a sign that said Evel Knievels jump site. It was the place where he had launched his rocket bike over the Snake River Canyon. He was the man, the real deal make no mistake. He brought more attention to bikes than any other thing including the cult movie Easy Rider with Peter Fonda and Dennis

Hopper. Two Harley riders who always wanted to ride their bikes to Madigra in New Orleans. They made it but things did not work out in the end. I have the original album of the movie Easy Rider. "Flow river flow on down my roads don't cry I am only bleeding". These words off the album stick in my head for some reason. The other major contributor to biking was a T.V series called, Then Came Bronson with Micheal Parks. This television show was a hour long and about a guy who rode a 1969 Harley 900 Sportster and his adventures on the road. He was the good guy believe it or not. It ran from September 1969 to April 1970 and there were 26 episodes. They also made a movie for T.V.. Then the series was canceled. I often wonder if it was canceled because it had to much influence on the younger generation. I know it did me. Funny thing is, one of the older men that I work with today on the Western Slope of Colorado, had a Harley Dealership they had started in 1962 called CM&H Motorcycles. The shop belonged to his dad. Apparently a movie crew came to town and needed a Harley. They where filming a movie about a Biker and his travels. They needed a bike for the movie, so CM&H supplied them with a 1969 Harley 900 Sportster. The movie was made right here on the Western Slope of Colorado. They called it Then Came Bronson. There is a Meter Man that works for the city here in Grand Junction. Co. You know the guy who writes you parking tickets except he just takes the money from the meters. Anyway, the movie crew gave the motorcycle back to CM&H and the meter man bought the bike from CM&H. Had it authenticated and still has it today in his garage. He wants to clean it up and put it in car and bike shows for the public to see. I am trying to get a picture of it but no luck yet. The owner of CM&H Motorcycles lost his son in a motorcycle accident 1983 here in Grand Junction. The man was in a pick- up, said I just did not see him. Even today if you think they can see you. You are wrong. You will be dead wrong. CM&H had done well thru the 50's, 60's and 70's but because of that fateful day and the death of his son they struggle through out the 80s and early 90's. Harley had given them a specially made bike and the old man still has it today. I have ask him many times to let me ride it to no avail. In 1994 they had lost there hearts and interest in motorcycles.

Hwy 128, Utah and the Colorado River. The best road you will ever ride

Sold the dealership and moved on. There was another factor that contributed to the biking world at this time in the early 70's. Harley was wining all kinds of races on the dirt tracks with there bikes and were always in the news and head lines. I think this help make there name. I believe they were riding Sportster 750's. If you don't know about these four people. You should look them up in the movies or on the internet. They are why we are Bikers today. Evil Knievel is dying today of Hepatitis C, I believe. He has been a major contributor to the foundation for the Make A Wish program. It gives children that will die within a short time a last wish to do or go or be what ever they wish. I heard in the wind that Evel may do a last jump before he dies in 2003. I hope so. We should never forget him. Micheal Parks is still making great movies and T.V. shows. Dennis Hopper is crazy as ever and still making great movies. Today Peter Fonda along with Evel Knievel are cult hero's at the bike rally Sturgis, South Dakota and we will talk more about Sturgis later.

I had just turned 18 yrs. old, moved out on my own and was sharing a apartment with a friend Ron in late 1971. Ron had just gotten back from Vietnam. One day his cousin David shows up on a late 60's Kawasaki 175 enduro. It was silver in color. Strange thing about silver and me. David suggested that we go next door to a empty lot and he really wanted to show me how he could ride. I had gotten a car, it had a stick shift and I was getting use to how they worked. I watched him and he was amazing on this thing. It was the first time I had really paid any attention to a motorcycle since that fateful day yrs ago. Although they had gotten very popular in the late 60's and early 70's but not quite in the main stream of the population. It was cool watching him throw dirt and do wheelies. When David pulled up after the show, we talked and I explained to him about what had happen with my first experience with a motorcycle. He laughed and said, that was then and I should try it again. Of course I did not want any part of this. David kept on and somehow there I was setting on a motorcycle again shaking my head. I looked at him and then the bike and then again at David. Gave it some throttle, leaned into it and let the clutch out. Bam!! the front end comes up into this giant wheelie, eased up a little on the throttle and down came the front end, shifted up into 2nd and hit the throttle, up came the front end again.

Humm I though. Down came the front end and up shifted into 3rd and bam!! the front end is in the air again. I was about 100 yards away by then from David and started to bring the bike to a stop, down shifting into 1st and turning around to face back towards David. I sat there for a second, said to my self, damn what is this it feels right to me. Hit the throttle and dumped the clutch and up into the air I went, 2nd then 3rd.and back towards David. Shutting the bike off and stopping in front of him. I sat their for a second as we just looked at each other. All I said was. I have got to get me one of these.

Not having much money I went down that weekend and found a used bike that I could afford. It was a pretty nice used 66' Bridgestone 200 street bike. It was made in Britain. Think I paid $200.00 for it. It was a really small bike but I rode it around for awhile and then went down and got my drivers licence on my Bridgestone 200. It was at this time that I learned that people in cars will run you completely over no questions ask. There were no laws really protecting Bikers back then. People had no respect and did not even think about looking for you or even trying to see you. Bikes and Bikers had a real bad name back then as well, due to the movies and some unruly bike groups. After awhile of trying to stay alive on the street I decided to take my hot rod 200 out to the dirt trails. As I rode through the trees and hills I found that this was much safer than being on the street. So I thought. So the first thing I had to do was put some kind of dirt tire on it. So I did. You know if you take the muffler off and put some knobbies on it and take the lights off of it, ahh, it is still just a small street bike. It was my first bike and in my eyes the greatest thing I had ever had. So off to the trails I went pretending I was a dirt Biker. At first I would go out with David to the trails and we would ride. Trying to keep up with him on his 175 enduro was more than a challenge. I spent a lot of time crashing into trees and running off into gullies and falling off and down hills. Avoiding other Bikers on the trails was a lot fun too and always trying to keep up with him. He would always come back to help me up and make sure I was ok when ever I crashed or went down and I did this a lot. David and I became the best of friends and went every where together. Did lots of riding and just had fun doing what ever was going on at the time. But soon all that changed. David met a girl and she did not like motorcycles and he spent a lot of time with her. Soon they were married. So we parted at this time. I kinda missed riding with David and riding on the street as well but this dirt biking was great. There where no rules of any kind. You could go as fast as you wanted or as wild as you wanted. So I did. I had seen some guys jumping out of some gullies and it looked like fun. Now you got to remember that this is an old street bike with no suspension. Maybe 3 inches in the front and 2 inches in the back. Dirt bikes today have 13 inches front and rear. At first just getting the front tire off the ground was cool. Then a little more speed and I had both tires off the ground. So there I was getting maybe a foot off the ground measuring height from the bottom of the rear tire to the ground. If you add a foot or so to the pegs from the bottom of the rear tire and then 5 feet to my eyes, you almost have 8 feet up and that is pretty high off the ground, well it was at that time. Not by today's standards but at this time I was thinking I am flying and looking for more on my Bridgestone 200. A week or so went by as I went out to the trails a lot and had a favorite place to do my jumps. I was learning how to ride and handle a bike and was feeling very confident. I had worked up to 2 or so feet off the ground by now. One day as I came out of my gully and looked up as I left the ground. I saw out of the corner of my eye, coming right in front of me, a guy on a dirt bike on the edge of the gully doing 50 mph. I hit him broad side. It happened so fast all I remember is hitting the ground and rolling several times to a stop. Pain was everywhere it seemed at the time. Just in case you want to know. I was not wearing a helmet or any safety gear of any kind. Ended up with tiny factor on my elbow and some cuts and bruises. The other dirt biker had a broken leg and some cuts and bruise as well. The bikes in themselves where relatively unharmed. So with my arm hanging at my side I managed to limp home. Had my elbow taken care of, it looked worse than it was. 2 or 3 weeks went by and I recovered quickly. It is nice to be young and heal fast. During that time I decide maybe it was the bike that caused the accident. Maybe I should try to get a real kinda dirt bike. Still not having much money I sold the Bridgestone 200 for $100.00 after 4 months to my younger brother Russell. He took it and put the street tires and lights back on it with my help. A short time later he was traveling down the freeway doing 50 mph, had a flat tire and went down hurting him and his girlfriend enough to make you think about it wearing some kind of safety gear. They were not. Mostly cuts and bruises and they recovered quickly. The bike in it self was relatively unharmed. Meanwhile for me. Back I went to the used motorcycle shop.

It was early 1972. Man what a year. Watergate, the beginning of the end of the Vietnam war. The men were starting to come home from overseas and bringing motorcycles with them and they where showing up everywhere now. When I was at the used bike shop I got a 1971 Suzuki 120 enduro. It was a fairly good bike. Part dirt, part street. Think I paid $300.00 this time for the Suzuki. By this time bikes where getting very popular with the general public and where showing up more and more on the street and out at the trails. I rode the Suzuki to and from work and out to the trails almost everyday and learned how to ride. Soon I became fairly good at riding and could hold my own with most. It had more suspension and was set up for the dirt as well as the street. I was doing wheelies at will, power slides and climbing hills with ease. One day I left the house heading to the trails and out of the corner of my eye I see two kids standing in the door way of there house with there dog barking at me. They smiled and let the dog out of the house. I was doing about 30 mph and the dog came strait for me. I had slowed down a bit and the dog ran up under my front tire throwing me to the ground. Because of my dirt biking experience I was not hurt and neither was the bike. The dog ran back to the house yapping in pain. I went over and knock on the door, there dad came to the door and I told him what happen, he said, So. Humm, got back on my bike and rode off. Now you know today if that was to happen, a nice lawyer would have me living in there house and them living on the streets but not back then. Harley's were around a lot more but Honda was the bike to have then, dirt or street. The other bike companies were starting to rise to the top and compete with Honda. The bikes got bigger and faster both on the street and in the dirt. Soon I new that my little Suzuki 120 was not going to cut it any more. The streets seemed safer than before and I wanted to try the street riding again. There was another factor that came into play, girls love fast street

Valley of the Kings on Hwy 141 along Dolores River near Naturita Co.

bikes but this is not a story about impressing girls. So I sold my Suzuki after 4 months and off to the used bike shop I went.

During that week I looked around at some motorcycles as I went about doing my business. I saw a late 60's BSA Victor 441 British made bike parked at a service station. Dropped by there one day and ask the attendant about it. He said that it belonged to a city cop and he stops by every now and then to check on it. He said that I should leave my name and stuff, so I did. The next day I drove by and saw a police car pulling out of the service station where the bike was. I motioned at him and pulled back around into the service station. The cop pulled up behind me as I got out of my car. Walking towards him saying I wanted to talk to you about his motorcycle, the BSA. He did not look pleased at all and ask me for my drivers licence and told me it was not his bike. Then telling me I shot him the finger and to get into the back seat of the police car. I tried to explain about the bike thing but he would have not part of it and told me to shut up and get in the car. I had no choice but to do so. I sat there in the back seat as he ran every check he could. Seemed he called everyone but the President. He found nothing of course. Then checked my car over really good. It was prefect and clean of any thing he could charge me with as well. At that time my car was always spotless and in prefect running condition. After 30 minutes or so he had to let me go. I pulled away ever so carefully and never ever went back to that service station again.

The weekend came and back to the used bike shop I went. While I was there I met a man from Kawasaki. He had some used factory production bikes for sale. I looked at them and saw a 1971 Kawasaki triple 500 2 stroke. It was blue with a shark colored tank. He told me that they had done some modification to it and that it was a pretty good bike. We started it and it really did not sound like a 2 stroke to me. I was impressed. It did not take long and a $1000.00 later I pulled out onto the street on my Kawasaki 500. It was the first factory production 11 second bike ever built. It was light weight, thin and 100 mph in 3rd gear. I was in awe of this thing. Wheelies where just a touch of the throttle in any gear. Every where I went was at 100 mph. Yeah I know, that is not good. I remember my dad came by and I took him for I ride. I remember telling him to really hang on. He laughed. I did a couple of wheelies and hit the throttle a few times and then back to the house. When we got back, white was his color and all he had to say was "get rid of that thing before it kills you". I laughed and said that I new what I was doing. I had started being a lot more careful than before, but still wild as ever. I was amazed at how fast this bike was. Everywhere I went friends and people would say that don't sound like a 2 stroke. I saw David a few times and he was still in love and she still did not like bikes or maybe me or both I am not sure. Some weeks and months went by dodging cars and trucks but still having fun. Also somehow managing to avoid speeding tickets. Traveling short distances anywhere I could up and down the main drag, highways and freeways. I learned some things during this time. When a semi-truck coming at you on a windy day on a light bike can actually lift you up off the road and put you in another lane. The other was when you are leaning into a heavy side wind on a light bike and a semi-truck passes you going the same way from behind, you have a tendency to change lanes as well. It really will suck you up underneath the truck. Promise. Been there several times. Some time later I was sitting at a red light day-dreaming. It was a very nice day. The light turned green not paying to much attention, off like a bullet I went, up into 3rd gear. This was a undivided four lane city street that led over a long bridge across a fairly wide river called the Trinity. In front of me a quarter mile from were I had taken off from the red light, in the middle of the bridge was a traffic jam. All four lanes were stopped except me. I was doing close to 100 mph and already on top of them. No where to go in the middle of a bridge. I locked down the rear tire, squealing, smoke flying. Then locked down the front tire, squealing and smoke flying from both tires now. I hung on watching as I slide forward at the stopped cars and trucks, seemed like this went on for ever. Maneuvering the bike as it slide with body english I managed to slide the bike between the cars about four deep. When I came to a stop. A guy in a car next to me rolls his window down and says "are you having trouble with your bike". I am sure my face was pale with fear and near death. I replied to him "No just out for a ride". The man in the car then explained to me that he had been watching me out of his rear view mirror the whole time and was amazed that I managed to get the thing stopped without killing myself. Shook his head and laughed at me. My pride laying in the street. I rode off trying to pry the motorcycle seat out of my butt and trying to make sense of what had just happen. There was no sense to be made. That night I came to the conclusion that maybe riding a rocket around town was not a good idea. So after 4 months that weekend I sold the Kawasaki.

Some more time went by 3 or 4 months without a bike but always on my mind. Late in 72' Remember the girl thing. Well I was seeing a childhood sweetheart off and on all this time since 1968. I had taken her for rides on the Suzuki and the Kawasaki 500 and she loved it. The word became love and so we move in together late 72'. We got a small apartment in Irving Texas. You know where the Dallas Cowboys play football. Funny thing is I use to play in the fields where the stadium is today. I was a little kid on my one and only bicycle that got ran over one day. Later I worked in a service station as a teenager across the highway from the stadium and watched them build the stadium from the ground up but really this is not a story about girlfriends, love, stadiums or football. On my mind was my next bike.

I decided that I wanted the best bike for both worlds street and dirt, well what I could afford. But now there was two of us. So I had to start thinking in that way. So I ask her if and what she wanted in a motorcycle. For her it turned out to be a new 1973' Kawasaki 350 triple 2 stroke. For me it was a new 1973' Suzuki TS 400 2 stroke enduro. It was starting to get cold out side but I still rode to and from work and out to the trails a lot even as winter took over. I spent some time with patient teaching my soon to be wife how to ride. She was a fair rider. She enjoyed riding but it had to be a nice day. You did not see many woman riders even at this time. In a bike world full of men she drew some attention. New years Eve night 1972 arrived. We went out and celebrated a little and then back home early. Both bikes and my car a 68' Chey 2 Door Capric were sitting in there normal places in front of my apartment. In those days arcades with pool tables, pinball, air hockey and primitive video games where a major hang out for all kinds of people adults and kids. One of these such places was right across the alley from my apartment. New Years day morning 1973 about 9 a.m.. We where sitting in bed talking, just in general. Outside a loud crash then the wall shook. I was up in a flash and into the living room to see a part of the front end of my car thru the wall. Yes I was just a little upset. But then it dawned on me. The bikes O' my the bikes. Rushed to the door to see both laying on the ground. A kid from the arcade, drunk form that night, lost control of his car and had broad sided my car pushing it thru the wall and into the bikes. The kid had taken off on foot and his car was still there slammed into mine. I immediately went over and got the bikes of the ground and checked them out. Other than a broken mirror and turn signal they were relatively unharmed. The police came and because it was on private property we had the option of pressing charges. The boys dad soon showed up and begged us not to press charges and that he would pay for all the damages and he did. So I did not press charges. I then fixed the bikes. Rode a little and waited for spring which came in March. At this time we decided to get married in the summer of 1973. Funny thing was we got our blood test 10 years later at the same hospital that President Kennedy died in that faithful day in 1963 but this is not a story about people getting married, arcades, being drunk or people getting blood test in a hospital.

Riding here and there when I could, sometimes out to the trails waiting on spring. The daily routine went on. Going to and from work on my TS 400 and I loved every minute of it. It was at this time early spring one day coming home from a little ride with my wife. She turned in to a parking lot on her Kawasaki 350 triple and slipped on some gravel. Down she went. Her feelings hurt more than anything. Lucky it was cold out and she was wearing lots of cloths which protected her. A few bruises and she was alright. Picking the bike up seeing that in itself it was relativity unharmed. She decided at that point riding her own bike on the street was not for her. We sold the Kawasaki 350 and for awhile she just watched. We picked up a Honda 250 XL enduro 4 stroke for her but she really never rode it and later I sold it. During this time I passed David on the street one day and he motioned me to stop and I did. Remember David he is the one that started all this. He was still married to his girl friend. We had a nice conversation about all that was going on. He really like my new bike and was in process of getting a new dirt bike as well. He mentioned that we should go riding as soon as he got his bike next week or so. I said sure but what about her. He said don't worry about her she does not mind anymore. I agreed and a phone call later we meet at the trails the next weekend and went riding. He had gotten a 1972' 250 Husky Varner a Swedish made dirt bike. It was a premier dirt bike for its day. We became close friends again. Now David was riding a pro type dirt bike and there I was trying to keep up again on a half and half street-dirt bike. Except this time I spent a lot of time almost crashing into trees and off into gullies. I had learned how to ride but still could not keep up with him. Trying to keep up with him meant something had to change. The answer was to take all the lights off and changed the tires to knobbies on the TS 400. Rebuilt the engine and put a high compression piston in it. With a little exhaust work and then changing the gears as well. With this turning my TS 400 into a full blown dirt bike. After doing this I could keep up with David most of the time. He was more than a average dirt biker. David and I went out terrorizing the hills and trails often. Jumps and wheelies were our favorite things to do. The other thing was to ride down streams and pop wheelies to fan the water up and out as high as we could. Then often surprising each other from behind with a fan spray of water on them. On a Saturday late spring the Texas National Hill Climb was held. Team Yamaha, Honda, Bulltaco, Suzuki, and some others where there. I decide to enter for fun. A helmet was required for the competition. I had on some jeans, a pair of old dingo boots and brought a old used helmet to wear. As I warmed up the bike and rode around. I felt the team riders making fun of me with all there fancy gear they wore. Ended up placing 5th over all, beating out most of the sponsored bikes. I remember hitting the top of the hill in this giant flying wheelie 5 or 6 feet of the ground measuring from the bottom of the rear tire. Then looking down from the air seeing the people standing at the top of the hill with there mouths open. The scary thing was this was the only time I wore a helmet or any safety gear during those days from the beginning and it did not change for a long time. Riding almost every weekend 10 to 12 hrs Saturday and Sunday. David, Ron and everyone were out early one morning and we were blasting thru the woods and streams. People used to cut down trees along the trails so they could see

My wife and Christy my English Setter who love to ride
as much as anyone

better. Some of the stumps were almost a foot tall. I was bouncing side to side along one of these trails and hit one of these stumps sticking up with my right foot. It folded my right foot up underneath the foot peg and broke my ankle. The pain shot up my leg and right into my brain. I folded over onto the gas tank as the bike came to a stop and we fell over. Laying there on the ground rolling around in pain. Soon David showed up and helped me back onto the bike at my request telling him I need to get back to the truck. Somehow I managed to ride the bike back to the truck where everyone was waiting and wondering what had happen. Went home where I tried to fight the throbbing pain of my ankle to no avail. A very long night and then to the emergency room that morning where a large cast was put on my leg. It reached from my toes to the top of my leg. They did not want any movement of my ankle. Of course I tried to go to work but with crutches it was out of the question. So a few weeks went by. David came by all the time to check on me while I laid at home. Somehow the conversation got on wether or not I could start my bike with this large cast on, of course there was no doubt in my mind that I could. He just laughed at me and out to the garage we went crutches and all. With the bike on the kick stand. Key on, gas on, holding onto the handle bars I lifted my self with a hopping motion off my left foot up to land my left foot on the kick starter and there you have a running motorcycle. This is where I am a really a bad boy. The next day or so I am out in the garage by myself and want to start my bike cause I really wanted to go riding. I prepared the bike to be started. I hopped up and missed the kick starter and down to the ground I went pulling the bike on top of me. The cast was broken a little and I told everyone that I was getting out of the bath tube and fell down, "R-I-G-H-T". The next day I was at it again but this time I got it started. There was a small field next door and off I went for a ride around in the field with my cast leg setting on top of the handle bars. A day later somehow I convinced David to load my bike into the truck and out to the trails we went cast and all. We rode around for a bit but I could not keep up with him and off he went on a little ride. While he was gone I went blasting around with my cast leg setting on the handle bars. I must have been doing 40 mph or so as I came around a corner. There was a 4 foot dirt wall in front of me and no where to go. Slammed into it flipping me and the bike head over heals right up into a small tree on top of the cliff. I then fell out of the tree, the bike then fell out of the tree landing on top of me. Man that hurt. The cast was pulverized and I had a few cuts and bruise as well, the bike in it self was relatively unharmed. I managed to get the bike up and started again and back to the truck and waited for David to return. He did. Told him what happen and back home we went. Did not say much to anyone. I had a appointment with the doctor to see about my progress a day or so later. He did not even ask about the cast. Just looked at me and put on another shorter cast on and off I went. I then was able to go back to work. Ron who had introduced me to David was around off and on all during this time. I remember him trying to teach his wife Karen a childhood sweetheart how to ride. David and I where there. He tried very hard to explain what had to happen to make it go. This looked very familiar to me. She kept letting the clutch out and it would die. I tried to stay out of it and let him work with her. Soon Ron's patience wore thin. She got frustrated and turned the throttle halfway open and dropped the clutch. The thing about bikes are when they take off they throw you backwards and intern that opens the throttle even more. Up into a giant wheelie she went, thru the yard, off the curb out of control. There was nothing I could do but watch. Out and down the street out of control and then down she went sliding underneath a parked truck. We ran to her. She was crying but so would you. We checked her out and with a few cuts and bruise she was up and ok. Embraced more than anything into the house she went. The bike in itself was relatively unharmed. We just looked at each other. Ron went into the house and David and I loaded the bike, got in his truck and left. We tried to make sense out of what just happen. What was funny, it was David's 175 that she was riding. She was not to fond of riding from that point on. Ron had come back from Vietnam in early 1971'. The story goes that he was out on some Ops in the jungle and a bullet bounced off his helmet. He was sent home early. Did not seem from that point on he was the same person. Little did we know. After awhile Ron got to where he rode our bikes and watched David and I ride a lot. Ron was not as crazy as David and I but loved to ride. Never talked about Nam much but he seemed to be getting more paranoid and recluse as time went on. We went riding all the time. Every weekend. In general we just had fun any where we went no matter what we were doing. There were motorcycle parks around in those days. One of these places was called the Flying P Ranch near Weatherford,Texas. Ranchers made there property available for Bikers.You would pay a small fee, 2 bucks usually. You would have 3 or 4000 Acers where you could just go crazy. Most of the time the ranchers would set up jumps, race tracks and trails threw out the park. All they ask from us was to leave the cows alone and we did. The ranchers also set up camping areas and for 2 bucks you could have a camp site or stay the night anywhere you wanted. Most of these parks had small lakes for swimming with beaches and out houses. While 5 or 6 of us where at the Flying P Ranch one weekend. We were riding up and down some trails along a cliff, it was a 5 or 6 foot drop to the bottom of this gully. I saw a small landing area so with out thinking I popped a wheelie and off the cliff I went. Landing in the bottom of the gully to look back up at everyone 6 feet above me. They shook there heads and a couple of them said, who the hell do you think you are Evil Knievel. I did this quite a bit from that point on mostly because it was fun to me. No one else would do it. Soon I would be known as JTEvil. Because at that time Evil Knievel was making news and getting ready for his attempt at jumping across the Snake River Canyon. Evel landed in the bottom of the Snake River Canyon and walked away again in 1974. A year went by and I rode hard and became better than most on the dirt. One day David and I were out dirt biking and doing our normal thing. We always tried to out do one another just for fun. We found a nice hill for jumping into the air on. I hit the hill in third gear catching 4 or 5 feet off the ground, I measure height from the bottom of the rear tire to the ground and about 10 feet in distance. David hit it in 4th gear low rpms and catching 5 or 6 feet in the air and 13 feet in distance. So I flipped around and hit it in 4th gear about mid rpms and 6 or 7 feet in the air and 15 feet in distance and nearly crashing killing myself. David watched me as he rode by headed to make another jump. I am not sure what he was thinking but here he came in 5th gear as he hit the hill, up was the word. It had to have been 20 feet off the ground, he was eye level with the top of the telephone poles.

He looked down at me and then at the top of the telephone pole. It was all happening in slow motion to both of us. His bike had a little more suspension than mine but not enough to cover this jump. He told me afterwards, he new this was going to hurt so he enjoyed the air while he could. The whole thing was in super slow motion, he must have travel 40 or 50 feet in distance. Unlike Evel Knievel he had no landing ram just hard flat dirt. Jumping off my bike and letting it fall to the ground. I ran towards him as he and the bike hit the ground, me yelling NO!. I saw him brace for the impact as he came down. The bike bottomed out the suspension and then David's body slamming against the gas tank. The bike going out of control and him fighting to control it. Flipping and bouncing off the ground side to side and then onto the ground they went. David and the bike now flipping end over end and separating. The bike stopped and David flip over one more time to be setting on his butt on the ground upright, legs apart with his head hung down. I ran up to him yelling David, David, there was no response. A few seconds went by and he fell over onto his side and came to, telling me, I messed up, I am really hurt here J.T.. In the middle of nowhere I was in a panic. Saying, were are you hurt, everywhere was his answer, can you move, NO, please David don't die on me. He said I want. A minute or 2 went by and me trying to figure out what to do. He said go get a ambulance, I said, no I will not leave you out here by yourself, can you move, let me see he said, a little. I said, You must get up I will not leave you out here. The bike in itself was relatively unharmed. I know this is wrong but I started his bike and picked him up and put him on it and told him to ride back to the truck. He said NO J.T. I cant, YES I said, you will and he did. I just could not leave him out there. Right or wrong. If you are wondering we were not wearing helmets or any safety gear. Then to the hospital we went. Rocks and dirt in bedded in his skin and a couple of broken ribs. A long painful cleaning process of his wounds and some tape for his ribs and then I took him home where his wife was in a panic. She said something about a hole and some kind of mother referring to me. I felt bad about the whole deal but two or three weeks later we were back at it again. It is nice to be young, you seem to heal so fast, not like today. I am always amazed we never wore helmets or any safety gear and somehow we managed to survive. It was at this time I thought I should get a real dirt bike. So I sold the TS 400 to a friend at work, another David. Then went down to the Yamaha shop and got a new 1973 Yamaha SC (scrambler) 500 MX. It was a close out and spring 1974 was on us.

I guess I wanted my wife to go riding with us as always. That is the way I am. So I got her a real dirt bike as well. A 1974 Suzuki TM (trail master) 100. They both were awesome bikes. The Yamaha SC 500 was silver with a line of red on the gas tank, it looks just like the Ghost my bike today. It was so fast all I could do was hang on. Friends would always say that I was just flopping in the breeze and on the edge of crashing most of the time. Did not take me long to learn how to control this beast. As I rode through the trees people said that it looked like some kind of ghost moving through the trees. All you could see was a flash of silver as the bike appeared and disappeared in the trees. They called it the Silver Ghost and with the eyes of a Biker, so did I. A week or so after I had brought the Yamaha 500. I was out alone at the trails. Riding along the edge of a cliff lined with small trees on one side and a drop off 5 or 6 feet deep on the other. I hit a tree 6 or 7 feet tall growing close to the edge with the left side of my handle bars. Which in it self is just the clutch. The problem was it drove the left side of the handle bars back and the right side forwards turning the throttle wide open. The bike jumped off the ground. Flips upside down with me on it and into the gully below. The gully was full of open roots from the trees and there I was laying in the middle of them with the bike on top of me upside down. Because it was late fall I was all but alone out there on the trails. Fighting and struggling with the roots. I pulled and fought the bike and a hour later I got it out. Back to the truck I went and home. After that I am not to fond of roots. This time somehow me and the bike were relatively unharmed. The TM 100 was a fun little bike as well. Everyone loved to ride it except for my wife. She had lost interest in dirt biking and that was ok. She loved to watch me ride and I only show off for my lady. I rode the TM for fun and did lots of tricks on it. My favorite was to pop a wheelie and then step off the bike and run along behind it while it was in a giant

Arches Natl. Park near Moab Ut. The wind has blown beauty into the rocks

wheelie. Usually people would freak out when I did this and think that I was out of control and about to crash. Soon I would let off the throttle and down would come the front end and back onto the seat I would jump. Hit the throttle and ride a wheelie while setting on the bike. Ron rode the TM 100 quite a bit and one of our favorite things to do was to go out on a rainy day. We called it muddy crossing. It was fun and we crashed a lot. David and I were out of control most of the time. Throwing mud on everyone and everything we could. We were really just a bunch of kids playing in the mud. Cleaning up was the hard part. We tried riding in the snow but that was just to hard and not much fun. Time went on. Did lots of dirt biking and raced a little here and there. Then I saw something on T.V. that changed my life. It was called Colorado. 1975 was on us and there was something else. A horrible sound that took over the whole world. It was called Disco.

Humm, I thought what would be the best way to get to Colorado. David and I were the best of friends still, although his wife was getting a little tried of us riding all the time. It became apparent that street bikes were in order. So we looked around the fall of 75' and bought a pair of identical 1975 Yamaha Twin 650's. Remember the T.V. series C.H.I.P.S, the two motorcycle cops. Well that is how David and I rode side by side every where and always. We planned our trip to go to Colorado in May 1976. Of course it was to be with our wives so we thought. Both David and I had some experience on the street and times had changed. There were a lot more motorcycles now on the streets but they were being taken down left and right by people in cars and trucks. People were still not ready for motorcycles to be a major part of the population in mid 1975 as it is today. This is were I met some real members of organized Biker gangs. I worked as I quality control inspector with a large manufacturing company that employed 250 people. Among these where three Bikers. Nice enough people really. Had there own way about them. One had been stabbed in the heart during a gang fight. He had a large scare down the middle of his chest as a souvenir form the surgery. The other had stabbed someone in the chest and nothing to show for it. The last was older and a nice enough guy that just loved to ride and was not much into violence. He told stories of a sophisticated monkey and of his bike days. I enjoyed his stories. They were always on me about buying the Yamaha in a nice way. They of course rode Harley's. They would say I would rather push my Harley than ride a jap bike. Then I would say, I would rather push my Yamaha up a hill in a rain storm than ride a Harley. This never went over very well with them but they tolerated me. I think they knew how much I loved to ride and respected that. Even at that time Harley's still did not have a very good reputation. Along with biker gangs being a popular thing to be apart of for Harley riders at the time. I would not own a Harley. I really did not want people to see me as a bad guy. This is true today. I would like for people to think I am there friend rather than there enemy. The best thing is most people do. I met a friend of these Biker guys and he was in a wheel chair. He was a Vietnam Combat Vet. He told me a story were he was going down the street on his Harley one day. For those of you who rode in those days. You know of the massive cars that the little old ladies drove. They would pull out in front of you and smile knowing that if you hit them in this tank they were driving that you would lose big time. So as Bikers back then we had to be aware of these little old ladies all the time. Anyway, he was doing about 50 mph or so down a street and out pulled one of these old ladies in a giant Cadillac Coupe Deville. He was already on her, He said, It was to late. Then she just smiled at me. He told me that he figured he was going to die anyway so he hit the throttle and drove his bike right threw the front door killing her and throwing him up and down the street for awhile. Broke his back and both legs and he would never walk again. After he had told me this I just stood there looking at him for the longest time with nothing to say. I guess we all have these horror stories and mine will come later. Colorado was on my mind and May was just around the corner. What will we do now, we ride because that is what I do.

Dream Of A Biker

Riding in the wind thru 1975. Waiting on May of 1976' and the Colorado trip. Riding dirt bikes thru the summer and fall of 75' David and I were still best of friends and rode all the time during the winter as well. His wife went a few times but got to were she had enough of us riding all the time. She ask me,why do you have to ride all the time. I said, because that is what I do, I am not trying to be a smart ass just the truth. He tried to live in both worlds. Riding with me and spending equal time with her. She became hateful and abusive towards me. Yes we tried to do the things that she liked to do. I was always very nice to her but still the whole time she was always trying to split David and I up. After awhile he got to where he recognized this and felt bad because of the way she treated me. I usually ignored her because of David. He was all that mattered and we still had one hell of a good time doing anything. David and my wife were best of friends and she loved us both and understood that we all were the best of friends. We spent as much time with her always, riding, talking and just having a good time. My wife knew what riding meant to us and would defend us when every David's wife said something negative about us riding all the time. One day David came to me and said that he was stuck between a rock in a hard spot. She had told him either he stop spending so much time with me or she would leave him. He did not want to loose my friendship. We were in a sense blood brothers. We had and would put our lives on the line for one another as well as our wives and did so many times. He was leaning towards leaving her and then I ask him, do you love her and does she love you. He said yes. I said. Then go to her, stay with her.

This is the best thing for you. In the long run to have love in your life is very important. So we parted again and I saw him a couple times here and there as time went on. A month later she had gotten pregnant. David was very excited and I was excited for him as well. He still had the matching Yamaha 650 Twin and the Husky 250. He soon gave up riding except to and from work and a small trip up and down a highway or two every now and then. He did not do much dirt biking from that point on. For the most part I left him alone calling every now and then to see how he was doing. Usually he was fine but sometimes he would say that he missed riding with me. I had met some nice people along they way and we dirt biked together sometimes. None of them could replace David or ride as well as he did but we had fun and I rode all the time. I knew at this time that David was not going to make the trip to Colorado in May 76' and as far as I know he never did. David had as much passion for riding as I do. He has the right to wear the name Biker.

My wife had gotten a German Shepard as I puppy before we moved in together back in 1972. He was a pure breed German Shepard about 100 lbs. and had turned mean because of some school kids teasing him all the time. I did not know what was happening until it was too late. He had tried to bite a little girl and scared the hell out of me. We sent him to a guard dog place. They used him to protect private property which was popular in those days before lawyers turned it into a money making deal. There is a fine line here but I do agree that dogs should not want to bite people under any circumstances. Heart broken of what had happen. We went out and got a pure breed English Setter. All white and a touch of tan here and there. Her name was Christy. Went to pick her up on the Yamaha 650 Twin. She was just a puppy 6weeks old but did not seem to mind riding on the motorcycle. My wife and I mostly rode the bike every where we went even in those days. Always taking Christy with us a lot as she grew to a forty pound dog. She would raise hell every time I started either bike and always wanted to go for a ride. It did not matter to her if it was on the street bike or the dirt bike. On the dirt bike she would jump up on my lap and off we would go. Did not matter to her up and down hills, fast or slow. She really loved to ride and looked forward to it. Sorry no pictures of this, which brings up a point, please take pictures. You have know idea how important they will be in the future. On the street bike she would ride behind me in my wife's lap and hang her head out in the wind. She just loved riding in the wind. Christy logged close to 10,000 miles in a 3 year span, which is more than most people did in those days. I only have two pictures of her on the bike. Both are on the Yamaha 650 Twin. One in Oklahoma near Cheyenne and there is a few buffalo in the back ground. The other is outside Wichita Falls, Texas with some deer in the field in the background. Most of her trips were within 200 to 400 miles from home one way. Most all trips were to Arkansan, Texas, and Oklahoma. Again please take pictures. I only have two to show you. One day when she was young during the summer, I looked over and there she stood frozen in a pointers stances. I called my wife over and we could not figure out what she was doing. She was frozen totally still for quite a few minutes. I walked over to see what was going on. I could not believe what I saw, there was a small butterfly on the ground. I stood there for a few minutes watching her watching the butterfly, frozen and then the butterfly flew off and she jumped around in delight. She did this quite often and people would freak out at the sight of this. She was a wonderful companion and very unique. 14 years later Christy had lost most of her sight and was a little senile. She was slow to get up and move around. We were living in Montrose, Colorado at the time. My son was 10 yrs. old and there were always kids over at the house. Christy had tried to bite a few of them because they would stumble by her. I tried to see that they stayed away from her. One day a 6 yr old little girl got to close by not paying attention and she bit her. Not enough to break the skin but enough to scare the hell out of me. On a cold and lonely day in September 1991 I had her put to sleep. In a true sense of the word Biker. Is the driver the only one who can be called a Biker. Is the passenger who logs as many miles as the driver on the bike and loves in the wind as much as anyone. Are they not Bikers as well, can they wear the name Biker and if they can, then would you consider that Christy in the true sense of the word, be called a Biker. Maybe.

First of May 1976 came and my wife and I started planning the trip to Colorado that we called the Dream. We were so excited. A long winter waiting for our vacation. We had decided to take a 5 day trip, 4 nights. I had bought books, maps and new exactly where we were going. All the roads that we would take starting from Irving,Texas to Colorado Springs the long way. Even where we would camp and had it planned out to the T. Got us some rain gear, sleeping bags, air mattress and a two man pup tent. As today and then we were a low budget ride. The one thing that I forgot was a good camera. In those days there were no good instant cameras that you could buy along the way. I had one of those 120 mm things but as you can see from pictures so far, did not take very good pictures. Think I was just way excited and did not put it on a priority. I packed the bike 2 days before and was leaving early in the morning. May 25th and a restless night. Woke up ready to go. Looked out side and it was raining. Not to hard but just enough to make it messy. No problem, put the rain gear on. It was 80ˣ degrees outside and off we went. As we left Dallas we were still very excited about the Dream. The rain was light and a dream was coming true, Colorado. Our destination that day was Buffalo Lake State Wildlife Park in northwest Texas 350 miles or so away. We loved animals and thought this would be a neat place to camp. In the wind on the road just out side Ft Worth, Texas on hwy 287 we stop for breakfast at a small café. It was still raining lightly. We went inside, set down and looked around. All you could see were cowboy hats. Now in those days my hair was a little long, about the same as it is today and with a beard I notice I was the only one that look like that. Kinda felt abused setting there. Felt like a rope tightening around my neck and ropes were hanging all over the walls. We eased up out of our chairs and slowly walked out the door. Now in hurry, got on the bike in the rain and drove off looking in the rear view mirror to see if they were following. Of course they were not. But still I drove with a purpose for awhile as the rain got harder and more intense. Basically all we had on were sweatshirts, a wind breaker and then a light weight rain suit. No helmets. Out side Bowie,Texas I had to stop at a rest area, it was raining so hard I could not see anymore. There were bathrooms and shelter tables there. Wet, cold and a little shaken about things we waited. Must have been around 11:00 am. The rain pored down for awhile and after 30 mins or so it slowed to a stop and off we went. The sky started to clear as we rode towards

The Rock House , my son almost two and the Ghost in the tree with me.

Wichita Falls. Excited once again in the wind on the road and things were looking a little better. We stopped and had lunch at a Jack In The Box. Funny name for a fast food place and off we went, a little wet and cold but still excited. The sun was now out and it was warming up. As we rode that day we saw a few bikes on the hwy. Mostly a couple of Honda Goldwings, a few BMW's and a Harley Glide of some kind. All headed for Colorado. Talked to a few for a second at rest areas and gas station. These are the best places to share a minute with others who enjoy in the wind as much as you do. It seemed all the locals along this hwy 287 were not so friendly. I felt like everyone thought we were the bad guys. The Bikers that we talked to were nicer and spoke of wonderful things in Colorado. There are lots of little cities along the way on hwy 287 headed towards Amarillo, Texas. Most supported a few local motorcycles parked here and there. I was being careful and obeying the speed laws.They went from 55 to 30 mph in a short distance in every city. I came around a corner into a city and was dropping off my speed. A Childress, Texas local city cop pulled me over. I tried to explain that I was slowing down, he said R-I-G-H-T and wrote me a ticket for a 40 in a 30 mph speed zone. NO, I was not speeding. Yes I was a little upset. As we drove off we where not as excited as we were in the begriming but Colorado was still the goal. So we pressed on. Buffalo Lake was a little off the beaten track about 100 miles and it was getting hot 85* or 90* about 2 or 3 o'clock med afternoon. Stripping down to t-shirts, hot and thirsty, out in what I would call a desert and no other bikes around. Came to the sign Buffalo Lake State Wildlife Park around 4 o'clock in the afternoon. Down a dirt road a mile or so and pulled upon a long hill looking out into nothing. There were a few covered picnic tables setting in a desert. Across the top of this hill was a sign. Parking the bike. We walked over to it. The sign said Buffalo Lake State Park dam. It was just a pile of dirt, no water, no animals, no nothing. I looked at my wife and said, what, there is nothing here, she said yes I know. I said a few choice words as I looked around. There was nothing. I wanted to be camping by this time and enjoying the water and the animals. It was now 5 o'clock. So I got out the map and looked to see what to do. Time was becoming a factor. North of Amarillo was this big place called Lake Meredith Natl Rec Park. We were tired and more than discouraged by this time. But we went on to Lake Meredith. Passing thru Amarillo because of time and planned to stop at Fritch, Texas right on the lake for a bite to eat. For those of you who have never been to northwest Texas. There is a whole lot of nothing. More than enough dirt and rocks in every direction and always looking the same mile after mile. We could see the lake off in the distance and finally got to Fritch. It was 7 o'clock. We were close to being out of gas and reserve was just down the road a few miles. In Fritch there was a bait shop. Across the street was a gas station and it was closed. That was it. Really. That was all there was in Fritch at the time. I said man is anything going to go right. The gas station would be open in the morning according to the bait shop guy and just down the road was our destination on Lake Meredith. We crabbed a couple of Pepsi's, chips and a box of Ding Dongs, my favorite, to hold us over till the next morning and we would get some breakfast along the way. What kind of name is that for a snake cake Ding Dongs. Anyway, off we went. A mile down the road and then had to switch to the reserve tank, which is about 25 miles before empty. As we drove down the road towards the lake we saw a sign that said our camp site was 15 miles away. So I added it up, 2 miles then 15 is 17 miles and then back to Fritch. That would be 34 miles. Hummm. Talk about a bad feeling, we did not have enough gas. Had no choice but to press on to the camp site. It had been a really hard day and just wanted to stop and relax. I would have to deal with the gas thing later. When we got there to the camp site. There was nothing, I mean nothing, except a bathroom and I felt lucky that it was open. For those of you who travel a lot, bathrooms are always a great thing. You Ladies know what I am talking about. As I looked around, nothing, I mean, no trees, no hills, no grass and worst of all there was no lake or water to stand and play in. No way to cool off. Just flat land and dirt, that is it. No other Bikers as well. One other camper there and it seemed they wanted no part of us. Shut there door and that was all we saw of them. Had not seen a bike since we left Amarillo and Fritch reminded me of that little café outside of FT. Worth. The lake as we could see it was a quarter of a mile away from the camp areas. Hot, tired, butts hurting, hungry and thirsty. We went down the road a bit and pitched the tent while talking about the day. We were very discouraged and on the brink of giving up our Dream of Colorado. After putting the tent up, we opened the Pepsi's and had some chips and was feeling a little better. I was thinking over at the restrooms there would be a drinking fountain of some kind. Now I am a chocoholic and know some of you are too. I got into the Ding Dongs having two or so because we had not eaten much that day. Finished our Pepsi's as I ate another Ding Dong. Still thirsty and a very dry mouth, now with ding dong stuck to my teeth. I went over to the restrooms for a drink of water. There was none. Nothing, no sink, the toilets were a out house style toilet. No outside facet either. Nothing. Ding Dong is now setting up hard on my teeth in my mouth. I thought ah, the lake, just walk out to the lake, wash off and get a little drink. Yeah that's it. So off we went towards the lake. The road ended at the camping area. So we started walking to the lake 200 yards away. As we got closer we started to sink in the mud and still 50 yards away. The lake looked more like a septic mud whole covered in bugs rather than a body of water. It was apparent that we were not going to be able to get to the lake and in the water. So back to the tent we went. Now at this time we were seriously considering ending the trip that night and going home the next day. It was so bad, no gas, a ticket, no water, beat down and harden Ding Dong stuck to my teeth. My wife was less discouraged than me. She was a pillar of strength and my best friend. All that I had planned had gone wrong and now having to go to sleep with harden Ding Dong in my mouth was just to much. I remember saying, what next, what will tomorrow bring. Can it get any worse. We decided when we woke up in the morning we would talk about if we should continue on to Colorado.

Another hard night as I woke from a restless sleep. There was a noise and the sound of people outside the tent. Unzipped the tent door and looked out. In the distance there stood an angel. He was six foot tall wearing green and a funny looking hat. On his shoulder was a patch that said National Park Ranger. He looked like hope in my eyes. We got up and walked over to him. In the back of his truck was a container of water and some cups. The Ding Dongs still pasted to my teeth. We ask, he said sure and I started to drink and wash the Ding Dongs off my teeth trying not to look silly. We talked to him and he explain that they were going thru a drought and that is why the water is not where it should be. Which explained Buffalo Lake as well. Some other people came up to him at this time and were talking to him about stuff. He picked up some flint and pulled a piece of deer antler out of his pocket and started making arrow heads as he talked. This was amazing to me. A few cracks and chips and there it was a arrowhead. He just handed them to people as he made them. The people talked to him for a while and then went on there way. Looking around and then at his truck, a 75' ugly green Dodge pickup, I remembered about the gas thing. So I proceeded to explain to him about what had happen and that if he had some gas it sure would be nice. He had nothing, no spare gas can of any kind. Being a mechanic and a machinist all my life I new this was a simple engine in his truck and all I had to do was unhook the gas line from the carburetor, start the engine and fill a bottle up that I had in my hand. A very easy procedure. The idea of doing this was more than he could handle and did not want any part of it. So I kept on and trying to explain to him how simple this really was. Popping the hood on the truck with him going I don't know about this. Then showing him as I am doing it what and how this would work. By this time all he had to do was start the engine and there you have it, instant gas for the bike. I think he was in aw of this and did not say much. Hooked the gas line back up to the carburetor and thank him very very much, went over and put the gas that I had taken from his truck in the bike. Packed the tent, loaded the bike and it was a new day. It was still early in the morning and the air was clean and fresh. The sky was a deep ocean blue and there were birds flying about in the sky. The lake had a shimmer of fog on it and it seemed that all the problems had been taken care of by the funny hat wearing angel. Things did not look so bad and we decided to go on for awhile and see what happens. Into Fritch, the gas station now open, filling up with gas and we were once again in the wind. Now we are looking for breakfast and headed northwest towards Colorado. Our destination for that day was the Great Sand Dune Nat Monument, Colorado, via Raton, Trinidad and Walsenburg, Colorado. Stopped in a small town Dumas, Texas at a Ma and Pa place and had breakfast. It was down home cooking and made us feel normal again. The people were very nice to us and wished us a safe and pleasant trip. We picked up hwy 87 there in Dumas that would take us thru northeast New Mexico into Colorado. This area was called the dust bowl back in the thirties. I guess the farmers had over used the land and the winds had taking all the good top soil away. The wind leaving nothing for them to farm in. Threw conservation and a understanding the land was almost back to normal at this time. Deep wells and irrigation were everywhere as we drove thru the open farmed fields. Very large silos along the hwy were not something we were use to seeing and added a bit of excitement to the trip. We had come 500 miles and still had seen nothing that would make you want to come down these roads in the wind again. Reached the New Mexico border, still nothing and wonder if Colorado would be all that we had dreamed of. 100 more miles of nothing but the skies were clear and blue and the wind was light. Near Des Moines New Mexico the terrain began to change and a small mountain came into site, it was Sierra Grande at 8700 ft. Mostly rocks, a black lava lawyer around it and along the Hwy. There were a few bushes and a few trees near the top. It did raise our spirits and we stopped for gas. Must have been 11:00 A.M. While we were there some nice local people told us of a old volcano just down the road, it was called Capulin Volcano Nat. Monument. They said all the lava laying around came from eruption's 1000's of years ago and it would be very interesting and we should stop there and take in the views. Of we went down the road a few miles, saw the volcano to the left and drove up to the top. Entrance fee was $1.00 including parking. Funny thing about those days, none of these places charged hardly anything to see what already belongs to you to begin with. Unlike today, where you cant even walk across the street without everyone sticking there hand in your pocket for more money. Anyway, at the top of the volcano found a nice parking spot on the west side. Parked the bike getting off trying to pry the uncomfortableness of my cloths away from my body, OK, adjusting my underwear and other things as well, my wife doing the same and looking around eastward facing the volcano. The volcano was very cool. We had not seen anything like this. The center was indented and black lava everywhere. It was just how you would think they would look and what it must have taken to blow this

On the road in Capitol Reef Natl. Park near Torrey UT. A prefect day.

thing out of the ground. With the eyes of a child and the wonder of it all I turned around looking westward. There they were, a post card picture of beauty, the snow capped Rockies. A long roll of peaks that look like heaven to me. The struggle and the long and winding roads that we had been on to get to this point disappeared. I felt privileged to be there. Tapping my wife on the shoulder and saying hey. As she turned I pointed, I could see the light in her face turn on in aw of what she saw. Some tears filtered from her eyes as we stood there looking frozen it time. Then a hug and a kiss. The Dream, the Dream of Colorado had come true. I look at her and said, Yeah the volcano is cool are you ready to go now. Mt Capulin was no longer in our eyes, all we could think about was getting into Colorado. More than excited, jumped on the bike and down the hill we went. Amazing that I did not crash the bike trying to get of the volcano and in the wild towards the Dream. It is now 2 o'clock in the after noon. It was starting to get warm out 80* degrees and off came most of the cloths. 80 miles later hit Raton Pass the border of New Mexico and Colorado on the eastern side. As we went up and over the pass, it was our first real experience with altitude temperature changes. A cold chill and stopped at the top to celebrate our victory. The Dream of a Biker had come true. The mountains in plain site but still not quite there. Walsenburg was down the road on Interstate Hwy 25 and that is where we would turn off to our destination for that night. The Great Sand Dunes. Stopping to eat, the mountains right there and we are so excited and driving up the road into the dunes and mountains. The mountains were so beautifully big, so majestic and the dunes were like the Sahara Desert dunes in a Egyptian movie. It was a unbelievable site to see come true. We reach the Sand Dunes around 7 o'clock. No other Bikers were around and a few other campers were about. We paid our entrance fee, picked a camp site and quickly headed for the dunes like kids would. Up and down a few times on the dunes as the night came and a real chill in the air. We were not use to this cold and really had know idea just how much the temperatures could change from day to night. At home the temperatures stay about the same day and night. Went back to the camp site and put on all the cloths we had, which was not much. Now freezing we put the tent up while trying to start a fire.

Good thing I remembered the matches, huh. The wood damp from the dew and the fire would not start, yeah, tried the paper thing but we did not have much paper. Then I thought the bike, drain some gas from the bike. Unfortunately we had no can or anything that would hold some gas in. The sand was deep and tried to push the bike near enough to drain some gas onto the wood, no luck. To dangerous. Did not want to drop or hurt the bike. Yeah well you were not there, I guess I could have took the wood over to the bike and soak them with gas but that did not enter my mind at the time. We are very cold and desperate at this point, "Must Have Fire". Over in the distance a little ways was another camp site with a fire burning. Off we went, when we got there it was 2 guys sitting in lawn chairs in front of the fire drinking beer. Normal hello's, them looking at me with that west Texas look as to say what do you want. I explained about the gas and can thing, they said, nope we don't have any. I stood there looking like a step son I am sure, but then realized that they were holding beer cans in there hands and said well could I at least have one of your beer cans. O' no, we are not threw with them yet. Then said, I just open this one and I am not going to waste it. I said please man we really need a can. He then said, well if you finish drinking the beer, you can have this can. Unfortunately for me I don't drink at all, I cant stand the smell of beer. Now I don't want to make anyone mad here but why would someone drink something that looks, foams and smells like piss. Sorry about that, anyway, I stood there and downed the beer in front of them and off we went back to the camp site. Drain some gas out of the bike and then pouring the gas on the wood and wallah, "FIRE". Uummm warm. After awhile of drying and warming up off into the sleeping bags we went with all our cloths on trying to stay warm. It was not to bad that night as far as that goes and some sleep. The next morning I woke with a voice saying, Sir, would you step out of the tent. Open the tent door and there stood another angel dressed in green wearing a funny looking hat and a patch on his shoulder saying Natl. Park Ranger. As I got out of tent thinking, two morning in a row, WOW, how lucky can you be. He started to give me the third degree on whether or not I new that there were no fires allowed in this area and in general treated me like a criminal. I tried to explain to him about the cold and if

I would have known I would not have started a fire there. R-I-G-H-T he said. He then ask us to pack up and leave the area and that is what we did. Went over and played in the dunes and set on the tallest hills admiring the views of the dunes and mountains. If you have never been to the Great Sand Dunes, you should but be aware of the fire thing. The bike was packed and we were headed for Canon City via Salida and to the Royal Gorge where the highest suspension bridge is. The Arkansan River running below in a deep canyon about 2000 feet at the Royal Gorge. Riding down Hwy. 50 with the Arkansas river beside you to the Royal Gorge. A very nice canyon ride. We came in the back way. In those days you could drive across the bridge and we did. Stopping in the middle setting on the bike to look off down below, kinda scary in away, the bridge sways a little bit but one hell of a view as you look down. Did the whole tourist thing all day. Buckskin Joe's is next door and well worth going to see. A lot of old western movies had been filmed there and they had shows and gun fights all day. A really Great time. Another great thing about these places at that time, they all had front door parking for the motorcycles and treated us very well. A lot like today but not really. Evening came and off to Canon City for the night. It was much warmer than it was at the Great Sand Dunes. A nice night and up in the morning taking a shower and on the bike. Destination, Cripple Creek via Guffey, Hartsel and Florissant. There were a few clouds in the sky but still a beautiful day. Headed north towards Guffey, just before we got there the road had turn to dirt, a post office was all that was there. The post office guy said there was a shorter route up to Glentivar a very nice drive and then turn onto a road headed for Cripple Creek. A very light rain began as we were leaving Guffey, higher in elevation it was cold. Some miles on the dirt road riding by Eleven Mile Res.. Very pretty and a little messy because of the rain and then into Glentivar. In Glentivar there was a very old service station and that was about it. My sun glasses and windshield messy from the rain, mud and stuff. So stopping to clean them off at the station. The station guy came running out and said hey, that stuff cost me money and for paying customers. I looked at him and said R-I-G-H-T then went inside and bought a Pepsi and a chocolate candy bar, said thanks. Cleaned my windshield and off we went to Cripple Creek. Turning at Florissant and down the road a little way, still lightly raining off and on. There is a place called Florissant Fossil Bed Natl. Park. If you get a chance. Stop. Interesting place and very nice people. Cripple Creek was down the road 17 miles, around 4 o'clock mid afternoon and the light rain as we got closer to Cripple Creek turned into a light snow. Fortunately the roads where still warm and not cold so the snow did not stick. Drove down main street in Cripple Creek and the snow began to come down in bigger flacks. By this time we were freezing and all we had brought to wear we had on. Sitting on the bike shaking and looking pretty silly I am sure. The snow was falling thick like a cloud looks but we were still able to travel on the streets. Realizing we had to get out of there we hurried toward a road that headed back to Canon City. Our destination for that day was Colorado Springs. Turns out the road is called Phantom Pass Hwy. 67 out of Victor at 10,000 feet. The road turned to dirt and the snow falling steady making me go very slow. We of course where all but frozen and I was not sure we were going to make it down of the mountain. Finally got down low enough in altitude that it stopped snowing and a very light rain was all that was left. We were so cold, I could barley move and had to stop. Leaving the bike running and putting our bodies and hands up against the engine to get warm. The bike is covered in mud and so are we. Thawed out as we stood around the bike and off we went down into Florence where we had hot chocolate for a hour. Wash up a little and the bike as well and on to Colorado Springs. In my mind at the time I though there was a reason why they called it Phantom Pass. It scared the hell out of me. We were headed for Manitou Springs a major tourist area. Arriving there around 7 o'clock always with Pikes Peak in our view. Picked a nice camp site at one of the local places. Cleaned up and off to dinner while studying the tourist pamphlets we had and planed out a great day so that we could see all the things in the area. Up early and right next door was a horse rental place. We had camped on the edge of The Garden of the Gods. A very beautiful day, warm and clear and blue sky in every direction. Pikes Peak always there to look at. We were so happy and felt so lucky to be in such a beautiful place. The horse rental guy came over and was very nice. Said can you ride I said yes, very well and my wife said I am fairly good. He picked out two totally magnificent animals, prefect in every way, there ears forward and looked happy to go. We got on them and he pointed towards the Garden of the Gods and said go have fun and be back in 4 hours of so. In those days you could ride horses all over the place in the Garden of the Gods. Not today. We rode off and thru the hills and valleys of the Garden of the Gods, Pikes Peak in the view with a little snow on top the whole time. The horses were prefect, they seemed to be enjoying themself as much as we did. Up and down hills and never hesitating, never looking back. Could have been a reflection of us I guess, they may have felt the over whelming joy inside the both of us to be there. I can not put into words how we felt that morning. We were in total aw of the whole thing. I am sorry that you cant experience the Garden Of The Gods as we did that morning anymore. Which brings up a point. When you are out there in the wind on the road, stop, do and see all that you can. Soon it will all disappear never to be seen again and for heaven sacks, please take pictures. Noon or so and back we went to the stables. The horses still full of life and we talked to them for a while. Thank the rental guy and back to the bike we went. Next stop was Cave of the Winds. Pulling up to be motioned to the front where there were special parking places for motorcycles. Kinda made us feel special. They were so nice. Inside we went and down into the cave. The other people with our group were all very nice along with our guide. A lot of questions and a half hour later out the other end. Amazing sights and knowledge is what we found in the cave. If you get a chance, you should go. Back on the bike and our next stop for that day was the Manitou Cliff Dwellings Museum. Pulled in and they motioned us to the front and special parking places for bikes. Wow!!. Inside we went. In those days you could walk in and out of all the rock dwellings, the ruins of the Pueblo Indian that lived here around 1100 AD. There was a Indian Tribal dance group there and fully dressed in authentic native cloths. They played music, sang and danced for us. We felt very special to be apart of this ceremony. I think it was there annual trip to there old home grounds. Spent most of the rest of that day there. Before heading back to the tent we rode up and saw Seven Falls in south Cheyenne Canyon at night. They light up the falls with different colors of light on each fall. We stood on a hill top so we could see the wonderful light show, you must go if you can. We were already planning to go there the next day and then back to the tent we went. The day was over to quickly and now we were feeling the wear and tear of the trip and wanting to relax. Stopped and had dinner and planned the next day which involved heading back in the evening for home. We would stay at Trinidad for the night in the south east corner of Colorado and then home. What a great day it was, up early and the day was ever bit as beautiful as the day before if not more. First stop Seven Falls in south Cheyenne Canyon. Again front door parking. A connecting stair case runs along the side of each of the seven falls right up to the top. I love water, it is life to me. It is were we all must go sooner or later. Wether you be an animal, bug, tree, plant, man, or any thing that is alive. Water is the life force. Everything must have it one way or another. We played and enjoyed the falls and then headed for the Cheyenne Mountain Zoo and Will Rogers Shrine Of The Sun. Will Rogers said he never meet a man that he did not like. I am sure he was talking about the people he would meet in his travels on the roads. Like him I meet so many nice people in the wind and on the roads. It seems the nicest people are in the small cities today, what I call the Ma and Pa places. Not so much back then. They always were a little hateful towards Bikers in the small cities in my eyes. But at the major tourist places they were always very nice to us at that time. Now it seems just the opposite. Small town people are very nice and the major tourist places are cold and unfriendly. We parked in front again and inside we went. Inside the Will Rogers Shrine, a tall tower, there is a spiral stair case wraps around the inside as you go up to the top. Along the way you can hear his voice talking and it gives you a warm feeling hearing him speak of rights and wrongs. He is never judging but always making a good solid point. Pictures are all over the walls of him and people he had meet as you climb up and the view of Pikes Peak and the valley below. After reflecting for awhile and our good fortune to be there on this trip. Down we went and over to the zoo. If you get a chance you should go. The Cheyenne Mountain Zoo right up the road next door and always front door parking for the bikes, amazing. Once inside, the landscaped mountain side of beautiful terraces and walk ways lined with trees, flowers and bushes. It was like no other zoo we had ever seen

and wide open spaces for the animals. We spent most of the day looking and talking to all the animals. I have spent most of my life trying to see as many different animals as I can. Now I try very hard to take there pictures out in the wild. Not wanting to go, 6 o'clock and time was up. Had to get on the road and thru Pueblo and getting a bite to eat there. Then stopping for the night, camping outside Trinidad. Happy and sad at the same time, being there and then having to leave. It was a very hard thing to do. Up early and only stopping for gas and a bite to eat, drove strait home. Arriving around 9 o'clock Sunday night. I did not realizes just how nice it was in Colorado until I got back to Dallas, in all reality a hell hole. A major part of my soul I left in Colorado. It was horrible, Dallas had never looked so bad to me. Up the next day and off to work to fall into the daily routine again. Always seeing Colorado in my eyes. Spent a lot of time telling the stories to those we had left behind and of our adventures in the Dream we called Colorado. Time went by and Christy, my wife and I rode all over Texas, Arkansan, and Oklahoma that summer and fall. There are some really beautiful places to see and be in those days in those states. The winter came, then 1977 and disco was still with us. The question was, were do we go from here. We ride, because that is what we do best.

Fishers Towers in Onion Valley on Hwy 128. Ut. A must do Scenic Byway.

Heart Of A Biker

In 1977 the year the Denver Bronco's went to the Super bowl the first time and lost to the Dallas Cowboys in January 1978. I had been a Dallas Cowboy fan since I was a kid growing up there. Played a little football myself but this is not a story about football. Colorado held a special place in my heart now and so did the Bronco's. We would dirt bike one weekend and then street bike the next always going to different places. The nice thing about the south are the lakes and rivers. They are warm water lakes and clear clean rivers and lots of them. You could spend your whole life traveling around these states seeing all the lakes and rivers, Arkansan, Oklahoma and Texas has to offer. Most of them beautiful but now taken over by population I am sure. There are lots of wide open spaces there but none that are as majestic as in the Dream. Anyway, In Hot Springs, Arkansas. Christy, my wife and I got caught in a helices lighting and rain storm. The bolts of lighting hitting everywhere around us as we rode into Hot Springs. I did not think we were going to make that day. Finally hiding in a lower parking lot under a large bank building. We were scared to death, the sound was deafening as the bolts cracked right in front of us. I new that we would be safe under the building but there was that small doubt and time were you wondered. A Hot Springs policeman came by and told us to stay there, this was going to be a bad one. There were sirens going off everywhere and ambulances running up and down the streets. A few people were killed and a lot others were hurt. Christy the whole time looking at me as to say are we going to be all right. We were headed for Lake Ouachita on a camping trip. We spent a lot of time in the Ozark National

Forest mountains and the Ouachita National Forest mountains in Arkansas. The forest were thick and had a nice green smell to them, always full of life and very beautiful. In the summer you would go along and when you got hot, stop and jump in to the river or lake which ever happen to be the closest to cool off. Christy loved the water, we would blow up air mattresses and float out in the lakes and down rivers for hours. She would swim and float right along we us never getting out of the water. At first I thought she would tire and drowned but she would swim along side us happy as can be never showing any sign of wanting to get out. The only bad thing about these states are, every mean and nasty thing that lives in the world lives in there. Every poisonous snake, poisonous bug, poisonous plant, poisonous spider and the meanest fish that there is in the U.S. lives there. Not like in the Dream where it seemed everything was prefect except the cold. It gets really cold there but in the spring, summer and fall the temperature stay the same day to night. Not like In Colorado where you can have a 50* degree temp change day to night. The fall colors there are as beautiful as they are in Colorado, but not as majestic. We spent the whole summer and fall seeing all there was to see in these states trying to stay out of the city as much as possible. Christy never hesitated about getting on the bike, she was always ready to go even after 500 or 600 miles. People would pull up along side us in there cars and take picture as we traveled on the road, her ears flopping in the wind and loving every minute. Soon winter came and 1978. Dallas was still a horrible place to live and it was wearing on me pretty hard. The people were so out of control even in those days. It was all I could do to keep from blowing a head gasket. A change had to happen. Not having much money as usual. We sold our house and moved to a little city called Troup outside of Tyler Texas. Yes, were they grow the roses. Earl Campbell of the Houston Oilers now the Tennessee Titans, grew up and played football there. Man that seems confusing, anyway, a nice little old house on one and half acres. With a couple of horses we brought that my wife had always wanted soon after moving in. It was neat having the horses in the yard and would always being hanging around trying to see what I might be doing as I worked on things. They had complete run of the whole place front yard and backyard and there was a little stock pond at the bottom on one end. A chicken coup with chickens we had brought right after the horses. A roster to keep them in line and we had fresh eggs every day. The roster tried to rule the whole yard including Christy. He would run up to her and jump on her like he would his hens, she would fight him off and then grab him by the throat and throw him on the ground with a thud. After a second or two he would come to and off he went looking for his hens. He was the yard boss and treated everyone the same. He soon learned that messing with me or my wife was not a good idea. On many a day you would look out the window and see Christy and him fighting and then her throwing him on the ground with a thud. She would just stand there and look at him, I am sure this made no sense to her. She really never tried to hurt the roster and soon he got to where he left her alone. In the front yard was a 100 year old pecan tree, it drop 500 or so pounds of pecans every fall. The pecans where prefect, sweetest pecans that you ever tasted. Every year in the fall you could expect pecans. People would come over and want to pick pecans off the ground and we would let them. Most thought we should charge $2.50 a pound but I never did. Had a nice work shop and in general a very nice place for us to life, but this is not a story about rosters, horses, nice places to life, dogs or 100 year old pecan trees or is it.

My SC Yamaha 500 threw the brutality of me riding it, had enough, I was more than it could take. I retired it 1978 and went back to Dallas to see about another dirt bike. Checking the news paper went to look at a 1977 YZ 400 Yamaha. It was a proto type factory bike and the guy had received a new 79' YZ 465 from his Yamaha sponsor. It cost me $1000.00 and I took it back to Troup. I do not know what they did to this bike but fast and furious comes to mind. Handling was unbelievable, it was the first mono shock bike ever built. It made the SC 500 look slow in comparison, later all dirt bikes would go to this style suspension. I continued to jump of cliffs and into gully canyons and became JTEvil to most people who knew me. Riding hard and a lot but now in a new city with no friends. Traveling to some of the motorcycle ranches when I could and meeting David and Ron for the weekend. We spent most of our time on the Yamaha 650 twin. Putting 35,000 miles on the Yamaha in three years. I was riding it 50 miles a day to and from work now and then on the weekends to all the beautiful places around us. I felt like it was time for a change. I wanted to move up to something a little nicer. Sold the Yamaha 650 and the YZ 400 because I needed more money than we had for the motorcycle that we wanted. I also had something else in mind, yes it was the Dream of Colorado again. I looked around, even at some Harley's and then bought a BMW R90-6 loaded with most everything, it even had a CB. In those days CB's were the bomb, every one it seemed had a CB. More so with the truckers. They made songs and movies about these CB's but I did not quite get it, so I took it off immediately and had no use for it. I also brought a used black leather standard motorcycle jacket that I would wear all the time form that point on. The BMW was solid black and that might not have been the best thing. It road like a dream quite and powerful compared to the Yamaha 650. While traveling on the BMW to and from work in 78' I meet a young kid really 19 or 20 yrs old, Craig. He was just married and loved bikes and to ride. He had 1976 Kawasaki 900, really kinda fast for its day. He could really ride this Kawasaki and also had a old 74' Suzuki 125 dirt bike that was out dated. He had just started to work where I was working in a plastic bag manufacturing plant. Funny thing was, one day out at a local dirt track, I had blown by him on the YZ 400 not knowing that we would meet later and become good friends. Craig and I became the best of friends along with my wife. We, being his wife and me and my wife road into Oklahoma and Arkansas a few times on camping trips. It seemed at work the biking thing caught on because I road every day rain or shine, hot or cold. I was somewhat the expert at the time on bikes and riding. So everyone around me always ask me about bikes and stuff. There were three or four guys at my work I would call want to bees, including my wife's step dad. He was cool, he had made a mistake as a young man and spent 12 yeas in prison. He was hardcore and nice to have covering your back side when things got rough. He understood what Freedom was and enjoyed life very much. We did not always agree on everything, but we got along very well. He had went out and bought a Kawasaki LTD 450, another guy got a 650 Honda, one of the real amateurs went out a brought the first new 79' Honda 1000 CBX 6 cylinder in 1978'. This bike was way to much for him. The seven of us, five bikes and two wives Craig and mine decided we would go into Arkansas on a over night trip about 600 miles. Even at this time late 1978, people still were not the friendliest towards Bikers and I always felt like that day outside FT. Worth in the rain storm. I always looking in my rear view mirror. Turns out the people in east Texas are the same as in west Texas, they don't want you around as Bikers. In my travels there many had tried to run me off the road for no reason. The people in general were better but not like today. A light rain the morning we where to leave and me convincing them that it would stop soon and off we went with our rain gear on. Riding thru the country side of east Texas is a pleaser. The rain stopped and with the sun slipping out form behind the clouds, the pines and flowers line the roads with a nice sweet smell. The birds and the animals coming out to say hello as we rode in the wind. There are some nice winding roads and rolling hills in east Texas and then thru Texarkana on the border of Arkansas never missing a interesting place to stop. The sky had cleared, blue with a touch of white clouds in spots. It was a nice ride up into Hot Springs always stopping where beauty was to be found. Riding east to our camping place on the Ouachita River on Hwy. 270. Christy was with us doing her normal thing and everyone was in aw of her. They could not believe that she loved riding that much. We stopped to eat in Mount Ida and onto the camp site we went. Night was close, I had told everyone they should bring a tent, sleeping bags and warm stuff to wear. Being a bunch of macho guys they did not. You probably don't want to know this, but unless it is totally freezing out side I sleep naked in the sleeping bag along with my wife. This is how we sleep at home so we feel comfortable this way and easier for us to rest. Most of them had a sleeping bag at best. One just had a blanket. Shaking my head at them and off into the tent we went for the night. Christy always slept at our feet in the tent and was never a problem. Had a very nice night, slept well and then up in the morning to find it had rained. Craig and another guy were over in the door way of a outhouse rest room shaking and freezing trying to start a fire with wet wood. Another under a picnic table with a blanket on him, saying some nice things about me. Not sure but there was a hole involved and a mother of some kind. My wives step dad lying on the ground in a sleeping bag with a tarp over him now waking up and laughing at everyone. Craig's wife agreed with the guy under the picnic table about me being the hole and a mother. Craig had brought a tent and stuff but they were not water proof and they got wet that night. I took some gas out of the BMW and helped Craig get the fire started and everyone warmed up as the sky's cleared quickly bringing a very nice day to us. Packed up our stuff and off we went. A little chill in the air but still a very nice and fresh day with the mountains having a slight fog on them. It is very close to a prefect morning and the one morning you are looking for Riding in the Wind. In Mena we had a nice home cooked breakfast at a Ma and Pa place. Then over into Oklahoma seeing the Winding Stair Mountain Natl. Park and some wonderful forest around Big Cedar, Oklahoma. On the way back home the Honda CBX just died and stopped. Took me awhile to figure out why. For some reason the alternator stopped working and the battery went dead. There were no Honda shops around, so I went down the road to a hardware store and purchased two pieces of medium wire about 8 ft. long with four alligator clips. Jumped my battery to his and it started. We let the battery charge off mine for awhile and off we went down the road. Soon there after the battery went dead again on the CBX and we stopped again. Humm I thought, twisted the wires together making a sort of cable and then attached one end to my bike and the other to his. We road off down the Hwy side by side with the cable between my bike and his charging his battery as we rode. Taking it off in the major cities to be safe. After a couple of hours of doing this and reaching the Texas border the bike seemed to be fully charged and we were able to make it back home that day. Funny thing is I don't remember any of those guys going on any long trips again. Craig on the other hand was different. He wanted more and had heard many times about my adventures in Colorado. I could see a sparkle in his eyes and the Dream of Colorado glowing bright. Winter came and so did 1979. We planned our trip that winter to be in June 79', that is when all vacation were taken for what they called a shut down period at work. You also had a week to your own and could take it any time you wanted. Meanwhile in the spring of 79' Craig and I with the permission of our wives decided to get some dirt bikes again and we all went back to Dallas. We looked and picked up a couple Maicos dirt bikes fairly cheap. They are hand made in Germany. His was 76' 400 and mine was a 77' 400. Somehow I ended up with another factory sponsored bike and back home we went after seeing the sights, the zoo my favorite, museum and the botanical gardens. We had fun riding and going to some of the ranches and spent some time out on the roads. Always with our eye on the Dream. My 2nd Dream of Colorado.

June came quickly. We were ready and very excited, five nights six days was the trip. Craig and his wife on the Kawasaki 900 and we were on the BMW. Christy stayed home for this one. Both were loaded with everything you can imagine. This time I knew about northwest Texas and was prepared. Being the middle of June the weather was nicer but really hot close to 100* mid day. Riding thru Ft. Worth with the purpose of not stopping and obeying the speed laws to a T and outside Amarillo on Hwy Interstate 40 for the night camping. From Troup about 500 miles. A long day but the excitement eased the ride. Taking a different route with the suggestion of Craig's wife. This time we headed for Sante Fe, New Mexico via Tucumcari and Las Vegas N.M.. Nothing, nothing but desert out there. There are some interesting things along the way but still nothing as we traveled down interstate 40 towards Las Vegas, New Mexico. By mid day the heat was so bad, my nose looked like Reudoah the red nose rain deer, my hands sun burned bad enough they were puffy and solemn. Covering up our bodies and somehow managing to get thru this. The heat felt like you were riding around in your car in the summer time with the windows rolled up. Outside Tucumcari we could see the mountains off in the distance and I think this is what keeps us going. The closer we got to Las Vegas the more excited we got and into the mountains were it was much cooler. Everything was ok now, the Dream had come true again. In Santa Fe a nice place with lots of history. Walked around and took in some sites and then thru the mountains onto Chama, New Mexico our destination for the night. The ride was prefect thru the Rocky mountains and all you can imagine. Seemed there were a few motorcycles here and there along the way but not to many. There was one thing I did not know about. In June there are mosquitoes, big suckers and lots of them. Guess what, no mosquitos repellent. It was so funny as we arrived at our camp site just outside Chama on the border of

Colorado near the rail road. Craig and his wife were so excited, got off there bike an walked away looking at the beautiful mountain scenery. My wife and I standing by our bike just looking around trying to take it all in. Nice very very nice. So beautiful. Anyway, I look over at Craig and his wife some distance away from us in the woods and they were dancing, well that is what it looked like to me. Then running waving there hands like crazy people and slapping themselfs in the face. Mosquitoes find you from your breath, your breathing tells them where you are and the mosquitoes were all over them. Guess what, they ran strait back to us bringing the mosquitoes with them. Now we were all doing the mosquitos dance together and slapping ourselves in the face looking pretty silly I am sure. Putting on anything long sleeved and feeling like mosquito dinner. An elderly couple from the camp site next door saw what was happening and came over and sprayed us down with repellant and all was normal again except for the occasional itching. I love people like that you don't even have to ask. None of this could take away from the beauty, the wonder and the Dream that had come true again, called Colorado. Night was here and off we went into our sleeping bags. What a wonderful morning as we woke up smelling like a mosquito repellent commercial. Packed the bikes and off we went on a ride of shear extassey into Colorado, Man, it doesn't get much better than this. Our state, Colorado is with out a doubt the most beautiful place on earth. It may not have the wonders of Utah and the animals of Wyoming but the Roads, the Roads are a never ending story of beauty and adventures. Our destination for that day was Crested Butte via Pagosa Springs, Lake City and Gunnison on Hwy 149. If you have never taken this Hwy or been in southwest Colorado. You have not been anywhere. Traveling in what I can only call and describe as a dream, my feelings were out of control, it was always the next place more beautiful than before, the next corner, the next pass, the next hill, the next road, the next city. Your eyes, mind and body are bombarded with sights that are hard to put into words. It felt like I could not absorb it all at one time, the word is overwhelming and that is what comes to mind. Trying to stop and gather it in constantly. I know there are some of you that cant see it and don't understand this thing called motorcycle riding. I feel sorry for you. I wish that you could see it thru my eyes and hopefully my pictures will be enough to let you know the joy that fills my heart each and ever time I go on a journey to the most wonderful and beautiful places on earth. Camping at the foot of Mt. Maroon, out side Crested Butte. Craig wanted to run to the top of this mountain. He did not know how big and wide open these mountains are coming from Texas and never traveling that much. I explained to him that it is bigger than you think and even to go a little ways up it would take every thing he had. In the first Dream, I had tried this and new that it was not going to happen because of the altitude thing. You got to be kidding he said it is right there. I said ok and off we went up the mountain. About a half a mile up the hill the altitude had us both by the basketballs and was kicking our jack assess. Setting down, the views looking like a postcard. Craig is looking at me, trying to breath and saying that is enough, lets go back and down we came. Night fall was close when we got back to the camp site. The girls waiting and a little worried. A camp fire and a nice conversation about the trip and all the things we had seen. A cool fog that morning in the valley and the next day our destination Royal Gorge and Buckskin Joe's, Via Monarch Pass and the Arkansas River canyon. Always stopping a lot to see everything we can. Craig's wife now getting tried, homesick and wanting to go home. Arriving at the gorge and buckskins late and we came in the back way and across the bridge. Craig's wife had enough of camping so we got a motel for the night and the next day spent most of the time at Buckskins Joe's. That morning leaving the motel, before heading to Buckskins Joe's we saw some deer on the road and stop to look. They seemed unafraid of us and I tried to get closer and somehow I did. We were able to reach out and touch them out in the wild. It was awe-inspiring to actually touch a wild animal as it walked thru the forest. Don't know why, they just did. Craig's wife now in better spirits and on to Buckskins we went. Had a great time there, did all the tourist things and we were to spend the last night at Trinidad and headed that way around 6 o'clock. We stopped at a gas station there at Trinidad around 9 PM. and decided with Craig's wife saying I want to go home. She was just a kid really. Off we went thinking we would stop somewhere along the way and camp. Out across northeast New Mexico and only stopping for gas each time deciding to continue on. I remember on several occasions, waking up on the bike a sleep doing 70 mph and looking over at Craig and seeing him a sleep as well, yelling at him to wake up as we pressed on thru the night. Each time we stopped for gas, we would just look at each other and get back on the bikes and go like hell. The girls were always asleep, waking up just enough to say were are we, then back to sleep they would go. 14 hours later and 1000 miles after leaving Buckskin Joe's, we got off the freeway and pulled into Tyler, Texas at a rest area 10 o'clock in the morning. As I got off the bike I fell to the ground looking over at Craig to see him fall to ground as well. Woke up, one hour later with voices saying get up. The girls had been asleep all night and were ready to go home another 40 miles away. Dragging my self off the ground and somehow onto the bike to get it started and then home with a shower and to bed. Three or four hours later I was up and dressed and back on the bike. Driving over to Craig's 15 miles away to see how he was doing, him looking like the walking dead and his wife saying something about crazy holes and some kind of crazy mother again. Then over to tell my wives parents 20 more miles, that we were back and got a bite to eat while we were out. Later the guy with CBX 6 cylinder, had almost killed himself on it and then sold the bike to Craig. This thing was fast, I mean really fast. I remember blasting down the Hwy at 115 mph on the BMW in front of Craig thinking I was flying. I hear this engine start screaming, then look in my rear view mirror and in a flash, he goes by me like I am setting still at 140 mph. Then he is off the throttle to fall back behind me again to hear this thing fire up again and pass me setting still at 140 mph. I rode this thing, it did not handle that well but when it came to going strait this thing would fly. Seriously. Some weeks went by and I went by Craig's to see if he wanted to go for ride because that is what I do. His wife very upset with me and telling me to go away. Craig did not like this to much and we went for a short ride anyway thru the country side of east Texas. Always a very peaceful ride.We spoke briefly about her and the rub between us. Weeks went by and it became apparent that Craig's wife had a real dislike for me now. He came to me one day and said that she was going to leave him if he did not stop spending so much time with me riding. He said I don't know if she is worth it. I said do you love and does she love you, he said yes, then go to her, it is the best thing for you. It is important to have love in your life. So we parted and a month later she was pregnant.

The old people next door in Troup had been there for ever and did not take kindly to me and my biking ways. I was always working on them and starting them seemed to irritate them for some reason. They hated the pecans and the pecan tree out front for some reason as well, why. Coming over to tell me what to do every now and then, me being head strong and telling to take care of there own business and leave me alone. I caught them putting salt water on the ground in front of the pecan tree one day, I was very upset but what I could do. Some time went by and one day there son came over. He was born and raised there and was talking to me. He said this is a small town and you have got to get along in order to life here. I said yes, but at the same time you have to have a little tolerance for other people. He left and I tried to do my things during the day so not to bother the old people next door. A few weeks went by and one day the old lady comes over and says the old man had died and would I like to come over and see him lying there in bed dead. Let's see, NOOOO!!!. But this is not a story about old people dying or pecan trees. As a Biker I had learned never to trust anyone in a car or anything around you when your riding on the street. I rode to work every day, rain or shine, cold or hot 50 miles on the BMW. There was a right turn at a red light that I took everyday for a year or so. I always did about 40 mph in this corner. Across the street was a truck stop on the loop around Tyler Texas. One day as I came around this corner, all the sudden the bike went down and I reacted quickly. I have a very nice adrenalin rush, always have from the beginning and I think it is what keeps me alive. Things seem to slow almost to a stop when I have one of these rushes. As the bike went down I crawled up on top of the side and rode the slide out as it came to a stop. Fortunately I had duel crash bars and they protected the BMW. I picked the bike up and started it immediately and back to see what had happen. Apparently a trucker did not close his gas cap and fuel spilled right in this corner. A Hwy Patrolman showed up and told me that he had chased down the trucker and sited him with vehicle endangerment and wanted to know if I wanted to press charges. The

BMW was fine and so was I, so I said no and went on to work. Now you know today with a nice lawyer, I could have been driving that truck and he would be walking, but I am not that way, never have been and never will. People make mistakes, don't they. Once on the way to work in a rain storm, the water was so deep around two feet, that people in cars were pulling over and stopping. I came by them on the BMW fanning water 6 feet in the air and seeing them look at me like I was the crazy one, Humm, now why would they do that. The summer was over and fall had come 1979. Craig and I were still friends but not as close and never rode together again. My wife and I rode a little and always on the BMW. I had seen David and Ron a few times during the year of 1979 dirt biking at one of the ranches. Ron had convinced everyone at the V.A. hospital that he was not stable and there was a real possibility that he might lose it and hurt people. They government gave him a full ride. A nice house in a secluded place in Arkansas and $1000.00 a month. In Vietnam he was a Navy Seal and ran special Ops into places they should not have been. In one of these places is where the bullet had hit him in the head. I guess that is why they gave him what he wanted. In between dirt bikes I had picked up a TT 500 Yamaha 4 stroke and took it up to see Ron on a short vacation. We rode and had fun but he would draw back every now and then and this bothered me. I went to see David one time and took the TT 500 with me then. His little girl was two and as cute as she could be. His wife now wanting to be a career woman and not a mother. She decided that she wanted a divorce and they were trying to work it out. Believe it or not she was still trying to make David and I enemies and even suggested that we have sex at the time. NOOOO!!!. I loved David as much as my brother that had died years before. The TT 500 was fun to ride but very heavy for a dirt bike and soon I sold it. Back home in Troup once again after a strange but nice visit. If you are getting a cold feeling here, you should. There was this small city called Whitehouse. It lies between Troup and Tyler midway and was a speed trap for most. Most of the time I would always go another route which is longer and avoid this city totally. One day going the short way to work, a Whitehouse city cop pulled me over and said I was speeding. I was at the back of a pack of cars and I always obeyed the laws in this city to a T. So I ask him, why would you pull me over and not them. I was not speeding and that is the truth even today. He said nothing and wrote me a ticket and said sign it. I said I don't think so I have done nothing wrong. He said sign the ticket. NO! I said I have done nothing wrong and if I sign that ticket I am guilty no matter what. He then told me to turn around and slammed me against the car hand cuffing me. I said ok I will sign it, he said to late and took me to county jail. They put me in a cell with about 20 guys. These were not the nicest people you would want to hang out with. One had killed his father, another had rape his mother and another had raped and killed his father. The rest were just drug addicts and armed robbers. Just a group of your average people hanging out in a jail really. I went and set down in a corner with my back against the wall. A few came over and ask me what I had done and did I have any drugs. NOOOO!!!. I told them that I had refused to sign a speeding ticket and they look at me strangely and moved away. Then me saying and resisting arrest creating a disturbance and they all came back over and we had a nice conversation about there crimes. As I waited on my phone call, which could not come soon enough. One hour later I was aloud to make my phone call and one hour after that the same cop came and got me. Hand cuffing me very tightly, I said is this necessary I not a criminal, I did not kill anyone I just did not want to sign the speeding ticket because I did not do anything wrong. The handcuffs were very tight and cutting off the blood in my hands. It was a 15 mile ride back to Whitehouse and to the court house we went. The judge and my in-laws standing there as I entered the room. Lucky for me my wives uncle lived there and had some influence being on the city council. I looked at the judge and said the cuffs are killing me, she said officer remove them. He did, then she told me to sign the ticket. Humm, looking at the judge, saying but I did not speed, she said sign the ticket. With a pen in my hand I just looked at the ticket for awhile, the judge said would someone please make him sign the ticket. My wife there watching all this, came over and told me to do so and I did. The judge dropped the charges and off I went vowing never to go that way again. Some time went by. I had worked all day and my wife and I decided to go into Tyler for dinner must have been a Thursday in the fall. It was a little cold that evening around 6 o'clock with a light rain earlier so we dressed warm and off we went on the BMW. Because it was cold that evening I had decided to go thru Whitehouse, a shorter route to Tyler. It was still daylight and the rain had stopped with a light fog in the low spots. The streets were wet and drying out in places. It was a wide two lane Hwy with very wide shoulders on either side and had traveled it many times. The traffic was light and we were the only motorcycle on the road. 2 miles outside of Whitehouse down at the bottom of a long hill one quarter of a mile away set a car with his turn signal on. I was doing about 60 mph close to the speed limit. For a long time riding on the roads I knew not to trust people no mater what. As I got closer to the car just setting there, my eyes thinking how strange why don't they turn. Now focusing on the car I saw that it was a police car and wondered what he might be doing. I thought he would be paying attention and his turn signal still on. Still doing 60 mph and my eyes focused on the car. I was now close enough to see the driver in the car about 30 feet away, he does a slow turn right into my lane in front of me. Remember the adrenalin rush I spoke of earlier, this was a big one. In a split second a 100 things went thru my brain. If I turned right moving away from the car he would hit us broadside and it would shear off our legs and probably kill us. If I jump off the bike, my wife will surely die. There is not enough time for the brakes and it would not help anyway the streets are wet. My wife will die if I don't do something. I know form experience, in all cases, it is the passenger that is thrown from the bike and killed because they are not prepared or hanging on to anything. It was apparent that I had to turn the bike into the car at such an angel as to throw us off to the side. I locked my arms ever so tightly against the handle bars to pin my wife against the backrest. My legs strand against the foot pegs to help pin her even more to the back rest. A light turn left and the words Damn It. This whole process happing in a split second. The impacted num me but still aware of all that is going on. I remember looking for her as I flew thru the air and landing in the ditch. Barely able to move my arm pointing in the wrong direction, num. I got up looking for her. Screaming Joan, Joan, pulling my arm down as hard as I could with my right hand to straiten it out with a snap and the pain. Then seeing her and falling down crawling over to her. She was just lying there, no movement and a light rain falling, me yelling NO!, NO!, please NO!. I did not know if she was alive or died. The cop ran over and was in a panic, saying O' my god I nearly killed you guys. I tried to get up, I wanted to kill him make no mistake. He said the ambulance was on the way. I fell back down beside her and she came too. Her words were, have you seen my wedding ring, I cant find it. Looking at her left hand bleeding form a 4 inch cut down her left hand to her ring finger was the ring that I had given her all those years ago. I had lost mine years before while dirt biking. That is all she said, do you know were my wedding ring is, I cant find it. I laid there saying, NO! NO! You Damned Asshole, looking at the cop. He went into the street and began to direct traffic. There was now a big seen on the Hwy. People were coming up and holding her and me trying to comfort us lying there in the ditch. Soon the ambulance was there, everyone running around seeing what had happen. I just caught a glimpse as they put me on the ambulance of the BMW. It was not relatively unharmed. It was setting on the hood of this Ford LTD 4 door, the front wheel against the windshield broken. The bike was bent into. My attention turned to the ambulance siren going now and my wife still saying the same thing, have you seen my wedding ring, I cant find it. I never lost conciseness that night the whole time. I was knocking on heavens door and he told me to go away. To this day I still see the bike and the car and the sounds of the horror of that night. We were lucky in away that it had rained and the gully was muddy, wide and no rocks that we landed in. A 5 stearin bard wire fence 10 feet away from where we landed, I new it was there and if we would have hit it, might have killed us. Once at the hospital both of us in the same room, they look at her, me saying is she going to be alright. They would say, lets just look at her. Me being wide awake and making since, they were concerned about her. All she would say is, have you seen my wedding ring I cant find it. I said, NO! Doc, is she going to be OK. Yes he said, I think she just has a concussion. What else Doc, I said. A small cut on her hand, He said. That is it I said. Yes, that is it he said. You on the other hand are not OK. My body was num but still there was pain and it came from everywhere. One hour of x-rays and then back to the room where she was awake and I was so relived and so happy to see her. As they rolled me in she said, James, James, She called me

James in those days, are you alright. Yes I said but I think I broke some more stuff. The doctor came in and checked on her and said good your doing fine. Then began to explain what they had found about me. A left broken ankle, left dislocate knee, left dislocate hip, left wrist broken, left elbow dislocated, left arm broken into, left shoulder broken and dislocated. My left arm had feeling but could not move it much. Dang, in my mind I did not hit anything, they did not realize this at the time. I did not hit anything, I did not hit the car or the bike or a rock or the fence or anything. Just landed in the mud that was it. The next morning after some nice drugs, they put me back together, solemn a little in each dislocation but not to bad, except my arm which would require surgery. Joan was up and doing just fine. All she had was six stitches on her left hand just above her ring finger and of course shaken a little. That was it. I had managed to save her life. But at what cost. Our cloths were hanging in the closet form that night in our room, she went over and was looking at them. She turned to me and said damn, pulling my leather jacket out of the closet and brining it to me. The zipper was completely ripped out, all the threads were torn apart. The left selves hanging by a thread, the sides of the jacket ripped apart. It was shredded and did not even look like a jacket. It looked bad and still I did not hit anything. It was then, that I new what had happen. As I braced my whole body against hers to keep her from flying in the air and dying. Then turning the bike slightly left to hit the car head on rather than a board side hit, where I thought we would surly die. The impacted of the bike against the car slightly left drove the left handle bar and foot peg with a shattering blow thru the bike and into my body. Tearing the jacket up along with the left side of my body. I never hit anything. It was the horrendous jolt of the impact that had done all the damage to me. The next day telling the doctor and showing him the jacket, he sat there and just looked at me. I don't think he could understand. A few days went by and it seemed a lot of people came to see me. Some I new, others I did not. Most all looked at me like you would look at a hero with thankful eyes and a smile. Four days had gone by in the hospital my body still hurting and I am not a big fan of drugs so I did not take many while I was there. They did not like this and it made me very uncomfortably. The city of Whitehouse and the police insurance company had came to me and told me that everything would be taken care of, not to worrier about money, hospital or anything. I told them that I would not sue them or the officer and just please take care of me and that is all I want and they did. I was tried and hurt. So I got up after four days asking my wife to get the car out front, I am leaving, she left to do as I ask. She knew how much I was in pain, not just from the broken bones but from being in the hospital was more than I could take. Home is where I would be more comfortable and she knew that is were I needed to be. While she was gone I managed to slip on some sweat pants and a shirt. While hanging onto chairs and the wall went out my room door and was headed down the hall towards the out door. Limping and leaning against the wall to help me along the way bare footed. The nurse came down the hall and said what are you doing. About this time my wife walked back in grabbing me to keep me from falling down, the car out front now. The nurse said, you cant do this, you are not ready, go back to your room. I said, yes I know but I am leaving anyway. She said please, don't go as another nurse came up along with a doctor saying Mr. Thomas please go back to your room. I said, I have got to go home just looking into his eyes. I think he understood. He then grabbed a wheel chair and helped me into it. All the time I am still headed for the door. They stood there in the doorway in misbelieve as I got into the car and we drove off and then home. A few months went by as my body healed. My job on hold and waiting for me. They wanted to do lots of surgery and put metal plates in me. My answer was NOOOO!. My left hip was messed up and my left arm even worse. Three muscles had been torn of my shoulder and the rotor cuff was factored from the impact that night. I had no choice but to let them repair it. My arm did not work right. I am telling them absolutely no metal plates. They had to do a cat scan thing in order to see what was wrong and this really hurt as they shot chemical dies into my body. Two days after surgery I was up and barley able to walk. Putting some sweats on and the orderly's saying Mr. Thomas you cant do this. Yes I know, I said, I have to, as I fell into a wheel chair with the help of my wife and then out the door to the car. A month went by back home with my arm in a hanging restraining harness as to keep it still and time went on. It was hard to drive around in the passenger seat and feared terribly someone hitting us in the car now. The insurance company had given me $4000.00 dollars for the BMW which was more than I paid for it. The cop who had hit us that horrible night was the very same cop that had tried to give me a ticket that one day and also was a friend of the son of the old people that lived next door. The ending of the movie Easy Rider comes to mind. Before all this had happen I was a black belt in Tae-Kwon-Do a Korean martial arts. I had been studying since I was 18 years old. I also was studying in Judo, Aikido and Jujitsu. I was 140 lbs of grace, speed and power. This all ended that night on a lonely Hwy in the rain. In one second every thing that I loved, except my wife, everything in my life that was important to me was taken from me. The Heart of the Biker was broken and it seemed that it would never be repaired again. Nothing had any meaning to me anymore. Hiding in the house like a recluse as time went on and I kept healing. One year had gone by and they had done all they could do to put me back together. The end of 1979 would be the last year Christy would ever go riding again and now it is 1980. There was no celebrating and the year going by so fast. I took the $4000.00 and went down and brought a brand new economy car in the summer of 1980. Brought this car with the soul purpose of going back to the Dream. It seemed this might help me mentally and raise my spirits. I could not be there any longer in the area where my life had ended. The angry that I felt towards everyone was very intense. David, Ron and Craig had all come to see me on separate occasions though out that year. This was the last time I ever saw Craig. You know how a dog when he is hurt really bad. He will growl and try to bite you because of the pain he is feeling, well that is how I felt at the time towards everyone except my wife. We went to Colorado and had a nice trip up thru the western side. Driving thru Durango, Red Mountain pass and then Montrose and decide that we should move there and forget all that happen. It had always been our dream after our first journey in 1976 to someday move there, have a kid when the right day came. I had a strong feeling that I would never be In The Wind On the Road again because of the fear I felt now. This was a very hard time for me. What would I do now. Where do we go from here. Riding was what I did best and no longer existed.

Will of a Biker

Late 1980 and I was on my way to being healed. My body did not work at all as it did before and this was very upsetting and hard for me. My mental state was not as it should be. I was still very angry and hated the world for what they had done to me. By the time the doctors were thru with me I was down to 120 lbs of nothing with all my cloths on and felt I would never be what I was again. 1981 came and there was no celebrating. In February we decide, as close as we were to dying that night, it was the right time to have a child and she should have her IUD removed and she did. In late March 81' she told me she new without going to the doctor that she was pregnant. There was some doubt in my mind that it happen so quickly. Shortly there after we settle with the insurance company April of 1981. I quit my job and sold the house and enough was enough. Put everything in a storage shed and went back to Colorado. By this time it was the first May again. Looked around and not having much money, brought 40 Acers in the middle of no where, 20 miles up out of Montrose, Colorado. Went back to Troup and loaded everything I own into the back of a U-Haul truck. I had traded the economy car for a 1977 Toyota Land Cruiser station wagon. It had a trailer hitch on it and with a old broken down horse trailer, loaded the horses. With my wife driving the Land Cruiser and me in the U-Haul truck, off we went towards Colorado leaving everyone and everything that had happen that night behind us. Not really. Even today, every time I move or lay down my body reminds me of that night. Christy and now Boo Boo a Doberman Rotwrilier we had gotten as a puppy to grow up and protect us, the horses, our cat, my wife and my child now a reality arrived in Colorado two days later the middle of May. The property was 12 miles south of Montrose and then left at Colona. Up 4 miles on the county road, then 4 miles more up a unimproved driveway to one corner of my property at 8000 feet elevation. The people who sold the property to me had plowed a road up to this point. We were not to smart still about Colorado and the only one we had talked to was the real-estate man. Be very careful with these people. My wife now 5 months pregnant, I pulled up to the corner of the property and unloaded the horses and tied them to trees with a couple of bails of hay and a bucket of water. Then unloaded all that we owned onto the ground, everything T.V.s, beds, dishes, couches, chairs, cloths, bathroom stuff, everything that we owned. First laying some plastic sheet down and then covering the stuff with more plastic sheet on top. I would not let my wife do any heavy lifting because she was pregnant. For the most part I did all of the unloading. I was doing a little better but still my body was no were near what it was before. Put up the same pup tent that we had used in the Dream, along with the sleeping bags and the same air mattresses. Spent two weeks in the pup tent as I built a horse shed that we would spend two months in as I built the Rock House thru the summer of 81'. There was no electricity, no water, no bathroom, nothing, just us and all that we had laying on the ground. I built the Rock House the same way the Indians did with a few changes. Lifting rocks that weighted as much as 300 lbs. Then like a jig saw puzzle, putting it together. I would go out along roads and any where I could and find rocks that look like I could build with. I would pick them up and load them into the old horse trailer. Then back to the property where I would unload them onto the ground and then pick them up and piece them together in a wall. Ok, try to build a 8' foot tall wall 50' feet long 9' feet wide and a wall 6' feet tall 50' long on the other side out of rocks. Then support all of it with logs that I cut on the property and drug over to the building spot. Somehow lifting them up on top to support the walls as I built the Rock House and trying not to knock the walls down. I did go buy some 2" x 12" x 12' feet long un plained wood for the roof. By September the cold was coming and my wife was showing our child growing inside her. The Rock House was 25' feet long and half done. Open on one end, I hung several sheets of plastic and a layer of boards for support. Moving everything from the horse shed that I could into the Rock House. Then put a wood burning stove in and all the comforts of home. A old style bath tube and sink. We had a old wood burning stove from the 1920 for cooking on. O' yeah I had gotten a job in July, the whole time carrying water up the hill in a 200 gallon tank in the back of the horse trailer to bath in and drink. In August I began to cut firewood and during all this time building the Rock House. You know what, we were as happy as a larks. My views were clean and without question the most beautiful. My nearest neighbor was a quarter of a mile away and they were never there. The next neighbor was three quarters of a mile away and they where never there as well. It was 20 miles to town and were I worked at a saw mill. I worked at a saw mill on the chain gang pulling boards as they rolled of the planner. The chain never stops, they just keep coming. I am not talking about 2" x 4" x 8' feet long, the big ones, 4"x 12" x 16' feet long. One day of this would kill a normal man, the wood just keeps coming. Going to and from work and shopping for food and supplies. I saw a few street bikes but not many. Dirt biking seemed to be the thing now. I did not have time to think about much, winter was coming I had to get ready. By October it began to get cold, not this chill stuff. Cold!. I had quit building the Rock House and was concentrating on fire wood. Almost everyday gathering and splitting firewood when I got home from work til dark which came quickly around 5 o'clock. The snow started coming down the end of October and there was about 6" or 8" on the ground all the time. The road's were still passable. We had ceresin lanterns for light and a old wood burning heater to try to stay warm. November and still even colder, cold like we had never felt before. 10* to 0* degrees at night and 20* in the day time. Sleeping with all the blankets on the bed that we had. My wife really pregnant now and caring a big ball under her shirt. The baby kicking all the time and I could feel it. First of December her dew date. Waiting as the cold increased now 10* to 20* below 0* and a heavy snow to keep the ground covered all the time. There had not been any snow there for two years. The real-estate person fail to mention the snow and the cold to us. I guess we did not ask, but he new she was pregnant. December 16th 1981, her voice 4 o'clock in the morning saying wake up I think its time. Up and into the Land Cruiser and down the hill as quickly and safely as I could 40 minutes away and to the hospital. She had been seeing a doctor and had it all planed out. A natural birth in a natural birthing room. Yeah the breathing thing. Labor was 12 hrs long and at 4 O'clock that afternoon my son was born. A C-section was the end result. They both were in good condition. He was a little ogen and 20 or 30 test, $5000.00 and three days later we went back to the Rock House with my new son. His name was James the Third. I had insurance but it did not cover it all. Still $2000.00 short and the hospital decided to wave the rest of the money. Christmas and the snow falling hard and lots of it. 20* below 0* now at night 10* to 20* during the heat of the day. Putting both sleeping bags on the bed along with everything else. Our heads under the covers all night long to keep warm and my son 3 weeks old right there beside me. Waking up every morning, the wood stove gone out and the inside thermometer peg out below 25* in the Rock House. Then getting up a hour before and starting a fire so they could get out of bed. Some nights I would get up and have to drive up and down the driveway packing the snow down so I could get out the next day to go to work. I am still on the chain gang, the wood never stops coming, wind, cold, snow, rain, the wood never stops coming. January 1982 a small celebration in the cabin and the snow keeps falling. We are now snowed in, 6 feet deep and no hope of getting out till spring. I had to use a snowmobile to get in and out, kinda a bike, not really. 36 feet of snow fell that winter. My son almost 2 months old and one of the lower neighbors plowing his road, sends a plow up to get us out late January. I decided to quit the chain gang, my land payment caught up for three months. Secured the cabin and took the horses down to a pasture. Then took my son to see the people we had left behind in Texas the first of February 1982. Our first stop was Ron and his wife in Arkansas. When I got there having time to think now. I looked into the mirror, I was 140 lbs of harden steel. I was back, it was the old me in the mirror except there were a few things that did not work the same anymore. But still strong as ever. It never entered my mind as I built the Rock House, chopped wood and dragging those logs of the chain what it was doing for me. Ron and Karen were excited to see us, but there seemed to be a hesitation in Ron's eyes. He showed us the sights and a week went by. Karen came to me one day and said that Ron was getting worse and very paranoid. That he felt like I had been sent there to assassinate him. This really hurt my feelings and we left the next morning without saying a word. Ron loved to ride but he was never a Biker. This was the last time I ever saw Ron. Our next stop was her parents outside Tyler, Texas. Spent a few weeks there and on to David's. His wife had walked out on him and his daughter, choosing career over family. Leaving David to raise there daughter. The 650 twin now gone along with the Husky 250. He had a young new girl friend 10 years younger than he was and rasing his daughter and that was about it. We spent some time there. It was mid March 1982 now and we headed back home to Colorado. This was the last time I ever saw David. We were all different people now and that was that. Excited to get back home. The snow was bad when we left but now it had turned into something even worse, MUD. It packed on every-thing, trying to drive up to the cabin slipping off into ditches and runts. It was terrible. A month of deep mud and spring time came mid April 1982. By May things were good again and everyone was doing fine and started building on the Rock House. One day got out the old Maico 400 dirt bike and went for a ride. I was a little shaky at first. Guess who I found, an old Biker. J.T.Evil was alive and kicking. Two minutes on the bike and there I was, back, the feeling, the feeling of it just feels right. It had been almost three years since I rode. With the wind in my face feel-ing so good and the will of a Biker to ride once again in my heart. I rode like a bird flying thru the air, happy as can be, doing all the things that I love to do on a dirt bike. We had name the cabin, Triple J Rock House for James, Joan and J.T.'s Rock House. JJJ. My son now 6 months old and was my biggest concern. I wanted to raise him and to see that we were all safe and happy. I would not take any chances of leaving him alone with-out a dad. Thru the summer I finished the rock house and cut firewood for the winter. We went around in the Land Cruiser seeing all the beauti-ful things in the area. There is so much to see and do here and I have not seen it all yet. Soon fall was here again and I cut more firewood still working in Montrose doing odd jobs and hauling water up the hill always getting ready for winter. Thanksgiving 1982 as I said before we went up to Idaho to see her dad and back to see that the winter of 1982 was not much different than 81'. In December I decided it would be safer for my family if we came down of the hill as the snow fell and began to get deep again. So we looked after a small ranch for this lady in Ridgeway that winter. Cold is the word during the winter in Ridgeway. Spring came and back to the Rock House we went April 1983. I got a job working in a print shop running a press in Montrose in May. My job in Montrose having to drive so far to work every day 45 miles and gas prices being so high. I started thinking of the possibility of another street bike but it would have to be an enduro of some kind because of the roads to the cabin. After some real thought, I went down and brought a close out new Suzuki SP 500 enduro. It was a very nice bike and the first time back on the street in four years. Every car that got near me I would pull over to the side of the road and freak out for a second. It took me awhile to get over this. It was a strait shot to and from work, most of it on the county road and the 4 mile driveway. So really I did not spend much time with cars on the road. I never rode it on the street for pleasure. But did go out dirt biking on the SP 500 a few times. The one thing I was always doing is cutting firewood and getting ready for another winter. Hauling water and hay all the time and still seeing the sights when we could.We would melt snow in the winter for water and brought fresh water to drink. December again and the snow deep. I decided again it would be safer if we got off the hill. Taking all the important stuff we had and rented a 8 foot x 30 foot trailer in a trailer park in Montrose. I worked in the print shop still and we spent the winter there and 1984 began. It was very nice and then back to the cabin in April of 84'. Still working at the printing shop I rode the Suzuki SP 500 for a little while back and forth that spring and summer but it made me very nervous to be on the street. Dew to other problems I decided to sell SP 500 and I did. My son was still my main concern. I think I did not want to get to comfortable again on the bike riding on the street yet. There was still something there and did not feel comfortable yet on the street. I took care of my family and time went on. The fall 1984 and now knew that the best thing for my family was to move off the hill into the valley below. Took a $1000.00 and brought a 10 foot wide x 50 foot long mobile home in a trailer park 8 miles south of Montrose. Spent New Years day there and 1985 was here. My son was now 4 and school became the word and so was 1986. A interesting story here. Like today and then I loved taking pictures of all things that I see. I loved trying to take photos of birds and animal. One day along the Uncompahgre River out side of Montrose. There was this bird in a tree late fall. I did the best I could to get the birds picture. It was a tough day, light was wrong and cloudy. Did not think much about it at the time and went on my way. One week later got the pictures back and trying to figure out what this bird was with my bird book. I told my wife that it looked like a Perigon Falcon. They were an endangered species at the time and did not think they excised here on the western slope in Colorado. So not being sure as to what it was I took 8x11picture down to the DOW, Division of Wildlife. Went in and showed the picture to one guy, then he left and got another guy. He looked at the picture and said where did you take this. I said a few miles form here on the Uncompahgre River. I said, it looks like a Perigon Falcon to me. He said yeah it is a Perigon and ask me if he could keep the picture. He wanted to take the picture to Denver to use as evidence to prove that Perigon's existed here on the western slope. He was trying to get the main office in Denver to release 60 pairs of Perigon Falcons here on the western slope. 6 months later they did and that is why you are able to see them here today on the western slope. So the next time you see a bird and it might be a Perigon Falcon remember I had something to do with it in a small way. I spent most of my time between 1981 and 1996 taking car of my family. Everything I did, all the money I spent, everywhere I went, my whole world rotated around them. Did all the family Dad things, coached soccer, baseball, basketball and football. In 1987 Sold the old small trailer and moved to the north side of Montrose, Co. on a nice 2 Acer lot in a 14 foot wide x 74 foot long trailer that was mine. This is where Christy had to be put to sleep, a sad day. When my son turned 11 years old, he could not walk and chew gum at the same time. I spent hours and hours everyday and on the weekends teaching him all that new about sports, "I heard that", you said, that must have not taken long, HAH, but it did. He had told me that he wanted to be a athlete when he turned 11yrs old. So I did all I could every day for years.

Sent him to all the best sport camps, sent him to the best tournaments in three states and every where I could so he could become the athlete that he wanted to be. Spent tons of money. Brought all the best stuff for him and in general did everything I could. In the end he became an Athlete. In 1993 we sold the 14 foot wide trailer and brought a house here in Grand Junction, Co. He set 6 school records the first year in JR. High and I am not sure how many records in high school. He was a premier Athlete and time went on. In 1996 after playing it safe all those years doing all I could for my family and now the bicycle laws protecting Bikers as well. Sometime in the 90's they passed a law making bicycles like cars. They had all the rights of a car and the laws as well. For a while the they killed a few bicycle riders on the roads here and there and soon it became safer as more bicycle riders rode on the streets. They were still killing Bikers left and right but I think that it was getting better. At that time as it is now, bicycling is a favorite pass time for a lot of people who love riding bicycles which is fine with me. During all this time I had been dirt biking a little but nothing serious and somehow managed to were out the Maico 400. I saw a cheap Maico 450 in the paper and bought it to play with. Taking the best of both bikes and making one good one. Even tried to get my son and wife involved again but it was not his thing and she had no interest in dirt biking at all. Along with the sports thing that took up most of our time and money. I saw lots of bikes always up here in Colorado during the summer. Have you ever seen a kid standing at a window in a pet store looking at the cutties puppy you have ever seen. Well that was me every time I saw a motorcycle on the road go by. Biking had gotten very popular and much safer thru the 90's and Harley had found a giant hole in main stream of society. I felt like I had to do something. I thought that it was time and the fear was gone. I had the will of a biker to ride again. It had been 15 years since I rode on the street for real. I went down to the Harley shop and looked at a nice purple Custom Sportster but it was way to much and just a look see really because as always, not having much money. Then I went down and brought a 1981 Yamaha XS 1100 dressed street bike for $1400.00. I still have it today and use it to go to and from work on. The Ghost and I are not interested in

Castle Rock and the Ghost on the road near Moab Ut. Just off Hwy 128

going to and from work, we ride in the wind and on the road because that is what we do best. Working as a mechanic at a dealership most of the time in the 90's. I really wanted to ride again in the wind and wanted my wife as always to be apart of this world. She made it clear that she wanted another way of life and no part of mine. In late 1996 my son decided that he no longer wanted to listen to me and my wife now agreeing with him for reasons I do not wish to discuss and decided to move out. If you want to know you can ask me and I will tell you. I did the best I could. But it was not enough. I lost it all again, everything that was important to me no longer existed. I am sorry to be telling you all this but I thought you should know why and how I got to this point. I know this is not a story about moving, people having babies, children growing up, Rock Houses, going to visit old friends, dads, sports or athletes. I was not happy about it at all. So, now what would I do. I am empty of feelings with a heart that is broken. Now can I ride because that is what I do best. There is nothing left and I miss my family.

Soul Of A Biker

With my family now gone, a long hard winter and the spring of
98'. I looked into the mirror, there was not much left of me and
this was a rough time for the soul of a Biker. I spent Thanksgiving,
Christmas and New Years Eve alone that year 1997. Will the land
slide take me down. I had been with my wife for 30 years always
faithful. Seen and done so much with her and then one day she is
not there along with the son that I had devoted all my life to. It is
funny how the night moves so slowly. Bringing the cold hearted
Orb that rules the night always reminding you of the mistakes
that you have made. You get to where you cant tell what mistakes
are real and which are illusions. There was this nice old lady,
Arlene,down at the shop were I worked and she helps with the
books. She gave me a jar of jam she had made me for Christmas.
It was the only present I got that year and I still have it setting out
in plain site. Arlene was a kick to mess with. She is what I think a
grand mother should look like and be. Later on I told her that I
wanted to get her on the back of my bike and she would be my
Bitch. She said, if I was 20 years younger that would be just fine
with her. Arlene was a caring and wonderful woman and had to
move on because of the death of her husband and a friend of
mine. She writes me ever now and then. Again I went to the mirror looking and I ask myself, where are the eyes, the dreams, the
heart, the soul and the will of a Biker. The answer my friend is
blowing in the wind. He is 10 steps just out the door where a
motorcycle is waiting. I went out the door and got on the Yamaha
XS 1100 and was in the wind and on the road again. The problem
was I knew no one who rode, nothing that was going on in the

bike world. I was in a sense starting over. So I went down to the bike shop and saw a flyer on a ride called the Turtle Run. It is a charity fund raiser for children without parents outside Glenwood Springs, CO. in New Castle. It involved leaving Grand Junction CO.. Riding down the old Hwy. 6 that was built before the 1930's. The bike run ((Run is what we call a ride to somewhere and back.)) is about 160 miles round trip to New Castle with a nice picnic and a lot of good people. While there eating and then a auction, now it is a raffle. The auction was fun for everyone. Some from Utah and others from all over. We would bid on stuff and just have a good time, OOing and Ahhing at all the stuff that people would buy and then the money was taken to the kids. I did not know anyone but still had a great time 1998 on the Turtle Run riding my XS 1100 Yamaha. One of the loudest, funniest guys there is Eddy. I did not know him then but later he was our Santa Clause for the 2001 Toys Run put on by the Western Slope Hogs here in Grand Junction. There were a lot of people there that I would meet in the future and would ride with and become friends. Hwy. 6 came out of Denver heading up thru Eisenhower Tunnel or Loveland pass, then thru Vail, and one of the neatest designed canyons around. Glenwood Canyon, a engineering wonder really. Down the road into Glenwood Springs, Grand Junction and on to Cisco, Utah, thru Green River and on to California before the interstate 70 was built somewhere in the 70's I think. There were a lot of great towns cut off by the interstate and soon became Ghost towns. Cisco,UT is one of them. It is a small town between Grand Junction, CO. and Green River,Utah. This is a great old Hwy with lots of history and many, many things to see and do. I have ridden down this Hwy many times and even now as I wait on spring of 2003 I cant wait to ride it again but I will talk and show you all these things later. I had work with this guy, Dustin at a car dealership and one day he came by on his bike a Yamaha V45 late1998. He was going for a ride with some friends and said if I wanted to go that would be fine, so I did. They were very nice people and treated me well. They were mostly weekend worriers and one you might call a Biker that would be me. With my bike made 5 and we rode the back roads thru the orchards of Palisade, CO. Down the Hwy thru Cameo on interstate 70 and the turn off on Hwy 65 to the Grand Mesa National

Forest. Which is one of the many scenic byways here in Colorado. Down a winding and nicely banked canyon called Plateau River Canyon that heads up to the Grand Mesa. Which is the tallest flat topped mountain in the world. There are a 1000 lakes up on top, goriest forest of aspens and spruces mixed with birds and animal thru out this paradise in the clouds. Riding into Mesa city a small town. This is a very nice place for lunch and then back thru the De Beque cut off road. At De Beque left and on to interstate 70 again and thru De Beque Canyon along the Colorado river which is where they filmed a movie call Vanishing Point. The movie is about a car delivery driver and how things stopped making sense to him. He is driving a hoped up 1970 Dodge Challenger. This is a very nice loop ride about 70 miles that a lot of local people do here in the valley of G.J. and back home for me. Later Dustin lost his licence, his car, his wife and his bike because of alcohol and Winter of 98 came. One weekend early 99' I went down and looked at some Harley's again, the same pretty little purple Custom Sportster 1200 setting there calling my name. But that is all I had at the time was my name, not much money as usual. Even so, I am still not quite sure if that is what I wanted to do yet, buy a Harley. There was that reputation thing as well and it seemed that was disappearing as time went on. I did not really have the money for the Harley anyway. So I put off buying a better street bike for awhile. I had wore out the Maico 450 dirt bike and had not ridden on the dirt for a long time 2 or so years. So I thought it would be nice to get back into dirt biking. Early 99' looked around and spent $1200.00 on a KTM 500 MX dirt bike, it is an Austrian made bike. Tall and very fast but a little heavy for a dirt bike and still have it today. I had gone out a few times and was getting back into the flow of dirt biking, riding, jumping and flying as much as possible. You have heard the saying I feel a need for speed, well that's the KTM. When I first got the KTM in 5th gear it would do close to 90 mph on the dirt. That is if you can hang on and keep it on the ground without killing yourself. I soon changed the gears and slowed it down to about 70 mph top end. At this time I meet a nice woman and took her out to the trails with me one day. My lady told me to take it easy, I said ok. Somehow the first time I got on the KTM 500 I popped the clutch and into a strait up and down wheelie, just on the edge of going over backwards doing about 20 mph. I turned around riding back to her and she said something about, you call that taking it easy with both hands around my neck. That is they way I ride on the edge, always have and always will. I love flying in the air, it feels right to me. Today I don't take as many chances as in the past but still ride on the edge. The kids today on there modern dirt bikes make the old guys like me look slow and with out ability. I watch these kids as they fly threw the air 25 feet up and 90 feet out, getting off there bikes in mid air. They don't know about people like me, David, Malcolm Smith, Evel and tons of others who made the path they now follow. We where the first to fly, I guess that is the way it is always, no one remembers where they came from. Today I still ride hard as every on the dirt but my main life desire is in the wind and on the road with the Ghost. At that time we rode every weekend on the dirt and made a day of it with my new family. Yes I had met a nice girl that spring and she had family and moved in June 99'. We got along good enough to make it as a couple for awhile. I think I was in over my head, but that is another long story and this is not a story about girlfriends and being in over your head. Funny thing was, I did not know she knew nothing about motorcycles. She had lead me to believe she did. One day I ask her if she had any desire to ride a dirt bike, her answer was yes that would be fine. Turns out, she is from Ohio and believe it or not she had no idea what a dirt bike was. She had never even seen one or knew what they were for. Yeah I know. How can this be. She had seen a few street bikes but really never payed any attention to them. She had brought two young boys into my life along with a lot of other things and I had to make an adjustment. I love dirt biking, so I got the boys some dirt bicycles and I went out to the trails all the time with her and them, always having fun. Problem was the soul of a Biker needs the open roads and the wind in his face to feel alive. Also during all this, she had mention she wanted to learn how to ride on the street and someday have her own street bike. She told me later she had no idea what she was talking about when it came to motorcycles. Even today and then I could not believe that anyone could know nothing about motorcycles. You have got to know what I did by now. That is right, I went out and brought her a 77' YZ 125 dirt bike, it cost me $700.00. A nice little bike and then began a long processes of teaching her how to ride. She new nothing, never even drove a stick shift of any kind. It was me starting the bike and then her killing it trying to take off and this went on for several weekends. I would hold her and the bike up and then push her and the bike a little in a rolling start so she could ride. For the most part she just puttered around in first gear and this was fine with me. All the time I am patient and teaching her all she needs to know about riding in the dirt. As time went on, street riding had been put on hold again through that summer of 99'. I took my new family every where, Water World in Denver, the zoo, sea aquarium, Elitch Gardens, swimming in Delta, Montrose, Glenwood Springs and dozens of trips to all the beautiful places I know around here and always having fun. I was doing all the dad things as well. Never riding the XS that much and only to and from work. Still having the desire to ride in the wind and winter just around the corner. My new girl friend and I rode the XS 1100 in my first Toys Run Christmas of 99 " early December. It was at the old Harley house on Hwy 6&50 before the building burned to the ground. We stood around there in the parking lot for awhile by the XS as the Bikers came in with toys strapped to there bikes and dressed in a Christmas theme. I think there had to have been a 1000 bikes there that morning. It was awesome to see this for me. All these bikes, every kind and make and all walks of life. A picture was taken of all the bikes in the parking lot and I tried to get one of the pictures but I guess you have to ride a Harley to get one or the fire had them side tracked. I never did get a picture. We road thru the city, I cant remember the route that well but it was down a lot of streets and one of the main drags here in G.J.. I am sure we were looking like we were important and we were. 100's of people lined the streets and waved at us as we drove by. Dropped off the toys at a place called Partners for children and back home. The old Harley shop was a real nice friendly place with a old dinner inside. Had one of those old timey shooting galleries and lots of memorability on the walls. I think a stove or something caught fire and the whole place went up in smoke soon after the Toys Run. Now they have a state of the art place out on the interstate but it seems they left everything that was good about them in the fire of 2000. It was very cold out and that was the last time my lady rode the XS.We were having a lot of fun dirt biking and she learned quickly how to ride. She once pulled up parking the dirt bike, lifting one leg over the seat to lean against the bike. She had felled to put the kick stand down and there she was laying on the bike on the ground me laughing at her saying you know they make kick stands on those things. She is yelling at me and trying to get up and then starts chasing me around calling me some kind of hole near a jack ass. Her feeling where hurt for a second but that was it. She soon became as good as most ladies on the dirt and began to learn to fly in the air. Always trying hard but somehow not quit there. So one day I started teasing her about the baby jumps of 6 inches to a foot in the air and 2 feet long that she was doing. Her telling me to shut up. I kept on about this and looked up as she came up our jumping hill into a 3 foot flying wheelie in the air about 7 feet long. Wow!. Her face lite up and the word became, We Fly. We did this all the time and with friends as well who rode on the dirt. I worked with a guy named Sam at a local tire shop and I am at the same place today. Sam had a brother named Tracy and they were close to being dirt bikers but no really. The one thing they loved to do was to fly and so do I. We would meet out at the trails and find places to jump in the air. This went on for awhile and the year 2000 was here. OH yeah there was something about a melt down and the world coming to an end. I think they called it Y2K or something. The computers were to shut down along with the world I guess. Computers only do what you tell them to do. Still lots of people were freaking out and really doing some silly things. I new this guy who was actually barring things in his back yard and buying up all kinds of stuff. There were so many rumors going around, it was to much and I guess I did not get it. Funny name for a melt down Y2K, huh. But you know this is not a story about melt downs and Y2K's. Early spring 2000 the XS 1100 was old, heavy and big but more than that it did not have the look that I wanted. Just being me, even today I don't like a real big motorcycle. I am not a Ultras Glide kinda person or Road King or any of the big touring bikes. I don't want to make anyone mad here but radios don't belong on motorcycles, I know, I know. OK!!!. I hate to admit this. I really wanted

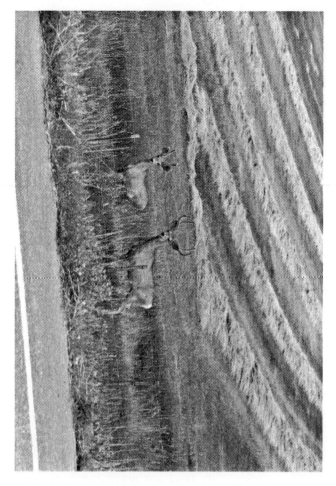

Setting on the bike riding down the road. How beautiful can it get.

a certain look for being in the wind and on the road again. Some kind of V-Twin was the look I wanted. I had bought a nice 1970 Camaro Z-28 in 1996 and had planned on giving it to my son when the time was right, another long story. Ask me if you want and I will tell you. Anyway, I decided to sell the Camaro and did so. My lady did not like this to much but there were other reason as well, I had bought a 1991' Olds Slhoutte station wagon type thing to hall my new family around in and still have it today. So I took the money that I had left over and then some I had saved. Looked around at some bikes, again I looked at the purple Sportster Harley and still more than I could afford. So I went down and brought a 94' Suzuki 1400 Intruder for $3800.00 in late summer of 2000'. I am not a big fan of the jap bikes but did not like the looks of any of the European bikes that I had looked at. The Intruder has that nice shape to it and a V-Twin as well. I began a new life in the wind and on the road. My lady rode behind me on the Intruder two times on short local trips. Soon after buying the Intruder my lady felt that she deserved her own street bike and no longer wanted to ride on the back of mine. Should have seen this coming, huh. Again the street bike had been put on hold. Ya gotta to know what I did. She pouted for awhile that summer me trying to come with a plan to get her a street bike and as usual not having much money. I had spent it all on the Intruder. She had no money and did not make enough money at her job as well to pay for anything let alone warrant an expensive bike. I had already brought her the dirt bike for $700.00. We looked at a few street bikes the summer and fall while dirt biking all the time. While looking around we saw a 95' Yamaha Virago 535 with 4000 miles on it. A very nice little street bike that fit her very well. They wanted $3500.00 for it and way to much for me to afford for her first bike. I do not even know if she would like riding on th street that much. I did not have that much money anyway. She would have to wait for another and now she is really pouting. The problem was I really did love her. It was now the end of 2000 and we rode in my 2nd Toys Run that Christmas early December 2000 on the Intruder 1400. Somehow we ending up on TV as well on the Intruder riding in the parade of presents. The Toys Run began at the newly built Harley shop out of town by the interstate on I-70. This time there had to have been 800 bikes there that day. We road down one of the main drags on 7th street strait to the new Partners place downtown. I though that somehow the city had abandon us on the parade route. A really short ride and very few people to wave as we drove by. This time we went inside and handed the present that we had brought directly into the hands of a beautiful little girl with the light of joy in her face. Of course I just melted as she passed thru the soul of a Biker and so would you. Looked at all the kids and most got to the heart of this Biker. Some did not and back home. Damn man its 2001 now, can you believe that. I went by the place that had the Yamaha Virago 535. They came down to $3000.00 and someone was looking at buying it. They put in the back of there shop on hold. I still do not have that much money anyway. By late spring 2001we were out on the Intruder looking around and I went by the place just checking on her a bike again. There set the Virago 535 out front again. Stopping and the people never came back to get it. How much I said, $3000.00, dang it, I am sorry I only have $2500.00 and that is it. Got on my bike and started to leave. The salesman came running out of the store and stopped me saying do you have $2500.00 on you right now, I said yes, he said you just bought yourself a Virago. Well guess who got all the loving they wanted for the next 2 months. That would be me. But you know what I always got good loving from my lady all the time. The beginning of summer I was so excited and so was she. Now we could be together in the wind and on the road and this made me very happy. I was planning trips with her and with the two boys to some nice places on the bikes. Most without the boys because I don't think kids should be on the back of motorcycles, just to dangerous in my eyes. I went out and bought her a used leather jacket that was in prefect shape, some boots, a helmet, gloves and everything you can think of to make her riding on the street everything it should be. I got her a book to help her pass the motorcycle licence test and she studied it all the time. I am telling her to take the test as they say and ride as I say because what they say is not how it goes on the Hwy. Of course she had her own ideas and failed the test twice. The first time coming out crying, me feeling very bad for her. Three times a charm and she passes the test for her beginners licence and what would I do now. Two bikes, two licences and we ride because that is what I do best.

Desire of a Biker

May 2001 and all is well. I began the long process of teaching my girlfriend how to ride on the street. Because she had spent so much time on the dirt bike, she was close to being ready. Which in my opinion is what ever street Biker should do with a new rider, you should start them in the dirt. It teaches you so much. How the bike will handle in different situations. What speed is and how to fall without getting hurt. Also how to react faster in all situations. The only thing it will not do is help you with cars and trucks on the road coming at you at 70 mph. So all she had to learn was the rules of engagement against cars and trucks on the road. Something I know a lot about. She learned quickly and her first trip was to Cisco, Ut. 60 miles away on the Yamaha Virago 535. Of course I was afraid for her the whole time as we rode. My eyes always on her in my rear view mirror. It is a simple ride and I would suggest if you have a beginner that you do the same. At Cisco we stopped and I ask how she was doing. Her answer was,what are you talking about. She was and is a very good street bike rider and a fair dirt biker as well. So at Cisco I took a picture and then back home about 120 miles round trip. We talk about the ride and she had no problems and was ready to go again. So I planned a over night trip to Moab, Ut. first of June about 120 miles away. Had someone look after the boys and down the road we went. From Grand Junction down the interstate 70 to Cisco. There is not much to look at but once you turn onto Hwy 128 and then thru Dewey, a old gas station there, that is it. The gas station has been closed for many years do to the interstate taking all the traffic. At Dewey, there is an old suspension bridge that was built in the 1910's or so.

In 1986 I took my first family driving across it in a V-W Bus. I was taking my family on a vacation to Moab. Today you cant drive across the bridge anymore but you can stop and get out and walk across it. Very nice place and lots of history. Just do it. The road is without question one of the best hwy's you can ride a bike on. The Colorado there beside you all the time in a canyon of wonder. To date I have made 30 trips to Moab and it always fills my mind and body with the true feeling of what riding a bike is all about. Here is what you should do. On a clear day with very little traffic. Ease out of Cisco and just take a slow ride down thru the canyon, stopping and taking it all in all the way to Moab. Then turn around and go back slowly the same way you came because it is as beautiful both ways. Stopping all the time to look and see the wonders and beauty of this canyon, it is magnificent. Once back at Cisco then turn and back the way you came except this time take a real ride on your bike. Just feel the wind and ride the road. Take the corners hard leaning into them, feel the corners, fly like a bird thru the canyon, just seeing the road. The road is banked just right. The ups and downs give you that feeling in you stomach like your on a roller coaster. Some of the corners disappear form your eye sight making you hesitate a little as you drop off left into a valley. The rock hill sides are right there beside you giving you that real feeling of speed. At Moab turn and back to Cisco the same way you came. Head back with the same attitude towards the road, ride, fly and feel the road as it was built with curves and lots of them. Always being safe the first priority. Here are some guide lines for riding down curvy roads that I use and in general really. You should always follow the speed signs to a T, this means, if it says a corner is 30 mph then that is what you should do. No question asked. But if you decide to push a little then this is what I would do. First what kind of bike are you riding, a jap bullet bike is going to handle way better than a dressed Harley Ultra Glide. So if I am riding a motorcycle that can handle corners and I was a novice, just above a beginner, no faster than 5 mph over the curve speed limits. Don't be stupid, people die out there all the time thinking they can handle there bikes in corners. R-I-G-H-T. If I was amateur two steps above a beginner, then I would stay around 10 mph over the curve limits. If I was a very experienced Biker on the right bike then 15 mph over the curve limits will give you a real good thrill and maybe put you in a ditch. Wouldn't that be fun. I of course never do this sort of thing. My fingers are crossed. Please never exceed the speed limits, it is just not safe and I don't want to hear that you got hurt. Really you are my brothers and sisters out there on the roads and I do care. O' Yeah, I failed to mention this earlier, For Pete sakes don't drink alcohol and drive. Riding a bike takes all of your senses being totally aware of everything around you. Alcohol, slows your eyes and mind down to much and you can be killed very easily out there on the roads. Please be very careful. Once you have ridden the Cisco to Moab road in the two separate ways, you will thank me I promise. Back to her first real trip. We stayed that night at Motel 6 in Moab. Spent some nice time in the hot tube, it really does help relax you and makes for a nicer trip. There were a lot of bikes there and on the roads that day. It was amazing that most of them were Harley's. My eyes always watching them with a light on. Back home the next day thru the canyon again. It is just as beautiful one way and more the other it seems each time. Excess me for a little bit here, I am going for a little ride. November 2nd 2002 Saturday and they have a Toy Run in Delta, CO., about 40 miles away. It is about 38* outside, clouded and the wind is blowing about 15 mph. Guess I will dress warm and give it a shot. There is a 10* change between here and there. Made it about 30 miles and the clouds looked like snow and turned back. Not much out there between Junction and Delta. Even still I had I nice ride and took a few pictures along the way, it was freezing. Today, Sunday the 3rd and I am going out the old Cisco Hwy 6 and take a few pictures of a old bridge built in 1931. It is the last of bridges as they tear them down and put up new ones. It is sunny and very nice out. Not to warm still 40* but the sun is out and it will be a nice ride around 50 miles. I will let you know how the ride was. Well, just got back and a real nice ride. A little cold though. I took 3 friends out, Jim, Tom and Lindsay on the old Hwy 6, all Harley's. Turns out the lady I went with today, when she was a little girl, rode down this Hwy with her dad and family all the time to Moab and Green River back in the 50's and 60's before the interstate. She had not seen or thought about this road for along time and was grateful that I suggested it. I would like to bring up a point here, please take care of the wonders of our world. I cant believe people still destroy things without thinking. There is a great state line maker built back in the 20's on the old Hwy 6 at the border between Colorado and Utah. It has been damage terribly, almost to where it is hard to read the words on it. This is not necessary. Anyway, as I ride down this two lane blacktop Hwy 6. I can see a 1938 Chevy two door going down the road and hearing the kids in the back seat saying, its hot, I am thirsty, can we stop. Stopping at the old border line to rest and celebrate the crossing into another state. The kids playing and the parents walking about stretching there legs. In the summer it can get to be over 100* out there in the high desert. In the winter below freezing. On the way back we stopped, had coffee and talk of our adventures in the wind and on the road and now I am here.

In June 2001 my lady and I rode a few times locally and dirt biked a lot. One day I went down to the Harley shop and the "H" is in my eyes. I am still not a big fan of the jap bikes. There were so many Harley's now on the road in 2001. It seems every one was riding a Harley. Every kind of person, age is not a factor young or old. Life style was not a factor as well and it seemed that it was time for me to move into the Harley I had always wanted. People had a much nicer attitude towards Bikers now and they almost can see you. "Not really". They are still killing Bikers left and right out there, so please be careful. Selling the 1400 Intruder in one day believe it or not and put my name on a Burnt Orange 1200 Custom Sportster, not really my favorite color but the only custom they had at the time. It was on display from Harley for 2 weeks, setting up on a self 10 feet in the air. I would have to wait this time before I could get have my Harley. Yes, Now I can here ya, "Sportster", but the Sportster was the bike that started it all going in one direction. Remember, Evel, Bronson and also the twins in 1970 thru 73' on the dirt flat tracks winning lots of races and world championships. The twins were always in the news media and on the front sports pages, magazines and T.V. all the time till 74'. You have to admit the Sportsters are very nice looking when they are done up right and back then they were very affordable as today. I would like to share a little history here that I have learned. I don't set around reading Harley books and don't plan on it. H-D was and is known as The Motor Company, I call my bike the Silver Ghost returned before I knew any of this. The first H-D engine was designed in 1899, the first production bike ever sold was called the Silent Grey Fellow developed in 1900 and built in 1903 until 1908. It was the engine that was the focal point of the bike and it was grey. In 1909 they changed there design. Close but not quite. The Silver Ghost and the 88 engine was developed in 1999, 100 years after the Old Grey Fellow. Ok I can here you. The Old Grey Fellow was called a F head and the Ghost 2002 is called a Fat head. Just me being silly here. The Super Glide 2 was the first factory custom bike built by Willie G. Davidson Jr. a design engineer after they took it back from AMF and his grandfather designed the Old Grey Fellow all those years ago. Ok I will stop. Don't yell at me. But you should know this is not a book about Harley's. When H-D was almost down and out AMF (American Machine and Foundry) bought them out in 1969. It was not a good time for "H" and there riders. Most of the bikes were not as they should be. From what I understand lots of problems. AMF made bowling balls believe it or not and some sports equipment. WHAT!!!. 12 years later 1981 Willie Davidson and some executives at H-D got some money together and bought H-D back from AMF. Here is my point, you will never guess what the longest production bike made, the most manufactured and sold by H-D. Nope, it is the Sportster. But you know that this is not a story about the Harley Family or the Davidson family or even Harley motorcycles. Anyway, my Sportster was very pretty in my eyes and the sad thing is you cant ride your Harley until you buy it. So as I was waiting I would go down and look at it with the desire of a Biker to ride the very thing he loves the most, his motorcycle. I was hoping they would get it down off the self early. NOOO! They never did. So one day walk in looking an wanting my bike and there sets the purple Custom Sportster that I wanted in the beginning 3 years ago. They had just taken it out of the crate, so I walk over and said to my friend Gary a salesman there, who I new before he worked at H-D and a very nice guy. A Preacher believe it or not. Can I have that one I asked. The answer was yes, July 1st, 2001. I am not sure but somehow with his help I got the Sportster for $9,500.00 a $ 1000.00 under there list price. As you can imagine I was so very alated with my new Harley and could not wait to ride in the wind. Man, I was so excite and you would be too. I called my

Jim waves at me as I take his picture doing 70 mph. Coming back from
Sturgis

new bike Passion, yeah I know, how silly, but not to me. In my eyes there are always two things worth doing anytime of the day. One is riding Passion and the other is making love to a woman with Passion. The truth. But wait there is more, if you buy now, you get a bonus plan. Seems that things were not going to well anymore between my girlfriend and I. So we broke up July 4TH 2001 and we would stay friends. I think she did not like the idea of me getting a new bike so soon after getting the Intruder 1400 and her eyes were on a new Sportster as well. I think you call it jealousy but I could be wrong. I guess there were other things as well, ask me and I will tell you. Alright, I heard what you said, jack ass setting in a hole. I really am a nice guy and I do the best that I can, I really do. I guess I am too nice of a guy sometimes and if you truly need help I will be there and with the heart of a Biker but I am no fool either. But ya gotta know, what will I do. I ride because that is what I do best and now with the desire of the Biker and Passion, I rode a lot, every where and every weekend. Joined the local Harley Hogs club and went on short runs with them. Just looking around it seems to me that 50% of the Harley riders today are in some way Veterans who have served in our military which is fine with me. So the next time you see a Biker, remember that he or she may have severed in some way to protect your right to say the word Freedom. Although I did not quit fit in with these people in the Hog club. I was and still am a low budget rider even today and most of them are not. It seemed they were very interested in my money and other peoples money as well to fund there charity activities. Which is a good thing for some but for me I just want to ride because I have a real desire too. Believe it or not survey says the average Harley owner makes $80,000 a year. Which puts me below poverty level in there eyes and mine as well. They are kinda strait laced and a little stiff as well and that is ok. Some Bikers are I guess. I am not that way and I am not so sure that is how Bikers should be. I am loose and can handle most anything that does not involve hurting anyone or anything. I just want to ride and have fun. The Colorado Harley State rally was here in G.J. July, 2001 and at the Adams Mark Hotel. I cant even afford a cup of coffee there. I did not have much to do with this as well, it is to stiff for me. Biking should be fun and I like to be friendly towards everyone. Jap bikes or what ever. I am not a fan of jap bikes. During the state rally the Hardly Angels (a procession riding team of woman on Harley's) were in town and I saw them for the first time. They were very exciting and good at what they do. They take a lot of risk in there show. Funny thing was, they did tricks that I had been doing for 30 years along with Evel and never thought to ask them if Evel had some kind of influence on them as he did me. One of the neat things the Hog club does, is called a breakfast run. It is where you go to 3 different peoples houses. The first is coffee and donuts and then a little ride to the next house for the main breakfast, eggs, beacon and stuff like that. Another short ride and to the third house and brunch, with coffee and cake. Kinda nice really but not much riding, which is what I like to do. A lot of riders are A to Z getting there type stuff. I guess I am a ABC and all the letters in between kinda rider, stopping and seeing all that can. Learning and talking to all that will talk to me. I love the small town people and there way of seeing and doing things. It is so different today from when I started riding years ago, everything is reversed. The people are nicer and are always willing to talk in the small towns but the big cities are cold and without feeling. I guess this is OK. It seemed to me most of the Hog club members are A to Z riders which is not me at all. They go from point A to point Z most of the time. Not me, I stop all the time, looking and taking pictures because in my mind without pictures why go. 20 years from now you will have forgotten some of the special things that you saw. I hate the idea of this. Sometimes I will stop and look at a possible view, old house, valley, mountain, tree, animal or just a picture that I thought was there. Then see that is not and move on to stop again. I see so many beautiful things doing this. I wish you could see them with my eyes and the Passion I feel, maybe some of you do. In between riding with the Hogs, taking pictures of them constantly. I met a guy named Jim at one of the Hog meetings. I noticed he had a real fire burning in his eyes for riding. We spoke of riding one day together and thought we should soon, more on that later. At this time I did a lot of riding by myself, taking pictures of what I saw and do you know why because that is what Passion is and what I do best.

The Return of a Biker

There was a nice ride that I did late July on my Purple Sportster that I called Passion, my girlfriend was no longer in my life. Leaving G.J. and down the old Hwy 6 riding thru De Beque Canyon and many small cities like Parachute and Rifle from years past towards Glenwood Springs. Which is a neat little city in its self. There is a nice Harley shop there and lots of history though out the city. A great hot springs pool and a really nice old hotel right next door called the Hotel Colorado from the 30's. I hope in the future they leave this hotel alone and the way that it is. It seems they always want to tear things down. Which brings up a point. They are taking and tearing down our beauty, wonders and history leaving nothing. Taking it away from us left and right out there on the roads. If you don't get out there and see them they will not be there in the future. There is so much that is already gone. Believe me. Once in Glenwood Springs, left on Hwy 82 and head towards Carbondale. Mt. Sopris will be in plain site, a 14,000 foot hill. Man what nice mountain and then left thru Carbondale on Hwy 133 along the Crystal River in the White River Natl. forest. Wow, so much beauty. You can hear, see, feel and smell the beauty of this Hwy as you ride along it. There is a lot to see and do, so stop. You will come to a road that says Marble that way, take it. This is where most of the marble that you see and have everywhere in your house and places. Statutes, table tops, chess pieces, lamp bases, side walks and all kinds of stuff made of marble come from this quarry. Stop and get yourself a piece but don't tell anyone, kkk. Back out on Hwy 133 and up the hill to McClure pass. A great view at the top, don't just drive by, stop and take it in. Down the hill thru Hotchkiss and into Delta. Yeah I know, there are lots of side trips here so lets take the one over the Grand Mesa before you get to Delta. "Are you happy now". Go north on Hwy 65, uumm, up a long winding road to the top of the Mesa with views of Cedaredge, Delta and the valley below which are wonderful. Into Grand Mesa Natl. forest, yeah baby, paradise in the clouds. So many lakes to see, miles of the most awesome forest, trails to walk, birds and animals are all around you singing and playing. To me this is what biking is all about. Local riders flock to the mesa on the weekends in the spring, summer and fall. It is a prefect ride down a nice road and so much to see and do. On the other side is the town of Mesa still on Hwy. 65 and a nice place for lunch or just a break. I don't want to stop here so lets keep going. Take a back road Hwy 330 into Collbran and up to Vega Lake State park, "yeah you gotta pay". But if you want just turn around and back down to Mesa and Hwy 65 thru Plateau Canyon that I spoke of earlier. There are very nice banked curves in the road and the river running beside you. Ahh man, nice. Wait a minute here!, lets go back to Delta where we turned of to go up to the Mesa on Hwy 65. Lets go back up to Hotchkiss a few miles and take Hwy 92 east for awhile. Do you remember who Joe Crocker is, yeah the singer, remember the song With a Little Help From my Friends. He started his singing career late 60's and was at Woodstock in 1969. Then thru the 70's and even in the 90's with some woman singer, Up Were We Belong. Cant remember her name, but this not a story about singers. Anyway on Hwy 92 in Cawford, Joe Crocker owns a restaurant called Mad Dog Café. It is a pretty nice place and the food is pretty good too. You should stop, have a bite to eat and with a little history here to see as well. I was there this summer 2002 with my old girlfriend and my riding buddy Jim. Jim and I have been ridden together for 2 years now. We have been to some great places and I will speak of them later. At Mad Dogs we stop and had lunch. While we were there my lady and Jim filled out a questioner for the Mad Dog Café. Of course this was a waste of time, lets ride in my eyes, just kidding don't yell at me. I was there to have fun and really I am never in that big of a hurry. You had to take the paper up a hill and to the Mad Dog curio shop, so we did. Nice short walk thought a nice garden eating area. Once inside we looked around at some neat stuff of Joe

Crocker's on display and they had t-shirts and stuff you could buy. My lady and Jim turned in there papers and the lady behind the cash register handed both of them this real nice bandana with the Mad Dog stuff printed all over it. Humm, I tried to explain to the lady that I had filled out the questioner but lost it coming up the hill. R-I-G-H-T she said and if I wanted to go get one and fill it out that would be ok with her. We thanked her and out the door with Jim and my lady saying, my what a nice bandana we have and asking me where mine was. I said something about jack asses with a hole and proceeded to show them my 2002 Cripple Creek pin and 2002 Ignacio 4-Corners pin on my tool bag mounted on my bike the Ghost. They said, yeah waving the bandana's in my face, but these are very nice, as they talked to each other about how nice there bandana's were. We were all laughing and having a good time as always. I did not get a bandana that day, maybe later. Headed east out of Cawford on Hwy 92 still and Lake Cawford state park there on the right. A nice place as well but totally empty of water because of a drought happing at the time. Along the north side of the Black Canyon of the Gunnison with a great road, hills and views of the Gunnison River below. Across the Blue Mesa lake dam. Humm, damn which way will I go, left or right east or west. One just as beautiful as the other. Lets go left back to G.J. on Hwy 50 headed west from the Blue Mesa Lake dam. A very nice high plains mountain ride to Cimarron where there is a old train depot display and the Marrow Point dam. A must see. A small pass and by a sign saying the south entrance of the Black Canyon of the Gunnison. If you have time this is with out a doubt a must do. It is 10 times the beauty of the Royal Gorge Canyon. It is a pay area, but well worth the trip up to the canyon walls. Back down the way you came and west into Montrose still on Hwy 50 heading west towards G.J. You will go thru Delta again and a interesting story here. A nice old city and was voted Americas Most Beautiful one year. They have painted lots of murals on all of the store building walls as you drive along the main drag downtown. Most are very well done and of all kinds of things. From animals to Indians on horses, corn fields and forest. Anyway, it seems back in the 80's, remember the Quait war. I guess some ambassador from there came thru Delta and was so impressed with there murals and the city in general donated

Grand Canyon. A Lady Raven above me with a rainbow. Now I see this.

one and half million dollars to the city. They were to build a park and a swimming pool. Which is one of the best around. Stop and see this park it very nice. You will never guess what the next city is called. Whitewater. Yes this a little to close to Whitehouse for me, but this is not the same city in any way. Just a street sign in the road. I tell you what, you should turn left here on Hwy 141 headed south to Gateway and Naturita. You climb up out of the valley in a nice tight canyon onto the Uncompahgre Plateau, the longest running plateau in the world. The Grand Mesa across the valley being the biggest flat topped mountain in the world. Ladies and Gentlemen, Evils is in the building and it don't get much better than this. Silent running comes to mind thru a valley with nice old farms and a little history along the way. A pleasant little store and lunch place with nice people in Gateway and that is about it. Still heading south on Hwy. 141 and in a valley I called the Valley of the Kings. Prefect is the word and the road thru the deep open valley into Naturita. A nice small town. Are you tried yet. "Not me". Lets go back a mile or two and take Hwy 90 west into Utah. Going thru Bedrock, Paradox and coming to Hwy 191 just south of Moab,UT. There are certain times of the year I have to say in Utah when it is as good as it gets. They have some of the nicest people and most majestic places to go, see and do. No question asked. The roads are well maintained and it seems they all start in Moab Ut.. So lets go north out of Moab. Just outside Moab there is a little known Hwy 279 on the left that is worth riding down. Taking you along the Colorado River with Pot Handle Arche along the way there on the road and ending up at a old salt mine. A gorgeous ride both ways and back to Hwy 191. Lets turn left one mile to Arches Natl. Park. Yep, it is a pay area, but if you have time and some money still in your pocket, you must drive this road thru the history and the winds of time. There are fantastic rock formations and of course the arches there as well. You can spend the night or turn and come back the way you came. Getting back to Hwy 191 headed north for 15 miles and the Dead Horse Point, Canyon Lands Natl. Park cut off. Turning left onto Hwy 313 and up thru a terrific valley onto the high plains. You wonder what on earth could be up here worth looking at and worth riding all this way to see. I guess it really is a nice ride out across the open plains on top. It gives me a real feeling of freedom. It feels very good up there with no fences lining the roads. It is a feeling of being one with the essences of the area that surrounds you. I can feel the Indians on horse back riding there beside me. I guess I feel that way about everywhere I go. But still Utah is a wonderful place to ride in. The nice thing about Utah is. There are separate fee's for motorcycle's at most of these places you go. It is usual $2.00 to $4.00 for a day pass. At the end of Hwy 313, left to Dead Horse Point or strait to Canyon Lands. Both equally above the rest of the world in the wonder of there beauty. The first, second and third time I saw Dead Horse Point. I was standing there looking out into the silent air that surrounds you. I took a step back in total aw of this view each time. As you stand there looking off into her majesty wonder of time. The Colorado river flowing 1000 feet below as it has for 1,000' s of years. I can feel it draw me in, lifting the heart of a Biker out into the open spaces of time and beauty. The Grand Canyon is a wonderful place and I will talk of it later. Dead Horse Point has the power to control your heart in my eyes. Words or pictures can not do Dead Horse Point justice. Standing at the point if you look down below, over to the left of the Colorado River you can see the Ghost of a horse laying on the valley floor below. It is more than clear to see. There are some stories about this place and I am not sure which is true or maybe they all are. For me I would like to think they are all true. I cant say enough about this place. It has a hold on me and want let me go. I think if you see Dead Horse Point it will have a hold on you as well. Back out to Hwy. 313 an right strait to Canyon Lands Natl. Park. You can stand in one place there and look back at Dead Horse Point. You should ride over to a old volcano called the Upheaval Dome. Really a very neat looking place and then out to Grand View Point. Very nice but Dead Horse is the place in my eyes. So back down the hill on Hwy 313 and right on Hwy 191 almost to Moab. Then lets go left on Hwy 128 down the Colorado River road, Dewey Bridge that I spoke of earlier and then to Cisco but I want to stop at Castle Rock first. 20 miles out of Moab and right on a Hwy they call the La Salle Mountain loop. You can almost go to the top of the La Salle mountains before the road turns to dirt and I turned back because of the wash board road at the top. Even still it is well worth the time to go up because it is just as majestic one way as the other coming down. A little history as well. There was some kind of Indian battle there in this valley years ago. Castle Rock views are beautiful and remind me of the movies. I see the Indians setting on there horses all around me. I can hear them too singing songs of greatness. Once back out and down the road I talked about before Hwy 128. I would say this is the best river ride you can do on a motorcycle and back to Cisco. Is anyone tired yet, never. Out of Cisco lets get on the interstate 70 and head towards Green River. An oasis in the high desert. Better get some gas it's a long way to the next stop from here almost 100 miles. Green River really is an oasis. The people are nice and that is about it there in the high desert. The waters of the Green River flow thru the city and there is a little history here as well. Something I forgot to mention. The rest areas in Utah are with a doubt the best that I have ever seen or relieved myself in. Ok, I have to pee a lot when I am on the road and know what I am talking about when it comes to outhouses. "Happy now". You ladies know what I am talking about, come on ladies back me up here. The old Hwy 6 goes thru here as well and you can still see a little of that era around the city for awhile. They will tear it down soon I am sure. Back to the interstate70 down about 10 miles and take the turn off to Hanksville on Hwy 24. We are still in Utah Huh. This road leads to Lake Powell but I want to stay on Hwy 24 and head thru Capital Reef Natl. Park. There is no fee thru most of this park and is a dream in itself. The color, beauty, wonder, history is amazing and the road is prefect. Thru Torrey and Whipup on a high country mountain road Hwy 72 to Fremont Junction and interstate 70 again. If you fell like you are tired here I guess we you should go back to Grand Junction thru Green River on interstate 70 and see what the Hog club is doing back at home.Well they have decided to take a trip over to Torrey,UT. for a over nighter and about 12 bikes are going. I am still riding Passion. We stopped at Crescent Junction on interstate 70 just before Green River to split up because no one wanted to go the same way. 7 bikes and me took the Hanksville Hwy 24 and stopping in Hanksville for lunch. Thru Capital Reef and Torrey never stopping to see anything. O' My so many things to see and do. This was not me at all. Some of them refereed to me as being like a ghost always disappearing and reappearing out of nowhere. I am always stopping and taking pictures as often as I can. I do this a lot because I hate passing up anything to see and do. Torrey about 200 miles from where we started and a motel where there was some question about the rooms. 400 miles to me is a day trip so I decided to go back to G.J. and I would save some money. Always stopping along the way to see some things as I rode back. You really should do this ride. Next thing the Hog club had on there agenda was a poker run fund raisers and the next weekend a overnighter to Bluff Utah. There seem to be some question here as which way to go. 5 bikes took the interstate to Moab then to Bluff. 4 of us took Hwy 141 thru Gateway, Naturita, Dove Creek. Then Hwy 666 to Monticello UT. Turning heading south on Hwy 191 to Bluff about 300 miles. This is one heck of a nice ride. Stayed at a nice hotel in Bluff and went down to Twin Towers restaurant and had dinner then back to the hotel were we set out in front of our rooms. We talked about the roads and the things that we had seen over the years. Later I spent some time in the hot tube and then we were up the next day to ride back to G.J. stopping at Wilsons Archer right on the Hwy. This is a very nice ride and lots of wonderful country to see. It is now mid August and there is a well known but little known rally in Cripple Creek, CO. It is a Veterans Rally or salute to Veterans who have served. They meet in Woodland Park close to Pikes Peak on the west side. 2 to 3000 bikes strong and ride into Cripple Creek 20 miles away. It is a parade led by the flag that they gave apart of there live to. The Hog club is going and meets in Parachute, CO. 40 miles from G.J. We are 10 bikes leaving at 10:00 am Friday morning. Down I-70 and thru Glenwood Canyon, Ummm, now that is a canyon and onto Minturn just before Vail where we meet 2 other bikes and off we go right on Hwy 24. This road goes in a valley along the most 14,000 footers you can see at one time in Colorado. Over Tennessee pass, Leadville, Buena vista and take a right at Johnson's Village staying on 24 headed east. I like to stay at the back of the pack and sometimes stop and take pictures but one of the guys bike is giving him trouble. The bike had been giving him trouble since we left and we had to stop serval times while he was trying to figure out why. I ended up at the front of the pack which is ok sometimes. Doing 70 mph on Hwy 24 I looked up and saw a magnificent heard of Buffalo standing right on the highway. There was the biggest fricken buffalo buck I have ever seen standing right there on the road next to me. I can not stop because I am up front and if I do they all do. Even if I try to get to the back of the pack it would make some stop or maybe cause a problem. So I have to keep going. I am crying and making a promise never to ride in a large group again. It was the most wonderful thing you can see in my eyes and reminded me of the day when they roamed freely everywhere here in Colorado. The buffalo stands for wide open freedom in my eyes. This is a nice high plains ride and I looked up to see the old gas station in Glentivar from the first dream to Colorado. Is was where I had stopped to clean my windshield and sunglasses form mud and the guy saying those towels are for regular customers. The place was closed and garbage pilled around it everywhere. Now on the road that we took to Cripple Creek all those years ago in the first dream and the return of the Biker. Clouds were moving in fast and I moved on quickly to Cripple Creek with a real chill in the air. Not having a place to stay I was concerned about finding a camping sight. Its August and cold for pete sakes. There is a KOA up out of Cripple Creek over 10,000 foot elevation and there I would stay. $20.00 to put my tent on the ground on the side of a hill. "Wow". A lite rain and quickly putting up my tent and getting everything inside. The rain turned to hail and hiding from it inside the tent. The sound of the hail on the tent was loud and it was very cold. It seems with the Hog club, I was more or less like step child and not always a part of things. Turns out they have all gotten cabins here at the KOA. The hail stops and they tell me to drag my tent down next to the cabins and that is what I did. Setting it back up in front of one of the cabins. We took a shuttle bus and went into Cripple Creek. Had dinner and walk about to see things, very nice place with lots of history. Some gammbled and lost there asses. Then back to the KOA at 12:00 midnight and now it is very cold out 35*. Into the tent I go. I have a very old summer sleeping bag and good to about 40* at best. Trying to keep warm with all I have to wear on. It is a very long night and I am very cold with my lady easing into my mind. In the morning about 4 AM inside the tent, there is ice hanging down from the top and it is about 28* outside. I did not sleep that night and had time to think about things and soon missed my lady very much. Silly me, I happen to love her, even today. I have loved three woman in my life. She was the only one that I was totally head over heals in love with. The one lady that makes you relax just holding her hand. A kiss is not a kiss unless its from her lips. I will talk of this later. I got up around 5 AM. and over to the campers convenience building there at the KOA. Were they have a place to set down with coffee and a TV you can watch. I got warm and waited for the day to begin. Soon there after in walks one by one all these Combat Vets 10 or so. Who like me slept on the ground and were freezing but would not admit it. They just wanted coffee they said. One of them said, did anyone freeze there butts off last night and a complete silent's in the room. The sun came up and a warm welcome sight for me. Packed and loaded my bike and off I went by myself to take some pictures. All the time thinking about my lady back in G.J. After taking a few pics and 11 AM. in the morning Saturday, I decided to head back and try to salvage my relationship with her. Rode strait back 250 miles and stopped to see if I could get a picture of the buffalo to no avail. They had moved away form the road and I would have to wait til next year. Riding a different way making a loop thru Salina, Monarch Pass and Gunnison. Only stopping to get gas all the way home. I called her as I walk in the door form my house. The next weekend was Ignacio 4-Corners Rally September 1st labor day 2001. I wondered if she still wanted to go. Yes was her answer. I had promised her before we broke up that I would take her to 4-corners no matter what. I always keep my promises if I can. Here is a promise for you. I will be Riding in the Wind and if I see you I will say hello.

Ignacio September 1st
Labor Day 2001

The Hog group had left Thursday and made motel reservation in Durango near Ignacio. I had already planned the trip with Jim to go down and we would camp Saturday night. I did not know him that well at this time. Jim on Lady his 2001 soft tail standard looking like as classy as ever. My lady on her Yamaha Virago and me on Passion. We meet at a service station here in G.J. and off we went headed south on Hwy 50 thru Montrose, Ridgway and Ouray to Silverton, Durango and then Ignacio. This is a must do ride thru the San Juan Mountain's for anyone who rides a motorcycle. I know I keep saying that but this ride is just to much. On a clear day the views are the best in the world. They call it the million dollar Hwy and the little Switzerland of America. The roads are nice and curvy lined with massive walls of rocks on one side and a shear drop off's a 1000 feet deep on the other. Along with the tops of the most majestic mountains you have every seen or ridden thru. There are water falls, rivers, lakes and a forest unmatched by any in the world. The history is all around you and you can imagine how it must of felt trying to cross this massive area in a horse drawn wagon. We stopped in Montrose for breakfast and meet a guy on an old shovel looking like Captain America headed for 4-corners. We talked and I suggested he ride with us and off we went now 4 bikes. Stopped in Ouray because you have too. "Just do it". We are seeing all kinds of bikes and loving every minute of it. Then up and over Red Mountain Pass 11,000 feet, hang on to your sense's and your eye balls. It is a unbelievable ride. The clouds seem to be creeping in on us and into Silverton a great little city with a historical train ride that I have never taken but really want to someday. All this a must see. In Silverton the clouds are now on us with a lite rain. The cold is now a factor as well. Up over Molasses Pass and off in the distance is the biggest dark cloud full of rain and no where to hide. So I motioned everyone to stop as I am leading. I don't mind leading, I am a very good rider and my first concern is to protect the pack. Here is a good rule if you are the road captain or lead bike of a pack. Always ride to the level of you least experienced Biker. See the road with there eyes and everyone gets home safe. Something else here, if there is something that you question concerning safety, for pete sakes say something to somebody. You don't have to be rood, but you might safe someone's life, kkk. Anyway I motioned everyone to stop and we put on all the warm stuff we had along with the rain suits. As the cloud got closer and now almost on us and it is getting very cold. Jim had this new rain suit and he had never put in on before. As I set there looking at the clouds and the sky turning black. Then watching him struggle with this suit. Looking at my lady and then at Jim. Then the words from Jim's mouth, I messed up, I got in on backwards. My lady and I just cracked up laughing and the clouds now on top of us. Jim is hurrying as fast as he could to get the suit on and I am saying are you done yet. The cloud hits us and off we went in the rain freezing and I am still laughing. Now my lady is a warm day, no wind and hates being cold kinda rider so you can imagine how she felt. She never complained the whole time. Just had that puppy look in her eyes as to say, it will get better, right. I am saying yes always to her. Dropping off the mountain and down into Durango we went wet and freezing. It was 3 PM and we stopped to eat warming up and off to Ignacio. There were 1000's of bikes, all kinds every where in Durango. Harley's were the majority bike there and every walk of life was there as well. A sea of black leather and chrome surrounds you the whole time. A short trip from Durango and passing 100's of bikes coming and going to and from Ignacio. The sun had come out and it had gotten a lot warmer. The excitement had kicked in and all was well. Ignacio is a small town with a large county fair grounds and that is where everyone meets. It is the whole show. Vendors, bands, food, games, rides, everything you can imagine having to do with a bike or Bikers is there and my favorite the Gauntlet. Humm, should I say something, yes I have too. The Gauntlet is where the guys and ladies as well, like to set up a gauntlet of some kind along a road or entrance way. It is just as much fun for the guys as it is for the ladies. These are wonderful ladies doing what we want them to do and all in fun. As the ladies come in on there bikes or the back of bikes, they are ask to show there thinges, ah lets see, lift there shirts and show there breast. I am trying to keep from saying there Tits. "Woops!". I showed mine but they told me to put my shirt down and this hurt my feelings. I thought I had a nice pair, I guess not O' well. It is a hoot and everyone enjoys this very much. It might be against the law though but it is all in good fun. Most ladies don't show and some do. Of course I never look. R-I-G-H-T. My lady caught me looking and said how would I feel if she did it. Ahh, humm, thinking. Camping is free there on the fair grounds. So we pulled up and pitched the tent right there at the end of the gauntlet. Jim stayed with the other guy who had made a motel reservation in Durango and would meet us there later. I had the tent set up an was the best I had ever done, strait, tight and neat. There is a sea of tents and 1000's of people and bikes everywhere. You can hear the crowd yelling and screaming ever time a lady came thru the gauntlet showing her breast. Awesome site. It is 6 PM and I see this older man and woman stumbling drunk and coming at us and the sea of tents. I am sure they are camped near by. He zigs, zags and falls right on top of my perfectly put up tent collapsing it to the ground. I walked over and said, buddy that's my tent, he said in drunkanies, O man I am sorry, got up and went over fell on top of another tent. His I think. He broke one of my tent poles and I know that this is part of the deal when you are in a large group of people. So I rigged the pole and move the tent to a safer place with no traffic. With all this done, I addressed the issue of the gauntlet and her showing her breast. My lady is saying that if I am willing to look at someone else breast then I should be willing to let her show hers and I must say they are very nice breast indeed. Humm, she has got me there. I cant help but look. I tried, really. It is just fun that is all. Ask me and I will tell you why. Being so close to the gauntlet with the tent and alcohol being a major factor. I felt it was

The Hoover Dam on the way to Laughlin River Run 2002.

unsafe and she might be in danger if she was to show her breast. I told her if we were just passing thru that I would have no problem with it. This seemed to satisfy her and we where able to continue on with our trip. About this time Jim and the other guy show up and off to the event's we went. Lots and lots of Cops every where but still a wide open party with good people having fun and all with one thing in common. We ride bikes because we love it. Most all the people there are having fun and a few ladies are riding the mechanical bull topless as we listen to a live band. The next day we were to leave and up early talking about things and I decided if she wanted to she could flash those beauties and she did while I took a picture of her. Damn I loved her. Then we packed the tent and the bikes and we are ready to go. Jim had gone back to Durango for the night with the other guy and I told him that we would be leaving at 11 AM Sunday in the morning. If he was there fine if not fine. We had to head back because of the baby setter and the boys. Jim was not there and off we went. It was partly cloudy with blue skies and a very nice day. I wanted to do a loop as always. Which took us over Wolf Creek Pass 11,000 feet. Via Pagosa Springs, left at South Park on Hwy 149 thru Creed, Lake City, Gunnison and the Blue Meas Lake on Hwy 50 headed west towards Montrose and G.J. home. Up over Wolf Creek Pass cloudy and cold with a little snow falling. The closer we got to Creed the more the clouds surrounded us and the cold set in hard. Stopping in Creed to suit up for the darkness in the distance. It looked bad but had no choice but to continue on. Up between Spring Creek Pass 10,500 feet and Slumgullion pass 11, 500 feet we got caught in a storm. It was the worst that I had every been in. The cold drop to below freezing. The rain was so bad the road disappeared and all I could see was hope. I could not stop. There was no place to hide, nothing. Besides that if you stop you will never start again in these situations. I could see blue sky off in the distance and wanted to get there. Don't know how far but thought it was 15 or 20 miles away. My lady stayed right on my tail all the way. I am sure in pain from the cold and the horror of the road. The rain turned to a light hail if there is such a thing. Beating me in the face and on top of my head. As always looking in the rear view mirror to see if she is alright. Then and in the past I never were a helmet. Lucky for me my lady was.

The hail became snow and on we went. I was not sure if we would make it or not thru this hour long ordeal. On the other side of Slumgullion Pass and down the hill to sunlight. We stop for 20 or 30 minutes and warm a bit. We were like birds on a tree trying to get warm. Facing the sun and turning around so our bodies caught some of the warmth on both sides. Time had become a factor and out of nowhere Jim rolls up from the way we came about 6 PM Sunday. We talk and off we went towards Blue Mesa lake and Hwy 50. There is a gas station by the lake and there we would get gas and rest 60 miles away. Just before the turn onto Hwy 50 my lady goes on reserve. She is needing a gas station in a bad way. 25 to 30 miles is about it for her. I had not been to Blue Mesa lake for awhile and the gas station had closed down. There was a second choice down the road on the lake a little ways and it was closed down as well. Now I go on reserve and stop to talk to Jim about the situation. We are 25 miles from Cimmaron and she only has 15 miles left on her tank. I could make it to Cimmaron I was sure. So we told her to coast down the hills and ease up hills and maybe we would make to Cimmaron. Not much hope but off we went. I knew there was a Ma and Pa place 5 miles out of Cimmaron and I felt they would be close as well. Guess what, they were open. We pulled up getting gas and I walked in. The old lady came up and said Hi! With a big smile, how are you people doing I am so glade you stopped in. The old man came out and with the same attitude. These people make the difference in our other wise messed up world. I will never forget them. Looked around and bought a few things and off we went. We were thanking them and them doing the same to us. Gas and 8 PM outside Cimmaron. Over a small pass and the deer on the sides of the road and down into Montrose. There we stopped and it was 9 PM. My lady looking as if she had no more will to do anything and we grabbed a bit to eat. The whole time she is saying I am not getting back on the bike. She said, there is a motel right over there and I am not getting on the bike. I said, we are only 60 miles away from home sweetheart. She said I don't care I am not getting back on the bike and she was not kidding. So I thought humm, ahh, lets see what to do. I told her, sweetheart if ya get back on the bike I will give you the sweeties hot Calgon bubble bath you ever had when we get home. She has had one before from me and knows that I am very good at bubble baths. If you want to know just ask me. Up and on the bike she was and off we went home. It was a beautiful ride that night. The moon full and no wind and back to G.J.. She got her hot Calgon bubble bath. When we got back the Hwy Patrol reported 5 dead during this rally. Three were due to alcohol. 1 was a lady rider to hot in a corner with the sun in her face. The other was a lady rider who did not see her husband turn in front of her hitting him head on. Which brings up a point, always make sure you see that everyone knows what you are doing before you do it and everyone gets home safe. I knew when we left to go to 4-corners that my lady and I were not going to make it again as a couple. A week later we broke up for good and I thought I would never see her again. I let her have the Virago which was mine and in my name. She had paid about half of it off. I decided I would help her and pay the rest off and I still am today. I gave the bike to her signing the title over to her at that time. That was the way it had to be. This also was the last time I rode with Jim for awhile dew to his job out of town and family things going on. Have you figured it out yet, what will I do, that is right I ride because when it comes right down to it that is all I know and what I do best.

September 11, 2001

1st of September, my lady and I are no longer. The Hog club, as I am a member has planned a yearly event to Maney Height Retirement home. Ever year they take there motorcycles and park in the parking lot so the old people can see them. Remember Eddy, Turtle run and not yet Santa Clause for 2001. Anyway, he has a sidecar for his Harley and he would give rides to the old folks who wanted one. It was a plan and waiting a week for Saturday morning to do this. Monday I went to work and as usual I turn the radio on. It was my early week so I was there at 7AM. As I listen to music which I love. There is something about they crashed into the building. I thought it was a joke at first and then began to listen. I went up front were there is a T.V. and told the manager that something has happen, someone has run into the one of the twin towers in New York city. We turned the TV on just in time to see a repeat of what had happen. The jet plane ramping into the building. It was like a bad joke of some kind. I could not believe that someone had done this and could it have been an accident. About this time a second jet plane ran into the other twin tower. What the hell is going on I am thinking. It looked deliberate in my eyes. As you all know it was a horrible day for America and its people. You know the story and I have not forgotten even today. I am not satisfied with the resolve of our government as it stands today. This was an attack on innocent people, woman, children, old or young. I will not and can not see this as any other way but a cowards attack on me. I will never forgive those people in Afghanistan for what they did. They have no rights to be on our planet we call home. That week my heart was broken as it is today. Everyday I remember the horror all these people must have felt. All those inside the buildings and on the streets below. All those who watch on TV and listen on the radio as there loved ones died. I have seen more than my share of pain and death over the years but this was as bad as it gets. Saturday came and we meet at the Harley house. As I stood there I told all that I did not have the heart to go and have fun at Maney Heights because of 911. Most of them agreed. The story is, you cant let them win and make you crawl in a hole surrounded be sorrow. We decide to go and off we went. 15 bikes and me on Passion. When we got there they had lined up the old people in wheel chairs and beds outside near the parking lot. We parked our bikes and it seemed they were afraid of us at first. All dressed in black leather looking like a bunch of roughens I am sure. The ladies went over and started talking to the old people and so did I. We are asking them how they were doing and that was about it. Eddy showed and the long process of loading one them in the sidecar began. Eddy would ride off with me and or two other bikes as escorts on a short ride down the road and back. As I walked around talking to everyone and then went up to the manager of the place and ask if I could do some tricks for the people we had come to see. Yes was the answer. Someone took a few pictures of me doing this and I took a few of everyone else. Some of the tricks I do are laying down on the seat with no hands, standing up no hands, side mount, flying ornament, and some other things as well. When I was thru everyone seemed amazed that I could do these things. Just stuff I had been doing all my bike life. I know, I can hear you saying, you are some kind of show off,huh. No not really I loved to have fun and make someone smile or be happy even if it just for a second. I only show off for one person and that would be my lady. They were loading another rider into Eddy's sidecar and she was raising hell the whole time. I thought they were killing her the way she was carrying on. But they would ask her, do you want to go, yes she said, yes and off Eddy went with her. I went over and was asking some of them if there was anything that I could do for them. A 90 year man setting in a wheel chair looked up at me right the eye and said "Pepsi", that was it, Pepsi. So off I went to get him a Pepsi but first I checked with the nurse to see if he could have one. No was her answer. Humm, well what can he have I said. She said orange juice and I would have to go to the back and get some, so off I went. I took the orange juice back to him and he looked up at me and said Pepsi. I did not want to tell him that he could not have one, to tell him no was more than I could handle at the time. I said, here is some orange juice they are out of Pepsi. He looked at me and said "Root Beer", Damn to myself, he is still looking me in the eye. I said they are out of Root Beer, he looked me right the eye and said "Coke". Mmaann!!!, I was already having hard time lying to him and now I had to give up the truth. I told him that they said you cant have any, him looking me strait in the eye. I felt very humbled at the moment. He then took the orange juice and began to drink it as I moved on. As I looked around at the Hog group I saw most of them drinking Pepsi's and Coke's with them in there hands. I began to tell them that the old people cant have any and maybe we should not as well. Some put theirs down and others did not. One of the old men started screaming and I walked over to him asking him what is wrong. He said I don't want to go for a ride on the bike, yelling. I said you don't have to go, really you don't. He looked at me and then calmed down after me telling him serval times you don't have to and I moved on. Soon all that wanted to ride with Eddy had done so and off we went and then home for me. I think this was as good for the old people as it was for the Hog club. It lifted our other wise sadden hearts up a little because of 911.

Hwy 550 out of Silverton Co. Headed up Red Mt. Pass.

The Touch of a Biker

In late September 911 still on my mind. A day ride over to Moab for lunch on Hwy 128 out of Cisco along the Colorado river. As always a nice ride close to 100 miles from where we started and about 20 bikes with the Hog club. Once in Moab we had a very quite lunch and then it was well lets head back to G.J.. I said, woo wait a minute here, lets go for a ride to somewhere nice. I mean we are already here. I said, has anyone been to Dead Horse Point. Most of them said no what is that. So I explained a little but not to much and off we went now about 10 bikes. Some choice to head back home. Up the valley onto the high plains and I could feel as we rode across the high plains some were not sure if there would be anything out there. I think we paid $2.00 each to get in and down the road 2 miles to the main parking area. The Bikers were all very happy that suggested the side trip to Dead Horse Point and I think Dead Horse Point now has a hold on them as it does me. Then back we went towards home. We had to stop once on the way there because of a shift lever falling off and had to put it back on the bike. It was a Road King I think. On the way back it fell off two more times and we stopped as he put it back on trying to get home. As a group over 3 bikes I think you should travel no faster than 70mph tops on the freeway. 60mph to 65mph else where or the speed limit which ever comes first. Always use the 2 second rule between bikes and ride a staggered formation. I am not sure but time I guess, to some became a factor or maybe they just like riding fast. We got to the interstate and once on it, we were soon doing 85 mph as a group and 10 motorcycles deep. I believe this is to fast and at one point from my back position of the pack, I thought I should pull to the front and tell them to slow down. Now I can here, if do not want to drive that fast then don't but at the same time, if you care anything about the group or the people you are riding with, safety has to be one of your biggest concerns. I always felt like a step son and never quite fitting in. I am not here to judge anyone for how they ride. If I would have known things might have been different that day. I did nothing to slow the pack down. Are you ready. I am not. On interstate 70 headed east from Utah, the first of three exit to G.J. I was second from the back in front of little Bob, Me, Squint, Moses and his 20 yr old son packing (passenger), Sharon, Darrell, Gretchen, someone, someone, Curtis and Kathy, Harold, someone and someone. The thing about going 85 mph for a lot miles, it makes doing 70 seem very slow and you loose a sense of what your speed is. We were still doing 85 mph and Moses with his son packing, slipped right to exit and had slowed a little in his eyes and waved at the pack as we started to pass by. It was then the adrenalin kicked in me saying Nooo! as I saw him turn to see that he was to hot into the exit and lite up the rear tire. Then front tire is smoking and still to hot in the exit. All this is happening in front of me in slow motion the whole time. I am screaming Moses NO! Moses NOOO! He was headed for the V-shaped garde rail slowing a little but still doing 60 mph. I could feel him look up and have to make a decision, the bike still locked down. Now he is in a lite gravel and turned the bike left and tried to lay it down. The front tire dug in and flipped into the air throwing his son off in a flat rolling position thru the air 3 or 4 times to land on the Hwy and roll 3 or 4 more times in front of the garde rail to a stop. Moses flew up into the air 6 or 7 feet with a long flip and down he went right onto the back of his head. With another flip to land on the front of his head coming to a rest laying on his side almost up right like David years ago. All this time I am smoking my tire and coming to a halt, screaming Moses NO! Please NOOO!. I like Moses, one of the real good guys around. Kinda quite but that's OK. Stopping my bike and running at them. It was bad, I am trying to keep both of them on the ground so they want do any more damage to themself by trying to walk or move around there on the side of the interstate 70. Neither were aware of anything. I just keep saying please, please stay down with the touch of a

Biker, help is on the way. Soon Squint was there to help me contain them. Squint was trying to keep his son down and a real struggle. I was with Moses begging him to lay down, blood running from both sides of his head. The skin folded back from his head and I thought that I might loose Moses that night there on the Hwy. Sharon and Gretchen came just after Squint to help and a ambulance happen by at this time and they took over. Squint and I directed traffic away from them laying there on the hard two lane black top that we love so dearly. A short time and they were off to the hospital in the ambulance. I was not sure Moses was going to make it. We picked the bike up and it was damaged but the amazing thing was we were able to get it started and down the hill to a parking lot and a trailer to come and pick it up and to the Hog house. Little Bob and I stayed with the bike until it was at the shop. One and half hours later we were at the hospital waiting to see. His son had received very little damage but Moses had some things wrong. Lets just say some surgery, 128 stitches later and a few broken ribs with a punctured lung, he would be alright. The next day was the celebration of the end of the riding season called Mac Attack in Mac, CO. 20 miles from G.J. I did not go and went to see Moses and he was not awake. Probably from the drugs and I set there with his wife Nancy who is a sweetheart of a special kind. A touch of a Biker for awhile and then back home. I did not sleep well for three nights as the horror of that night repeated itself in my mind. I went to see him everyday until I knew he was going to be ok and October was here 2001. I had to think, a helmet not out of the question anymore, I guess I will just have to ride with a helmet because that is what I do best.

Adventures of a Biker

Moses was alright and the nightmares stopped. Another poker run or bake sale by the Hog club and a ride to Cedaredge for the Apple Festival. A nice cold ride in the rain but fun with some great people. October Festival downtown G.J. and a lot fun as well. Some short rides here and there all the time 911 in the back ground. Why, who, when, where, what are we going to do about it and the end of October, now a little colder. They are building a very nice memorial to the Veterans here in G.J. At the Hog meeting 1st of November. A representative of this memorial ask if we would ride with them in the Veterans Day Parade. The answer was yes from a lot of us. The day comes on a Saturday and it is very nice out and blue skies as well. I am there early as usual on Passion and we are to be close to the front of the parade. There are 20 or 30 Harley's there by the time the parade starts. Two days earlier I had gone down and bought 6 big bags of candy to throw to the kids lined down main street as we rode by. As always there was a large crowd at the beginning of the parade there at 2nd and main downtown G.J. It became our turn to ride and we pulled forwards towards main street. Most of us have flags on our bikes. At main street the crowd roared and clapped as we pulled into the line of the parade. There were 100's of people on this first corner. Kids it seemed by the 100's as well. I started to throw some candy and they were over whelming, cheering and clapping at the sight of the bikes with the flags flying proudly. Disparately grabbing as much candy as I could trying to see that all the kids got some. Then to look up an see the streets are lined 12 people deep on the sidewalks and kids by the 1000's. I looked and the kids were every where as far as I could see down main street. I new at this point that I did have enough candy for all of the kids. By 7th street I had thrown all of my candy to the kids and still they were 12 people deep as far as I could see. The people roaring, clapping and smiling as proud as anyone could. It was 911 they saw and me as well. Tears filtered from eyes with all the kids there, so many kids, waving flags as we rode by. The bastards did not win on 911. We are strong and it is time to kick some butt. We keep riding down main street and they are still there lined up all the way out to 12th street. It was the most people ever to attend a parade downtown G.J. and I felt honored to be a part of it. I am sorry I was riding and have no pictures of the parade to show you. There was something that I noticed as I waited downtown main street G.J. that day. I saw a lot of people on cell phones. Now don't get mad at me but I wanted to bring up something here that just kills me. Something I thought I would never see and now it seems this is all you see. As I ride around thru cities and towns every where I try to see all that is a round me. I was out one day and pulled up to a red light. There was a Biker setting there and I look over at him. He has on some old leathers with the usual Harley emblems all over them. Motorcycle boots and his bike is a old chopped out Harley 74 of some kind. He has a bandana on his head with long hair and a long beard. When I look at him I see he is setting there talking on a cell phone. Now common, in my mind this is just not cricket, you know I don't think this looks right. In my eyes it would be like someone wearing bermuda shorts, wing tip shoes, a white dress shirt with a bow tie setting on a Harley. But that is just me I am J.T.. You know it seems every where I go now, this is what I see and I have been lots of places. I see them as yuppy Bikers. One foot on there bikes and there ear stuck to a cell phone talking about business. Maybe I am wrong or not suppose to get it, probably so. I know cell phones are very good to have for emergencies and I do suggest that if you have one that you carry it on trips but don't show anyone. Especially if you are on your Harley. I was on a bike trip to Bryce Canyon 2002 which I will talk more about later. Jim and I had stopped and he wanted to try to cell phone home like E.T. which is ok but not while your setting on your Harley. So I said alright, we are out in the middle of Utah and I just fell of my bike. I have a fence post stuck up my butt. Can I get a little help here. Then I am saying to Jim, "Can You Hear Me Now". Every time he gets this cell phone out that is the first words out of my mouth, Can You Hear Me Now. So he gets on his cell phone and dials out. Nothing, he says I am out of coverage. I said, what about the pole stuck in my butt. Aah Jim's says I can get thru. I said O' I guess I will have to go on with this pole stuck in my butt. Laughing at him and him laughing at me and off we went. A little later down the road 50 miles or so we stopped again. He brakes out the cell again and I say, Can You Hear Me Now, laughing and saying you know I still got this pole stuck in my butt. He calls out again and out of coverage was his answer. I said I am glade it was not a telephone pole, laughing and off we went again. 50 miles later we stopped again, he tries again on the cell phone and he gets thru, Can You Hear Me Now. So now I am saying that it is alright I am kinda getting use to the pole in my butt. I will be alright. I guess my point is, something is only good if it works. Don't depend on these things to safe your life but I still would carry one if you have one. The Hogs had there Biker bash after the Veterans Day parade. It is a celebration and fund raiser for the Christmas Toys Run which will come on December 8th 2001.

A Veterans graveyard full of Hero's here in Grand Junction Co.

Toys Run 2001

Dec. 8th 2001 and the Toys Run. It is a nice day, blue sky and 35*. There are 800 bikes there to join in the parade of presents at the G.J. Harley house. I am on Passion. I had talked to Jim and we rode over together that morning. He shows up on his soft tail standard and I say man she is a classy looking lady. The bikes are covered in all kinds of teddy bears and toys for the kids. Santa Clause is there as well on his Harley. Please don't tell anyone but it is Eddy. He is and always will be a hero to me. As I walked around I took a few pictures of all that was going on. I swear 20% of the people are talking on cell phones. This is unbelievable in my eyes and then it became time for us to leave on the parade of presents. There is a lot that goes on behind the seines of this ride. Leaving the Harley house which is way outside the main city of G.J. Going out and down Horizon to 7th street about one and half miles, then down 7th street three miles to Petkins a one way street. One mile over to 5th street and across a bridge to the Eagles Lodge where the kids are to be waiting. My parade of presents 1999', we rode up and down the main streets of G.J. with lots of people that were out to wave and say hello as we rode by. Even in the 2000' parade we rode some of the main streets here in G.J.. In 2001 it seems to me that the city of G.J. was a little offish about the Biker toys for kids thing. As far as I know they have nothing to do with it and very little corporation towards the Toys Run as well. This parade of present coming up will be the 23rd Annual Toys Run 2002 believe or not here in G.J.. There were very few people to see and wave on the 2001' parade. The parade route went down Horizon ave and there is nothing there but tourist stuff. 7th Street is a short street going thru nothing that goes nowhere. Then across a bridge to the Eagles lodge. After parking our bikes at the Eagles. I wanted to say something here. The Eagles are a very good organization and are dedicated to honor and I am a member. We then carried our presents up some stairs and into a room. Thru this door and it was an amazing site, here set 250 to 300 kids. Eyes wide open and some very happy to see us and others a little afraid. You would be afraid too if 300 leather wearing, burly looking, long haired bearded Bikers walk in on you. It did not take long for it to become a wonderful thing for everyone as we passed out our presents to the kids as we saw them. All of them went home with more than presents. We also went home with a lot as Bikers. The joy came from both sides of the presents that were passed out that day. The love flowed all thru the room and you could feel it surround you. In my eyes all of these Bikers are hero's and I know they are to 300 kids that day that may have had nothing for Christmas if it were not for some Bikers who cared. David Bowie said in a song, "And We Can Be Heroes For Just One Day". I was walking around at the end seeing the kids as they were leaving, happy and so was I. They made me feel so very good because I could see in there eyes that we had done something good. A guy came up to me said would you like to do a interview on TV. I said sure grabbing Sharon pulling her next to me. She is a sweetheart of a woman and telling her that I am not going to do this alone. She said Ooo! I will get you for this J.T.. A bright light hits us in the face with a TV camera stuck against my nose. Close -up in your face kinda thing. Man talk about pressure. Sharon tells him one of the sad things about this is I have to turn families down because we do not have enough room for all them here at the Eagles. Then telling him how much effort goes in to putting this on. I told him as I look around and I see a lot love. A lot of happy faces and that we did something good here today as Bikers. If you get a chance and a parade of presents comes by your place, go out and wave, I assure you they will wave back with a big smile and a warm heart.

White Hog Christmas Party

It is now the end of 2001 and 2002 begins. I am looking out the window and waiting on spring. During a Hog meeting Laughlin River Run comes up and I would love to go. This would be my first Laughlin River Run and Jim wants to go as well. Jim and I talk a lot about the trip to Laughlin and with all the riding I do he thinks maybe I should step into a glide of some kind but money is always a factor for me. I went down and look at a Super Glide but decided that Passion would do for now. The Hogs have there annual Christmas party called the White Hog. Because of the holidays it is January on the 12th 2002. About 50 people show up and everyone brings a present. Then numbers are drawn to decide who goes first and they are allowed to pick any present form the pile that they choose. There is a 3 steal rule in affect and that is when it becomes you turn you can steal someone else's present and then they get to pick again. The most popular steal is a 5th of Jack Daniels. Which I got four of them and you know that I don't drink and everyone took my Jack away from me. So that meant I got to choose until I came across a very nice book on the History of Harley. I tried to hide it but a lady friend remembered me having it and then took it from me being the second take. So almost at the end of the drawing and I have another 5th of jack and someone takes it. I then took the book back from her being the third take. I love this book called The Encyclopedia of the Harley Davidson. It has everything in it that you might want to know about Harley, except what I do best, Yeppers, that would be riding in the wind because that is what I do.

The Olympic Torch

In January 2002 the talk turns to the Olympics in Salt Lake City right next door and if the terrorists of 911 will attack there. It also seems there is a battle in the motorcycle world here in G.J. It is over what the city of G.J. should buy, Harley's or BMW's a German made bike. They are to be for the Motorcycle Police department here. Humm, I think American tax payers money should buy American things if possible. But that is just me. Not all Police Departments ride Harley's but I would say most do. The story goes, they said this and he said that and the city is going to buy BMW's. WHAT!!. I listen to radio sation here in G.J. every day at work and sometimes at home when I am there. The subject turns to the BMW's on the radio by the DJ's and there seems to be a big controversy over what the city has done. So I call up the radio station and the DJ's and I have a 5 minute conversation about the BMW's on the radio. My point was this, are you going to lead our Veterans down main street during the Veterans day parade with those BMW's. I said, some who have actually went to war against Germany. On top of that the whole world will be watching because the Olympic Torch is coming right thru G.J. and not only that, right down my street in front of my house. So I said you cant lead our American Torch runners thru our city with BMW's. Two of the DJ's agree, the other says it shows that we are worldly by having BMW's lead the Torch. NOOO! If you go to Japan for there Olympics I guaranty you they will be riding a Japanese made motorcycles and not Harley's to lead there torch thru there cities. That also goes for the rest of the countries that make bikes as well. Humm, some people call into the radio station and say

129

yeah he is right. A few say who cares it is the Torch. I heard someone say it is just a stick with fire on it and I said yeah and the American Flag is just a piece of material with some patterns of color on it. Somehow I think it is more than that. I have always wanted to be apart of the Olympics and wanted to go try out even if I failed miserably. Never got around to do this. So the battle continued in the newspapers and radio stations. February 2nd 2002 the torch is to be here at 4 PM on a Saturday in Cliffton just outside G.J.. They will parade the Torch down the streets of G.J. to a large celebration that night downtown G.J. This party will start at 7 PM. The Torch it seems, after looking at the parade route will come right by my house. A short dog leg for some reason. I come home Friday night February 1st from work and there is a number on my tree in my front yard, # 154 along with a sign Olympic Torch Run and a Torch Flag. I thought it was a mile marker of some kind and then it dawned on me. It was the number of one of the runners of the Torch and they would be stopping in front of my house. I still have the stuff as I took down off the tree after the Torch left that night. The stuff is still hanging on my wall today. All that week before I had decided to see the torch come into Cliffton. I also decided for some silly reason to lead the Torch into G.J. on Passion my purple Harley Sportster. So I went down to were the torch would arrive around 3 PM. I waited along with 100's of other people for the Torch to get there. The sun is out and still a little cold 35*. All the Torch barriers are standing around waiting with us for the Torch as well. No other bikes around that I remember. At 5 PM 28*, the Torch comes into the parking lot and I feel very honored to be there. By this time there are 1000's of people lined up every where along the Torch route. Some say close to 30,000 people all the way to the celebration area downtown. The official flame is lite and off they go and so do I. I know this is kinda silly but I knew the parade route and out in front of the Torch about a half a mile ahead of it I went on Passion with a American flag flying. It is the same flag that I had during the Veterans Day parade. The radio crew had gone out as well in front the Torch and I rode a little ways behind them for awhile. The people waving signs, torch flags and cheering at all the front floats and me as I rode by. Don't yell at me but I felt that a Harley had led the Torch threw the city and it was Passion. Other than the BMW's I don't remember seeing any other bikes at all that day on the parade route. I went on quickly and got home to wait for the Torch to come to my house. Now it is 25* out and very cold. At first there are a few people waiting there in front of my house. As the time got closer the more they showed up. Around 7:00 PM Saturday, standing in my yard are the parents, husband and there little girl 7 years old of the lady who will carry the Torch from here to the next stop and we talked. They were very excited and I am too because in a small way I was apart of the Olympics a life long dream. They transferred the flame right in front of my house. A parade of police cars, sheriffs cars, official cars, some cars with mean looking men in suits in them and the BMW's arrived and I felt privileged to be apart of this. I took a view pictures before the cold got to my camera and 2 minutes later they were gone but the memoire remains as strong as the day it happened. I had put up some streamers red, white and blue on the tree next to the number 154 and they are still there today. By this time, thru the Toys run, 4-corners, and the White Hog Jim and I become friends and planned to go to Laughlin together in late April 2002. If I have not said this before, he is a excellent riding partner. There is no one that I would rather ride with then him. He has as much Passion for being on the road as I do, well almost, Haha. Along with my old friend David this would be a close call as who I would like to ride with best. I can only imagine just how much fun the three of us would have out there on the roads. We did a nice day trip to Moab middle of March and took a few pictures. A very nice ride down Hwy 128, the river road from Cisco. We talked, planned and were getting very excited about the ride to Laughlin and the River run. It is a miniature Las Vegas there in Laughlin. I come home and guess who calls to see how I am doing, My Lady. She wants to see me and I agree thinking I am over her and I will face my demon. I saw her and she had taken the Virago to Denver with someone and sold it for $900.00. It is $3000.00 motorcycle. She was now in trouble and needed my help. I agreed to see her and the demon had her way with me that day. I was not over her and she was in control. So I said I would help her when I got back and on my mind was the trip to Laughlin.

Laughlin River Run 2002

The Laughlin trip which would be 4 ½ days leaving April 24, Wednesday around 5PM.. Riding thru Green River Ut. to camp around the Hanksville cut off on I -70. The day comes and it was a very pleasant day. 5 O'clock is here and Jim is late and I am really ready to go. Now it is 6 PM. and Jim shows up and I can tell he is not to happy. It seems that Jim's wife is not to happy about him going. Humm. Does this sound familiar to you, it does to me. Anyway all that matters is he is here and off we go. Jim on his Soft Tail, Lady and me on Passion. About 50 miles out I stop and we talk for a second. He tells me that she was upset but he really wanted to go. He said he had told her weeks before that he really wanted to go. He then told me that it would be fine, lets go on. After a very nice ride out thru the high desert on the interstate. The air was nice and felt like freedom to me. In the spring everything seems fresh as if it is starting a new life and I guess it is. I love to ride in the spring I see so many beautiful things out there on the roads. We stopped in Green River for a bite to eat and he is still a little under but ok at the same time. Then we stop for gas because there is a stretch of a road to Salina Ut. about 100 miles where there is nothing but nice wide open spaces. There is so much to see out there, so better get gas in Green River. 10 miles out on I 70 is the cut off to Hanksville and we set up the tents out in a small valley of rocks. Very peaceful, there is no one anywhere within miles of us. The moon is full and playing peek a boo with the clouds that gently roll by over head. Jim is feeling a little better as we talk about things including my recent breakup with my lady and that she had called. You know I still love her even today and soon all that is left on our minds is the trip to Laughlin. I get in my tent and I am ready for a nice nights sleep. I hear zippers for 30 minutes coming from Jim's tent. He un zipped this and zipped that and re-zipped this and re-un zipped that, after awhile, I am saying are you thru yet, laughing out loud. A nice quite night and some sleep. I am a very light sleeper and it is always hard for me to sleep out on the road. The next day our biggest concern is getting across to Richfield without getting caught in a snow storm. There is only one pass we must do to get to Las Vegas our destination for that day. After 10 minutes of Jim adjusting his bungee straps on his bike, I am saying are you thru yet, laughing out loud. We were off and on the road again. A month earlier I had made a reservation at the Palace Station Hotel in Las Vegas and we figured we would be there by 6 PM. I had always had a dream of riding my Harley down the strip of Las Vegas and was hoping to achieve this goal. I travel a lot on my motorcycles and most people go like hell to get somewhere. They are doing 100 mile stretches before stopping. I think they miss so much by doing this and by the time you get there you are very tired and sore from riding. Jim was the same way. I came up with a new way to ride a long trip. I call it the 50-50. I found that you make the same distance in almost the same time and you are not as tired when get there. Also you get to see so much more and talk to so many more people. I guess it is all in the way you look at it. Anyway the 50-50 is 50 miles and take a break, just stop for a few minutes, talk and then 50 more and stop for gas, repeat this. It is very simple really and at the end of a 400 or 500 mile day I don't feel as wore out as I do when I just try to take it all the way. Try it once and see what you think. Enjoy your ride it is in my mind the best thing in life next to making love to My Lady. Up and out on I 70 and thru what is called the San Rafael Swell. A incline onto a high plateau thru some nice rock formations. There is some very nice scenery along the way and a steady climb up of 80 miles to Salina. Up over a pass about 8000 feet in the Fish Lake Natl. Forrest which is where we though there may be snow. Some nice mountains and dressing up for the cold. There are a few clouds and we are just missing a storm. It is a little cold around 30* but not to bad and there we are in Salina. There are serval gas station here and a very nice Denny's with a good breakfast with nice people. Still

On Hwy 141 in the spring of 2001 headed for Dove Creek Co.

doing the 50-50 and the ride is nice and a little windy along some mountain peaks in the Dixie Natl. Forest. We are on a busy Hwy I -15 to Mesquite Nevada. Lots of traffic and the road is not that good. In Mesquite we stop for a drink and a bite to eat. While there at the Oasis casinos we walked around looking at all the stuff they had inside. A very nice place. Back on the bikes and it is getting hot. So off with some the cloths we had put on to cross the mountains. Closer we got to Las Vegas the hotter it got. Now this is April and for us it is still cold most of the time in G.J.. I have seen it snow a foot here in G.J. in the middle of April not to long ago. Still a very nice ride and there we were in Las Vegas right on time 6 PM.. Now Las Vegas is real touchy about camera's and most places where there are casinos don't like you taking pictures. So there are not to many pictures taken here. In 4-corners I took a pictures in the door way of a casino and they were on me in a flash. I thought they were going to arrest me for taking a picture, damn that seems crazy. Anyway checked into our room at the Palace and a nice long shower. I Came out of the shower and look over at Jim. He is putting his stuff up so neatly. Hanging every thing up and laying out all of his stuff in a pattern of neatness. Then you look over on my side of the room and there are cloths laying all over the place, on the floor, in the chair, on the bed, humm my side looks like a mess but that is the way I like it. I started laughing and he ask me what was going on. I said O nothing really, you are so neat and I am so messes it reminds me of the Odd Couple movie Felix Unger and the slob. After everything was put up we went down to the Palace Station casino and walked around. Had a little to eat and now 8 PM. Thursday night. As you know Vegas has some of the most awesome building designs you will ever see. It is worth it to go there to just look at all the buildings and casinos. This place is amazing with sites and sounds that are like none you have ever seen. Now I am very excited and it is time to go ride the strip. This is another Dream that has come true. There are bikes everywhere and all kinds of makes and models but seems to be more Harley's then any other because of the Laughlin River run I think. As we rode up the strip, people would wave and smile as we rode by making me feel as though I had done something right. The streets and buildings are lite up like the 4th of July. All the colors of the rainbow and more. There is so much to see and do it is so over whelming. Up and down the strip three times and over to Fremont Street and the old strip where the 4 Queens, The Golden Nugget is. They have now closed off the street to traffic and is a pedestrians only place. There is a light show put to music on a large canopy 50 feet in the air above you. We stopped and walk around in total aw of this. Being back on Fremont street reminded me of the last time I was there. It was in 1969. A friend and I were hitch hiking to California for no reason and I was just a kid 17 yrs. old. I had long hair and looking a little like a bum I am sure. Going thru Las Vegas we stop while we were there and was walking around on Fremont street. My adventures then are a whole other book of stories and I will write it later. For now we were standing on the west end and a car pulled up. At this time you could still drive up and down Fremont street. Two men jump out of a black car shoving guns in our face and telling us to leave there city now. Of course this scared the hell out of me. I said ok would guys give us a ride it is 7 miles to the edge of town. They said no. I said well can we hitch hike, they said no. They said start walking and guess what that is exactly what we did. The stay right there following behind us in there car for two or three miles and then disappeared. We kept walking until we were out of town. We stay under a bridge that night and woke with 20 people around us that morning. This also scared the hell of me. Where did they come from. It was a interesting trip and would love to write about it someday. Anyway, back to the strip and we hit some of the major casinos, to many to list. You can not put into words what you will see in Las Vegas. It would take a whole book full of pictures and metaphors to even get close. Being there was all that I could imagine and all that any Biker could dream of. Las Vegas at night riding up and down the strip is the bomb. Just go and do it. Back to the Hotel and I am trying to go to sleep. Jim is a out like a light and a sleep. For me I am to excited to sleep and decide to go downstairs and play some Roulette. I came away with some extra money but not to much. I went back to the room to get some sleep around 2 AM. Still to excited trying to sleep and no luck. At 6 AM I decide to get up, taking a shower and went down and watch the old men playing craps (dice). They are a kick. They really know how to play and they know how to talk the talk and walk the walk.

This is a lot fun to watch and if you get a chance go watch them for a second. Back to the room around 8 AM and Jim is still knocked out. I start gathering my stuff form all over the floor and Jim is up and a shower. We pack the bikes and off we go to Laughlin which is a miniature Las Vegas in it self, via the Hoover Dam. Our plan is to take Hwy 95 down to Laughlin and a side trip on Hwy 93 to the Hoover Dam which was and is a must do ride if you are any where near there. Across the dam on the bikes to stop and walk out looking over the edges. It is so big, a structural master piece. You could spent all day there but we are headed for Laughlin. We did a turn around to head back to Hwy 95 and the wind picks up turning into a fairly stout head wind on the way back to Hwy 95. At Hwy 95 you look down a long road towards Laughlin and there are 100's of off bikes coming at us and we continue down the road a ways as people give us the turn around symbol. This is your hand in the air in a circling motion which means turn around. Let me say something here about hand signals. It is a good thing to know them when you are traveling with other Bikers. You should learn them and use them all the time. You know the standards left turn being left arm and hand strait out left, right turn left arm in a L shape, hand pointing up, stop is left arm L shape hand pointing down, or left arm hanging down. Object on the road in front of you is, left hand moving and pointing down to the road, to look or see something is left hand moving and pointing over your head in the direction of the place you wish them to see. To say hi to other Bikers coming at you, is left hand out with fingers showing. I think if you use these it is a easy way to communicate with other Bikers as you are riding down the road. This is illegal but if flash your headlight it means a Police car up ahead. These signals may help keep down some of the confusion that can take place in the wind and on the road. Anyway with all the other Bikers telling us to go back and the only other way to Laughlin is via Kingman, Arizona. We turned and stopped in Boulder City, Nevada for gas. There are tons of bikes around and all makes and models but mostly Harley's. While getting gas, up pulls this dressed out BMW around $40,000 worth. It looks like some kind of space aged rocket ship to me. It has a solid body and solid wheels. Jim and I are looking at it and thinking man this thing is probably catching the wind in a bad way.

I said hey, how is the bike doing. He said it is killing me. He said, when it comes to going strait this bike is killer. But with this side wind I cant keep it on the Hwy. doing 55 mph at best. He said I am trying to get safely home which is down the road 125 miles. So now we are going back across the Hoover Dam again on Hwy 93. The traffic is 30 minutes to go 5 miles because of all the extra cars and bikes do to what ever happened on Hwy 95. Turns out a semi truck was hit by a gust of side wind and flip over onto the Hwy destroying everything in its path. The truck and the destruction was blocking both sides of the Hwy, not sure if anyone died but there were a lot of injuries. They were saying there was to be a 4 to 6 hour delay on Hwy 95 to clean the mess up off the Hwy. So now leaving the Hoover Dam for the second time that day and headed south on Hwy 93 into Arizona. There is a very heavy wind coming from every where it seems. To me in Arizona the wind comes from up above you, strait down to beat on you the whole time you are riding no matter which direction you are going. At one point I am leaning hard into a side wind and it is coming over my sun glasses hitting my eyelashes shutting my eye lids so that I cant see. It is blowing so hard that you feel like you have a rubber face flapping in the wind. It is all you can do to keep the bike on the road and we are only doing 55 to 60 mph. I passed a sign that said, Please Don't Drink and Drive. I think to myself, hell man, I cant even keep the bike on the road let lone try to drink something. The clouds are all over us and it is cold. We pass a car right in front us that was lifted off the ground and rolled across the Hwy onto the other side, upside down, not sure if anyone was hurt, probably so, it looked bad but we continue on. This is one of the hardest 90 miles I have ever done. We start passing a lot bikes with California tags on them. Most have no windshield and Ape handle bars. The real high above the shoulder type handle bars called apes. Most of them are wearing T-shirts and that is it. As we pass them you can see the pain of the cold and there arms up high as the wind rips there ribs apart. There are tears running down there face from the cold wind beating there eyes. So Jim and I stop to put on some more warm cloths because we ant proud or cold either. We start to laugh at the humor of this, holding our hands in the air like Apes. It was just to funny. The wind was not so funny and we continued on to Kingman.

Downtown Durango during the Irons Horse Rally 2002

Out of Kingman and a long, long hill down into Laughlin and the wind stops. We check to see were to camp and end up at Lake Davis Friday night 6 PM.. This is a very nice place to camp and setting up the tents. Jim had told me what a great tent he had got as we started the trip that night outside Hanksville Ut.. He told me how it was made of space age type technology. I said but has it every been to Mount Everest in the Hymimalayas. You see my tent was made by Sir Hillary the first man to climb Mt. Everest and it says right there on the box that it had been to Mt. Everest. So boxes don't lie do they.

Anyway I set my tent up and look over at Jim to hear a snap of his tent pole and the words out of his mouth, I messed up. I could not help myself, I started laughing and saying, you know that space age stuff is good but it will never make it to top of Mt Everest. He is giving me this look like I am some kind of hole and a mother of some kind. So we repair the pole borrowing some tape and stuff from another camper. All is well and down into Laughlin we go very excited. 1000's of bikes every-where. It is such a small town and 80, 000 bikes are riding up and down the strip and parked in every parking spot available everywhere. There are 100,000 people come thru the town during this rally. It is more than a sea of bikes. It is a giant party of people having fun. Bands, vendors and display's are in the parking lots of the casinos everywhere.We are drag racing up and down this 2 mile strip on the main street of Laughlin. There is a gauntlet of 1000's of people lined on both sides of the road and the ladies are doing there thing, show me them tits. The police are there and they are nice and fun to be around. They were just part of the party as well.We rode up and down the strip three or four times to stop and walk around buying some thing at the vendors. Into a few casinos where we had dinner at the Colorado Belle. I usually order a chef salad because it is cheap and has all the stuff in it that I need to continue on my journeys. Yeah it is heathy. Most of the time they almost put some salad dressing on it. So this time I explain this to our waiter and I ask if I could have some extra ranch dressing for my salad, sure was his answer. Everyone in Laughlin that night was so very nice to us and in general everyone was having fun. A short time and the waiter brings me my chef salad and lays a bowl a foot in diameter and 3 inches deep full of ranch dressing beside me. I said damn man, now that is some extra salad dressing. I am not kidding this is a big bowl of salad dressing. He said yeah and you have to eat it all before you can have some desert. OO' Man!! Jim, the waiter and I laughing out loud as people looked to see what it was all about. There is no way I could finish this bowl off, but still I used most of it and did the best I could to finish it off. The waiter would come by the table and point at the bowl and we would all crack up again. A very nice salad and back out onto the strip. Jim and I went to see all that is going on. People were still riding and racing up and down the strip by the 100's. The Hwy Patrol had brought in some men and woman on mounted horses to control the crowd. They are big like the Clydes Dells but I don't think they were. It is now close to 12 midnight and some people are a little more routey but not to bad. The mounted police would move the horse into the crowds and with the rear ends of the horse just kinda bump people back onto the sidewalks because they are blocking the entrances of the casinos. It was so funny to watch them with there horses. It seemed the horses knew what to do and the horses seemed to like to do this as well. A couple of guys got out line and the mounted patrol would surround him on these horses and the two mounted police would grab him and drag them off to be arrested. There was no reason to act a fool we were all having fun. The cops were too and all was well. Now 1 AM. Saturday morning and we are tried and head back to the bikes which are parked between two casinos and back to the camp site. A very nice ride that night with the moon out and clear skies about 15 miles. A short talk 1:30 AM. and into the tents we went for a nights rest. But wait next door to our camp site there is a party going on with lots of yelling, hooting and stuff. So about 3 AM they settle down and I am just about a sleep and it is now probably 4 AM. As I am just asleep there is this horrendous noise outside of a helicopter. This thing is so close to the ground my tent is moving from the wind of the helicopter. Three or four times he passes over our tents and then he is gone as fast as he was there. It is now 5 AM Saturday morning. I drop off to sleep again to be awakened again by the noise outside of the motorcycles moving out for the day at 7 AM. I lay there thinking what the hell was that all about last night. I got up to see the party people next door. They were all dressed up in black leather and boots looking very biker types and none of them had bikes. They have just cars and one them talking on a cell phone. O Well, the adventures of a Biker. Jim got up and I ask him, man what did you think about that helicopter last night. He said what, I did not hear anything. I said you go to be kidding. He had told me at Hanksville that first night that he was a heavy sleeper but man that is unbelievable and he really did not hear anything. So as we packed and got ready to go we had borrowed some tape and stuff to fix his space age tent which has never been to Mt. Everest and wanted to take it back to the people. So we packed the bikes and went over to there camp site. This is were we first heard about the shooting. It had started about 1:30 right after we left that night. We were parked right next door to the place were 12 people were shot. 3 Bikers I think are dead. 3 are wounded and they are innocent bystanders. 6 more were wounded and they were Bikers. This was more than I could understand. We were all having so much fun and now this shooting would change everything. We pulled into Laughlin that morning about 9AM. Things seemed closed and tight. I felt a kinda pressure on me. No one was smiling anymore. The cops had riot shot guns and looked as though they wanted to shot you. Everywhere I look the faces of the straits and the Bikers as well had that look of doubt in there eyes. Just a thought here. I think if you want to kill one another that would be fine but leave the innocents out of it please. If you want go out into the desert and do what ever you want to do that would be fine too. Jim and I went to the Golden Nugget casino for a buffet breakfast and the waitress comes up to us. I ask her, do the drinks cost extra, she said, no just tell me what you want. Humm I said, you mean I can have some orange juice, milk, coffee coke, tea, she said yes. I said, alrighty then, coffee, orange juice and some milk thank you very much. She brought us everything that we wanted with a smile. She was great and I had three big glasses of the best orange juice I have ever had along with one hell of a good breakfast. I was feeling a little better and back out to the bikes we went. Still 1000's of bikes everywhere and on the road we went headed towards Flagstaff, Arizona. It is a very nice day out. Jim's brother lives just outside Flagstaff and we are to meet him there Saturday night. We drove down the old Hwy Route 66. On the way a couple of guys pass us with high ape bars on there bikes and are doing close to 90 mph. We travel near the speed limit about 70 mph most of the time. As they passed us I shook my head at Jim and he did the same. 10 miles up the road the Hwy.Patrol had them pulled over and was giving the third degree along with a ticket. We decided to stop at the Harley house outside Williams Arizona around 2PM.. Right next door is a Dinner and we have not had much to eat since breakfast. It is a very nice looking place inside with Harley stuff all over the walls. The tables are very tall with bar stools to set on and we decide we would get a hamburger. I look over and there is this big barbeque grill and some stuff to cook with. Jim goes to the bathroom. Some people had walked in before us and ordered. The waitress walks by me with two plates of raw meat on them. I am thinking, what the hell is that all about. So these people get up and go over and start cooking the steaks on the grill. Jim comes back and the waitress shows up, me asking her, do you have to cook you own stuff, her answer yes. I said even a hamburger, yes she said. Jim looks at me saying what are you talking about. I tell waitress that it will be a second and to come back. I tell him the story and Jim says, hell man I don't even cook at home let alone out here on the road. While we were setting there, he mentioned again that I should think about a Glide of some kind and I am telling him that money is pretty tight, maybe someday. I still enjoy riding Passion anyway. We decided not to cook dinner at this time, got something to drink and was on the road again towards Flagstaff. On the way these same Bikers with apes come by us again after there conversation with the Man still doing 80 mph or so. Jim and I are in the slow lane about 70 mph and there is a semi-truck in the fast lane trying to pass a slow car we had passed and is going around us as well. Behind us is a line of cars happy with our speed just cruising along. The semi makes the pass and is right beside us and is going to get over in our lane. Up comes the two Bikers and one makes the cut across in front of us and cuts the truck driver off. His buddy behind him comes up haling ass and expecting the semi to get out of his way. He cant because the other bike has cut him off. The Biker hits his brakes directly behind the truck. Whips out around beside the trailer and catches the side draft drawing him almost underneath the truck trailer. He is trying his best to get his bike under

The picture I missed on the way to Cripple Creek rally 2001.

control and with in inches of the wheels. Final getting control of his bike he proceeds on and Jim and I are looking at each other thinking man that was close what a fool. Some other cars come up from behind us and are looking at us like we are the crazy ones. I am shaking my head at them and pointing, saying no that is not me. Riding in the Wind should not be crazy or put anyone in danger. Especially yourself. Once in Flagstaff and then to get a room at one of the original motels called The Frontier on Route 66. Jim gets on his cell phone, Can You Hear Me Now and calls David his older brother. A nice shower and there at the door is David now 6 PM Saturday night. We go to a real nice place there on Route 66 for dinner and lucky for us it is cariokie night. I want to stay and see it because I have never been to one. Some of these people are serious about this and are there hours before hand to wait till it is time for them to sing. Wow. Some are very good and others are not. One of the ladies sings a Cher song. I start singing along with it. David looks at Jim and says he is worried about me, he actually knows the words to the songs. I said you think that is bad, I got the CD and the album as well and we all cracked up laughing. Funny thing is I really do. Off we went and decide to stop in for drink's at a local club called the Mustang Club. We walk in and to see a sea of cowboy hats. You know how I felt. There were lots of ropes hanging on the walls and I was wondering if by the end of the night I would be talking to one. So we set down Jim and David looking like just one of the locals and me with long hair. The waitress comes over and we order a drink, just coke for me please. It has been a long time since Jim had seen his brother and they caught up on what was going on in there life's. The waitress comes back with the drinks and she drops something off the tray and bent over to pick it up. I notice there is a tattoo on her lower back. Of course I am looking, I been told to look at the beauty of woman all my life. I like looking at women anyway. I cant see all of the tattoo as some of it leads down into her pants. She stands up again and I say what is the tattoo I could only see part of it. She said OOO, that will cost you a dollar to see all of it. By the time she said see all of it, I had slapped a dollar on the table. She came up to me, turned around and pulled her pants out and down a little as to let me see. Yes it was a very nice Tattoo. Don't ask me what is was but it was a very nice Tattoo. Anyway, Jim and David had some beers and talking and some more beers and catching up on things still. Now close to 1 AM Sunday and I thinking early up and 500 miles home. So back to the Frontier motel and still we talked til 2 AM. I noticed something going on outside. There seemed to be a lot of trains going by all the time. Lights out and clicked clack, train whistle blowing every 15 minutes. Sometimes the trains are going and another coming at the same time all night long every 15 minutes. By 6 AM I am train crazy up and waiting for Jim. In order for us to get home on time we have to leave 7 AM. Jim is up and half dead, the alcohol has him by the bowling balls and kicking his jack ass. But still he is up, packed and on the bike around 7 AM. In Flagstaff the elevation is about 8000 feet and in April very cold in the morning. Up over a pass and out across the Indian reservation northeast Arizona. Still a very nice ride to stop in Kayenta, Arizona for lunch at a Burger King. It is a funny feeling to be surrounded by Indians. You feel so out of place, like you don't belong. Anyway back out to the bikes and Jim's want start. He has had this problem before and for some reason the battery cable is loose, I don't why. We fix it and 20 minutes later down the street we go for gas. I get my gas, pay for it and push the bike off to the side out of the way. A Indian Kayenta city cop pulls up and says to me, I am going to write you up for speeding. I said what, he said did you not just come off the Hwy. I said what!!, no man I have been eating at Burger King for 20 minutes and the bike was broke down for 20 minutes more. No way was I speeding, I came from the other direction anyway. I said, what are doing to him, don't you know who you are after. He said well not really. Not really I said. Man if you don't know then don't do anything. He looked at me funny and went over and started harassing some other Biker saying the same thing, I am going to write you a ticket. Wow?!. Jim was inside all this time and when he came out, he said was that all about, my answer was, hell man I don't know. Told him the story and off we went towards the border of Utah thru Monument Valley. I was feeling a little like Custer and looking for the ambush. Long open roads and a nice valley. We had good weather all day and as you remember the wind in Arizona beats on you from above always. The day is getting long and now into Utah. Jim is looking pretty bad and worn but never says a word. I can see this and it worries me a little. 4 PM out side Monticello UT., still 200 mile's away from home and all that matters is trying to get home safe and before dark. I am beat down but not as bad as Jim. Pulling into Moab, what a good feeling that was coming off the hill into Moab. Now we are just a rock throw from home really 120 miles, 2 hours away. Stopped and had a burger and then thru the river valley on Hwy 128 into Cisco to stop. I can tell Jim is almost done, fatigue is on him hard and I ask him are you alright. Yes was his answer. A short ride now and home. This was an amazing trip 4 days, three nights and 1600 miles, no sleep and all I could think about was when and where would my next trip take me. It is now almost May 2002 and it would be Bryce Canyon UT with Jim. We have a trip planned for the end of May because riding is what I do best. But wait there are some messages on my machine when I get home from Laughlin. Who could it be.

The Feelings of a Biker

In spite of everything Laughlin was one hell of a kick in the ass ride of fun and adventures. I loved every minute of it, except that one thing, I know it is a big thing but lets not dwell on that ok. On my answering machine is my lady and she is still in Denver. She is scared and she thinks her life may be endanger from someone and in Denver that is not to hard to believe. I said well then you need to come home and be safe and she did. She was to stay with her mom and that was the plan. You got to know I still love her but I think I can face the demon and walk away. Wrong, Obe One Canoebee. After 6 months without seeing or hearing from her, I see her face and all the old emotion that I have for her come back as if they never left. I think things can be different between us and maybe she has figured it out or maybe I have figured it out. This is what I want to be happy with her. After seeing her a few times, I ask her if she would like to move back into my house for awhile. The answer is yes. She is just a little girl about 12 years old in a woman's body with three kids and I love her so. I don't blame her for our demise, she is happy when she is happy and if it always is about her. When it is not about her she is mean, hateful, vindictive and very destructive when she dose not get her way. Always saying things that go deep into my heart to hurt me. Doing things that she knows will tear my soul apart. I am hoping that she might see the light that is so beautiful in my eyes as I see her. She knows that I would never do anything to hurt her. If she ask for anything I usually tried to do for her. I think Meat Loaf said it best, I Would Do Anything For Love But I Want Do That and I love her dearly. She moves in middle of May and I have the Bryce Canyon Run planned the end of May before she came back with Jim. She thinks that she will be Ok and I should go. Jim and I talk about the trip on a short ride over to Gateway up the Una Weep Canyon the only river that flows two direction north and south at the same time in the U.S. With my lady on the back of Passion. It is a very nice ride thru Una Weep canyon with a wonderful road to match. All the time Jim is telling me that I need a bigger bike. You know I really love my bike Passion and enjoy riding her always and the idea of giving her up is a little un-nerving for me. The end of May and I am asking my lady if she will be alright if I go to Bryce Canyon Utah while she takes her mom to Denver to see a doctor. While she is there she will take care of some old business of hers as well. She would be back by the time I got back and it was settled I go to Bryce Canyon with peace of mind. Jim and I have planned for a 2 night 3 day trip and we are to do the same thing as on the Laughlin run. We would leave Friday night at 5 PM and stay at the Hanksville cut off at I-70. It seems that Jim's wife is not to happy again about this trip and he is a little down again when he shows on Lady. By the time we get to Green River he is fine or close anyway. Stopping to get gas on the west side of Green River. A van pulls up and out comes a family of six. I can see there pockets are not to heavy with money. As they walked by the bikes one of the littlest kids looks over and says, OOO bike. He heads strait for the bikes. I walk towards the kid quickly to keep him from being burned on the hot pipes, telling his folks what I am doing. They all stop and all the kids are looking and saying man those are some nice motorcycles, as we say, well thanks man. Standing in the parking lot we all had a nice conversation and the Dad told us of the days when he had a Harley and was in the wind. I never felt so good, I love it when people see me as there friend and just talk to me as if I was somebody to them. Down the road to the cut off we go now 9 PM dark and another inspiring night if not more at the Hanksville cut off I-70. This place is so quietly peaceful with 500 foot rock walls around you on three sides. Making you feel at peace with yourself and the world. No one can see this but Jim and I and it is just a simple place in the middle of no where. I ask Jim if he was going to do the zipper thing again before he settled down, his answer was probably so. Jim is very particular about things and likes things a certain way.

He will spend time making it so. This is fine with me because I am out on the road doing what I love best. The sun tops the rock wall and you can feel the warmth. The next morning it is as close to a prefect day as it gets to be in the wind. Jim has this thing about bungee cords and he always tells me you can never have enough bungee cords. When he puts them on his bike to secure his stuff he is never satisfied with they way they are. This always cracks me up watching him adjust these bungee's. Soon he is satisfied and off we go down Hwy 24. Stopping at Hanksville at Blonde's for a great breakfast and nice people as well. The road Hwy 24 from here is a must do for every one, even if you have to walk it. The day is clam, clean, clear blue skies and very little traffic on the road towards Capital Reef and Torrey Ut. In Jim's words, the best day I every had on a bike. It was that one prefect day in the wind and on the road that you look for as a Biker all the way across the top of Dixie Natl. Forrest on Hwy 12 out of Torrey. Down a long hill thru Escalante Canyon, Ummm, the air is prefect and the views are the best as usual in the world. We stop to make a call to his wife and I say Can You Hear Me Now, which I spoke of earlier, the pole thing and he could not get threw, out of coverage. We are meeting and talking to some of the nicest people on the road along the way and I enjoy this very much. There is a drought happening in 2002 here in the south western part of the United States. Utah, New Mexico, Arizona and Colorado are hit hardest by this drought. At one time there were 20 fires going on in Colorado at the same time at some point. Looking off into the distance, there is a fire happening in the Dixie Natl. Forest outside Cannonville Ut near the entrance of Bryce Canyon. It is getting late and we are excited to reach our destination for that night. Pulling up to the entrance of Bryce Canyon at 7 PM, the girl says $20.00, I said for a motorcycle, yes $20.00 a bike and $10.00 to camp. I said you are telling me I need to pay $50.00 for two motorcycles to camp on the ground in the woods, Yes she says. My blood begins to boil and Jim says lets go back to the small city Bryce Canyon that we passed and talk about it. I said yeah we better before I get into trouble. Small point here please. In my mind I pay a lot of taxes and have all my life. In my mind I have already paid to have the right to drive up a road to see something in a place that already belongs to me as a citizen to begin with. If you have a problem with bad people destroying things in this country, punish them not me. Let the bad guys pay for there destruction and let me enjoy my world. I take care of my world and so should you. Anyway Jim and I see differently on this subject but that is ok. I may not always like what you have to say, but I will fight to the death your right to say it, Promise. Really we had only planned to spend the night and had to leave early in the morning to get back home that Sunday night. To pay $50.00 to sleep on the ground at that time was more than I could understand. Point here again please. They are taking away everything that means anything to me and changing it into a rich mans world where he will be the only one that can afford to see things of wonder and beauty and it upsets me terribly. Most everyone buys into the dog and pony show that they put on, all the time lining there pockets with your hard earned money. Sorry about that but this really upsets me terribly. So we go back and there is a nice camp ground with a swimming pool and a hot tube for $15.00 for two bikes and we still get to sleep on the ground. That is where we would stay for the night, now 8 PM Saturday and starting to get dark. Looking for nice spot we stop and began to set up the tents. I set mine up facing a camp fire pit and the table with our stuff on it. Then to look over at Jim as he puts his tent up. I said what is the matter don't you like this camp site, huh he says. I said, well your tent is facing outwards away from this camp site towards the next sight, his answer, I messed up, me laughing at him. It always kills me when he says this, I messed up. I try to have fun all the time no matter where I am or what I am doing. You can look to the north and see the fire in the night air and the smoke lighting up the sky. We go back out on the bikes to ride and look around. I had seen a side road just up the Hwy that leads to the edge of Bryce Canyon and we ride down it because I am always couriers and want to see. At the end of the road is a very nice overlook into a small canyon of nice rock formation. On the trail that we walk down there are three deer, a young buck and two females which I love very much standing right there beside us. We marveled at there wonder and the sunset now happing as well. Dark becomes all that we can see and we go back to Ruby Canyon Restaurant to eat. This is the first time I talk about maybe writing a book. I tell Jim what I would like to do and he is very supportive about the idea of this book. I explain to him how I wish to mix pictures with words in a book call On the Road in the Wind a Bikers View. He thinks this is a very good idea. Then back to the camp site to talk of the prefect day on the road and a nice nights sleep for me which is unusual always thinking of her of course. I was up early as always and went over and took a few pictures of some ducks and birds playing in and near by a small lake. The morning is clean and fresh like something new. It is another prefect day to be in the wind. Jim is up and playing with his bungee cords as always and we are on the road once again. Making a big loop out of this trip like we do with all our trips. We turn and head towards Richfield Ut. thru Ruby Canyon still on Hwy 12. Great colors of reds in this canyon and pillow like rock formation. A must see ride. Turning north on Hwy 89 to stop in Panguitch a small city for breakfast. It looks like its right of the 30's. We travel a lot and always get a cup of coffee at most places we stop. I really don't drink coffee, just when I am on the road. Anyway a nice little Ma and Pa place just inside town. Walked in and they are very nice to us asking how our trip is going and would we like some coffee. Yes please as we set down. She brings the coffee and the taste is like how the guy on T.V. Quan with the donkey says it should be. The coffee goes down as if it had come from Colombia smooth and mellow to the taste warming us. A very fine breakfast and some very nice people. I guess my point here is, some times it is the little places that are the best and you should try them out along the way. Unfortunately not all places will be like this one but don't let this stop you from finding a dream of a place where the people are nice and the food is the best in the world. Down Hwy 89 headed north thru a long beautiful valley between two rolls of mountains in the Fishlake Natl. Forest. It is a little cool and I have on my warm stuff. I have to say prefect would be the word and very little to no traffic all the way to Richfield and onto I -70 headed home now 12 noon. Every and all trips I take or we take. We try to stick to the 50/50 I talked about earlier and it does work. At the end of the day I have seen so many great thing and talked to so many wonderful people and me fatigue is low. Richfield to Salina and the only small pass that we will go over and heading back thru the San Rafael Swell. Coming off the high plains and down a long hill, the sun is out and the temperatures change from 50* in the mountains to 90* the closer we get to Green River in the desert below. Stopping in Green River for gas and burning up from the heat and all the cloths we had on. We were pealing the cloths off as fast as we could that we had on from that morning looking pretty silly I am sure and now 4 PM. Sunday. Jim is still telling me how much happier I would be with a bigger bike like a Glide. Now I am saying, maybe you are right and I will look into when we get back home. Still on I -70 and our final stop in Cisco to say it has been nice riding with you and I will see you the end of June, Yeah that is right, another trip and it will be back to Arizona for David's 50th birthday his older brother and it would be 3 nights 4 days headed south of Flagstaff and the city Camp Verde. Near by there is a major fire going on in the Coconino Natl. Forest, Arizona. Once back in G.J. and my lady is there waiting at her moms for me to get back home. I love her and I know there is a small chance that we will make it as a couple. I want it to work out in my heart and mind and know that it will not. I hate the ideal of saying good bye to someone. I have said good bye so many times to so many who have meant so much to me to never see them again. So I am not to much on saying good bye. Some people may see it as being rood but it is not, it is just me. I am J.T.. If you are wondering what J.T. stands for it stands for Juvenile Telinquent. I graduated from delinquent many years ago. Some people say it stands for Just Thongs baby. Monday, the next day I go back to the Harley shop to talk to a old friend of mine who I think the world of, Hootie. We have known each other along time but never do anything together because his world is on a bullet bike. Our paths cross a lot and I consider him to be a brother. Hootie is now a salesman there at the Harley house and I tell him that I really would like to step up into Super Glide. He says OK give me your numbers. I had saved a little from my taxes and pinched a little here and there. I wanted and was looking at a plain 2002 Super Glide for $12,000.00. All he has is a dressed up Super Glide around $17,000.00. I said, ahh man. NOOO, I don't have that kind of money Hootie. He says man, that's all I have and not sure if we will get anymore because of the 100th anniversary bikes going into production. So I call around and there are none to be found anywhere in three states. A few days go by and Hootie calls me and says

Mt. Sniffles is the pretties Mountain I have ever seen. Out Ridgeway Co.

there is a Super coming in 1st of next week, do I want it, YES!! Hootie I do. 4 months before all of this happen I had looked on the internet and found a picture of a nice plain Silver Super Glide and I have been using on my computer as my desk top picture since then. The bike comes in Thursday and I go down to look at it as they get it out of the crate to be prepped. It is the same bike as on my desk top. It is the Silver Ghost Returned. It looks like the old Ghost from years past. I love this bike, it feels like it has been a part of my soul for a long time. Every time I look at the Ghost it brings me so much hope and joy for a future that is full of nice people, great places, desires and adventures in other wise messed up world. So many people have patches all over everything that say Live to Ride. It is on there jackets and the side covers of there bikes. For me I don't live to ride, I am not alive because I ride. I Ride To Live. It is the only time I really feel like I am alive. If you take away my right to ride I might as well be dead. The idea of this scares me to death and at the same time helps me to appreciate what I have and the ability to enjoy what I consider to be the best thing on earth. The Ghost does not have all the fancy stuff on it and that is fine with me because as Jim said you know you can do all that stuff to your bike. He said, you can do this and that to it and put this on it but really in the end I just want to ride in the wind on the roads. This is also how I feel, I just want to ride. Funny thing about this, the end of June 2001 I brought Passion my Sportster from a friend Gary at the Harley house. In a years time I put 12.000 miles on her and loved every minute of it. We had seen so much together and I was very hesitant to trade her in. In a since saying goodbye to something that I had shared so much with good and bad. The end of June 2002 Hootie a friend of mine at the Harley house sold me the Ghost and I have more Passion for this bike then any other bike before in my life. Even today the Ghost is still plain and I would not trade him for any other bike. So a new bike and now what, yes sir I ride because that is what keeps me feeling alive. The run to Arizona for David's birthday is three days away and I have 80 miles road time on the Ghost, just out of the box really. I would have to break him in on the road headed for Arizona.

The Ghost and the Biker

The Ghost is five days old and if you really think about. It is almost the 1st of July and Arizona in the middle of summer would not be my first choice as a nice easy trip. If it was not for my friendship with Jim, I would have gone to Yellowstone Natl. Park instead. Jim like me has a long back ground in a world full of bikes and at one time he owned a 1400 intruder like the on I had. He did the same thing I did, sold his Intruder to buy the Harley of his dreams. The drought is still burning everything up in sight in all four states and no relieve is coming. My lady deep into my life now again and completely moved into my house. I talk to my lady a lot as time gets closer to the trip to Arizona. I am having a hard time with the idea of leaving her there alone for 4 nights 4 days. She is telling me that it would give her a chance to catch up on some things that she likes to do and that I should go and have fun. So this becomes the plan. Jim and I are very excited but that is the way we are anytime we get to ride out there on the roads. This time we will go out Hwy 50 east to Hwy 550 heading south via Delta, Montrose, Ridgeway, Telluride, Lizard Head pass, across the desert and the Indian Reservation. Into Kayenta across the desert to the Grand Canyon and down into Flagstaff the next day. Still going south to Camp Verde where David lives about 1400 miles round trip. It is Wednesday evening around 5PM and we are ready to go. I had spoke to my lady about how when it came time for me to leave she would break down and not want me to go. She would just laugh at me and I teased her a lot all the time. I was trying to prepare her for that day when she would have to stand there and see me ride off. Always she still laughed at me, telling me that it will not affect her like I think it will. Ok my love if you say so. The Ghost has my tent, sleeping bag, all the gear that I might need and it is time for me to go. Jim shows on Lady and I crawl on the bike firing him up. I then turn to kiss her as to say I will see you as soon as possible. I am not to good at saying goodbye and I never have been. I am thinking she is fine but she is not and the tears flow from her eyes. I looked at her and said, I want go if it is going to hurt you this much. Now I am with a few tears in my eyes and my lady is saying, no please go I miss you already that is all. Kissing her serval times and then looked at Jim as I rolled out of the drive way on to the street. Always turning to see her face as long as I could pulling out and down the road. My heart is already missing having her there with me to be on the road and in the wind. It was a long ride to Montrose about 60 miles, always seeing her face and the tears. We stopped and had a bite to eat at Wendy's and talked for a second about how she was alright and at the same time not alright with me leaving on this trip. The funny thing was that Jim's wife was not upset with him this time about going on this trip. The Hwy from Montrose to Ridgeway and then just outside there we had planned to spend the night. This is a very peaceful ride and lots of pleasant views along the way. The San Quan Mts on one side and the Uncomphgre Mts on the other. All time the river flowing beside you riding in the wind. We pass Lake Ridgeway State Park and it is empty of water because of the drought. It is getting late in time somehow and dark is coming around 8PM. I know this area very well and know we have over a hour crossing Dallas pass. It will be very cold and in the dark before we get to a place were we can camp. Thru Ridgeway and 5 miles out I stopped to discuss the situation with Jim near a bridge. As we talked I looked down in a swampy area below to see my first Beaver in the wild. The animals hold a very special place in my heart. We decide for safety reasons that we should go back to Ridgeway and a place I know for the night to camp. A nice old man 80 years comes out that owns the place and says you got $10.00 and go pick yourself a spot. We did. Very nice and peaceful place and met some interesting people there as well. I love talking to people and to hear a few of there stories. Soon after we had put up the tents I call my lady, Can You Hear Me Now. She is still very sad, crying on the phone and I try to ease her sorrow. I miss her as well and it has only been 4 hours since I left her standing there crying. I tell her that I promise that I will never leave her alone again and if I have to I will change my way of seeing things and she is fine with this. I tell her I will see her as soon as I possible can and I love you hanging up the phone. A very nice night thinking of her and a morning of peaceful clam to start the day. Up and out on the road headed on Hwy 62 towards Telluride, Lizard Head pass and just on the other side of Rico a nice little place for lunch on Hwy 145. These people at Stoner's Café are very friendly towards Bikers and you should stop for a bit to eat. The food is great and they have15 Hummingbird feeders on the outside deck where you can have lunch and watch the Hummingbirds come and go.The Hummingbirds make a wonderful sound and they stop sometimes to look at what you might be doing setting there eating. I love this place and you should stop. This ride over Lizard Head pass is equal to any that I have ever done. Coming out of the mountains a little cold but clear, clean, fresh air and views that are the best as usual and riding down into Cortez, Co. Just out side 4-corners Monument on Hwy 160 headed into Arizona and you can feel the heat out across the desert on the Indian Reservation. Most of the reservation is sand and dirt and has a beauty of its own. The thing that inters my mind is this was the best we could do for these people. I had a hard time riding this stretch of Hwy and find it hard to understand. There is nothing out there but sand and dirt and that is about it. The wind starts blowing 20 mph as we hit the border of Arizona. It is like someone opens a door as soon as we crossed into Arizona. The wind begins and never stops as you ride the roads there. There is blowing sand storms and it covers the Hwy in spots. As I said before the wind comes from above you and beats on you the whole time you are there. Now 2 PM and we are in Kayenta AZ. for a bite to eat and some gas and I am wondering if the ambush is just ahead We are still 150 miles away from our destination the Grand Canyon for the night. A very nice ride as we get closer to the Grand Canyon and you can feel some real heat drying you out. Turning right on Hwy 64 at Cameron AZ and up a long beautiful hill onto a high plateau and the entrance of the Grand Canyon close to 8000 feet. $30.00 for two motorcycles to camp on the ground and a very nice place. There is very little water because of the drought and everyone has to conserve while we are there. We put up the tents and there is a giant Raven over looking us from a tree top. I am some what mystical due to a little Indian blood in me and believe the Raven looks after me when I am on the road. They always seem to fly along beside me as I ride down the hwy's and appear out of nowhere at the strangest times. I guess I like to think someone is looking out for me and so far I think they have been. Jim always laughs at me about this in a nice way. He see the Raven in the tree watching us and wonders if it is coincidental. The one thing Jim likes to do is eat. So after the tents are up, food becomes the subject now 7:30 Thursday night and the wind stops like the door was shut. The closes place to eat is Grand Canyon Village 25 miles away and off we go stopping to catch a view of the canyon with a very nice ride thru a great forest. In my mind the Grand Canyon is bigger, wider and longer but still not as powerful as Dead Horse Point. The road to the village has a sweet smell to it from the pines along the way. At the village this is where I call my lady Can You Hear Me Now. She is a little upset that I did call earlier now 8:30. I tell her that in some places I cant get thru and I miss her. She is now mad at me for leaving her there alone. I tell her I love you and I will see you as soon as possible hanging up the phone. Eating some really expensive food that is not that good or enough of. It is a wonderful dark cool ride looking for animals on the road and back to the camp site 25 miles. There is and has been since we left a no burn situation in all states. So there was no camp fire. We talked and the moon comes out and a very clam night with some sleep thinking of her always. In the morning there are two ravens setting in the tree by our tents. I looked at Jim and he looked at me as to say surely a coincident. Packing and off we go. The fires have clouded the skies with smoke in all four states making it difficult to take long distance pictures. One of our first stops is a rock tower built buy a lady back in the 1920's or so. It is a wonder in it self with drawings of history on the inside walls. It is worth walking up a spiral stair case to the top for some great views. The canyon is wonderfully big and has a silent beauty about it. We stopped at all the turn outs to see the canyon and getting some breakfast to eat at the Grand Canyon Village. Down off the plateau into Williams AZ. and you can feel the heat on us. I can feel it drawing my strength out of my body and we are trying to drink lots of water. Up until this point we had missed most of the heat because of being up early and crossing high heat areas in the morning. Clouds and elevation has been a factor as well as we rode. It is 20 miles to Flagstaff 8000 feet elevation and now 2 PM. We are on interstate I-40 looking for somewhere to eat having nothing since 9 AM that morning. Picking up I-17 headed south to Camp Verde and nothing looks like a place we can eat at. Going thru a lot of forest as we travel and everything is burned up. There are no green trees hardly to see at all. The trees are more a dark brown and looking like a match stick ready to catch on fire. All the roads are blocked off headed into the forest and some have armed guards in front of the entrance ways. In my eyes it looked like they where at war with someone and I guess maybe they were. It seems that people were starting a lot fires out of meanness or stupidity. Again I don't understand. It is 85* a little hot but very nice as we head down out of Flagstaff. This is a 25 mile hill into the valley below and Camp Verde on I-17. It is a 3000 foot drop in elevation to the valley below. 15 miles down the hill the temps climb to 100* in a flash and having to stop removing everything except a T-shirt to try to keep from burning up. Still headed down now 105* and the wind is blowing 20 mph. You fill like you are standing in front of a blow dryer on high but you cant turn it off. The heat is so bad, when I left Flagstaff I needed to go to the bathroom and by time we got to Camp Verde, there was no fluids in me at all, completely dried out. I was almost dehydrated and near a heat stroke. The heat feels like your in a presser cooker and you are almost done. This is the way I felt and almost nauseated to the point of being sick. We pulled into Camp Verde at a gas station and I run in store to get some Gatorade trying to revive. I am thinking if I just get to David's, there I can have nice long shower and a cold glass of ice tea. Then set down for a while under the water cooler and try to recuperate and this is my plan. Arriving in Camp Verde at 4 PM and very hot 105*, Jim breaks out the cell phone, Can You Hear Me Now. He calls his brother and all is well in my mind I think. David pulls up, me saying, man I cant wait to get to the house and a nice long shower setting under the water cooler. Jim and David look at each other and then Jim says to me, I guess I failed to mention this, there is no water cooler or a shower and really there is no house either. I am looking at them in disbelieve, saying REALLY. Jim and David say he has been working on a house now for two years and it is not quite done yet. Humm, I am burning up here, I have not had anything to eat, my lady is mad at me, there is no shower, no water cooler, no ice tea and all I can do is start to laugh as we get on our bikes headed for what ever is there on David's property. 10 miles and turn right down a dirt road a short distance to see more dirt and a narrow tree line with a dug out spot where David's house is to be someday and that is about it. There is no electricity, bathroom or anything that you might consider convenient. The small tree line is supported by a irrigation ditch that is clean and fresh water that comes form somewhere. David has old septic tank near the ditch and a hose leading into the tank from the irrigation ditch filling it with water. I was a little set back for a second but that is where my shower will be in the septic tank. Off with my cloths and into the tank I went feeling so very good to my body and helps me revive a little. Still not having any food now 6 PM Friday evening. I call my lady, Can You Hear Me Now. She is still a little mad but now misses me very much and I talk to her for a while. Telling her that I love her and I will be home soon but we had one more night before I can start back. Saturday night being David's birthday and a small party with his friends. I want to head home Saturday morning because she is very unhappy and I don't like her to be sad especially because of me. She knows I will be headed home on Sunday but does not want me to wait that long. It actually is not to bad at night down there after 8 PM because the heat dissipates quickly. Friday night at 9 PM we go and get something to eat finally at golf corse restaurant of all places. It has been 12 hours since we ate. Very good food but when you are starving to death anything would be good to you. I get up from the table after ordering and I call my lady again now 9:30, Can You Hear Me Now. I tell her that I will never leave her alone again and that I love her and I will see her soon. When I come back to the table they are making fun of me because of her and that is fine with me. Back to David's and a nice nights sleep out in the desert in a small shed with a wood floor and no roof. Up the next morning and a very nice day to go see all of David's friend's and letting them see Jim once again. Mid day and temps are up to 105* and the heat is like standing in front of your oven set at 650* with a fur coat on. It is amazing how fast you dry out down there in the heat. By 4 PM Saturday we are back to David's place and long bath in the septic tank trying to cool off and it is very refreshing. At 7 PM Saturday night people arrive for the party out in the woods and a nice Bar be Q with shrimp and steak in the night with very little light. In my mind I know that Sunday on the way back will be a long day 600 miles and Jim is hitting it hard til 2 AM with David and all his friends. The next morning the party is kicking Jim's jack ass and we pack the bikes to say so long for now will see ya later to everyone as we leave. Which reminded me of song and I am singing it as we pull out onto the road loud enough for all to hear. So Long For Now, -M I C-Will C You Later-K E Y-Y Because We Like You, -M O U S E-, MICKEY MOUSE, MICKEY MOUSE, HIS A FRIEND TO YOU AND ME, MICKEY MOUSE, MICKEY MOUSE, M I C K E Y M O U S E will see ya later. It is 9 AM and I wanted to be out on the road a little earlier but it was a great party and lots of nice people. Back on the interstate I - 17 and thru Flagstaff and across the Indian Reservation around noon and you can feel the heat start to build up on the Hwy. Still doing the 50/50 and crossing Monument Valley where a lot of great John Wayne movies were film all those years ago. Utah just ahead and the heat is there with us. We try to drink lots of fluids keeping up our strength. This is a very nice Hwy really and certain times of the year it is a must do ride. Hwy 163 picking up Hwy 191 thru Bluff, Monticello with a nice cool pass and Moab never looked so good coming down off the hill 110 miles away from home. Stopping to get a bite to eat there and then home. I was very glade to she my lady and I knew that in three weeks or so was Sturgis. My lady and I did a short trip to Denver and the Mile High National Drags in Morrison on the Ghost together. Going thru Glenwood Canyon, Vail Pass and then thru the Eisenhower tunnel about 600 miles round trip. If you have never been to the NHRA National Drags, go, just go. Harley is making a effort to compete with the jap bike in Pro Stock class and I think in time they will give them a run for there money. These bikes are 7 second quarter mile at 200 mph. The Top Fuel cars are more than you can imagine, 4 seconds and 330 mph and will stop your heart when they take off. You need to go once. While I was there at the Mile High Natl. I saw a live long dream. I have always wanted to see the Budweiser Clyde's Dell horses. They are a wonder in themselfs and as beautiful as anything you might see. Denver has a lot of great things to see and do. If you have the time and money do some these of things. Casa Bonita a restaurant with cliff diving and shows all around you. The Zoo, Museum of History, Botanical Gardens. You need to just drive by the new Bronco Stadium on I-25, sea world, Elictes Garden amusement park with lots of roller coaster, Water World a great water park, just to name a few things to see and do in Denver. Back home during all this time I am looking for a motorcycle for her to ride because I wish for her to go to Sturgis with me the first of August. Riding around town always looking and we come a cross a nice little Intruder 750 that fits her perfectly. I buy it for her to ride knowing that someday she will get the bike of her dreams as I do. If I have not said this before I really love my bike the Ghost. I had a Intruder 1400 and I think they are a fine bike for being Japanese. The 750 was a very nice bike and very nice looking. It was well maintained and she loved the bike. It is two weeks to Sturgis and time to make plans. We did a Una Weep canyon run over to Naturita, Co. about 200 miles round trip to see how the Intruder 750 felt to her. Then a short trip that I talked about earlier to Crawford and the Mad Dog Café. Riding along the north rim of the Black Canyon of the Gunnison and then crossing the Blue Mesa Lake Dam to see that it is empty of water because of the drought as well. We are on the road Hwy 50 that we took coming back from 4-Corners Rally 2001 and remembering that night where gas was the issue and seeing all the places along the way back down into G.J. about 350 miles round trip. In the end she says the bike is great lets go to Sturgis next weekend. It is my first run to Sturgis 2002 and her second rally that she has every been to. It is also the longest ride she has every done and I am a little concerned for her safety and the distances of the trip close to 1400 miles. Sturgis, South Dakota a Dream in it self for me and we cant wait to get on the road and in the wind. Jim and I have planned this trip since January and it is his first trip to Sturgis as well. But you gotta know by now that riding is what I do best and with my lady, Sturgis is the third Dream.

Veterans Rally in Cripple Creek 2002. All I can say is Wow!!

Sturgis, South Dakota 2002

Looking at a map and seeing the route that we must take to get to Sturgis. Jim, my lady and I decide that 4 days and 4 nights is what we have in time to make this trip. Leaving Wednesday afternoon to stay at a motel that night in Denver and we would share a room. Then camp for two nights Thursday and Friday in South Dakota near Sturgis seeing all that we can. On the way back we would stop in Denver again at a motel Saturday night sharing a room for a nice easy ride home. For me I love camping out there on the roads in the forest and parks along the way with what I consider to be the real Bikers of the world. There always is a lot of very nice strait people no-bikers and Bikers at these places. I enjoy speaking to them about there days and mine in the wind on the road. Talking to Jim it turns out that he has a friend that would love to go to Sturgis and has made a reservation at a motel for two nights in Rapid City S.D. very close to Sturgis. So now our plan is, my lady and I in one room and Jim and his friend will share a room in Denver Wednesday and Saturday night. In Rapid City we would all share a room for those two nights and that camping was no longer a part of the trip. So this becomes the plan and Wednesday is here ready to go on another Dream, Sturgis. Now 4 we meet at my house around 12 noon, a little clouded but a nice day and as always we are very excited. I always do something before we leave on our trips. I ask my lady, Are you excited, as I slap her on the shoulder and me saying, man I am excited, are you excited slapping her once again. She always gives me a little dirty look when I do this. I do this to Jim as well all the time and he laughs at me saying, Yeah man I am excited. Are you excited. I get excited just thinking about riding the Ghost on another trip to anywhere and I am more than ready to go. Jim pulls up with his friend who has a cell phone stuck to his ear. Can You Hear Me Now. I am on the Ghost, my lady is on the Intruder 750, Jim's is on Lady his soft tail and his friend on a chromed out wide glide. Damn man are you excited and off we go headed east on I-70 to Denver. Going thru Glenwood Canyon which is always a very moving feeling for me. The Colorado River flowing there beside us as it has for 1000's of years cutting a time lines of wonder thru the rocks. There are nice hill sides of trees and rocks surrounding you looking and feeling old in time. A light rain starts but not enough to warrant rain gear. At Vail the clouds become darker as we head up Vail Pass. I am watching the cars in the other lane coming down off the pass. I am checking if they have there windshield wipers on and for rain drops on there windows. Half way up the pass and the clouds are looking heavy with water and then to see all the cars wet and wipers going like hell. I motion everyone to stop and we gear up for the rain and the cold that will follow. Vail Pass is 11,000 feet and I have seen it snow up there in July. Remembering all the great rain storms I have been in and saying something to my lady about Jim, how I hope he gets his rain suit on right this time and the rain starts to hit us. My lady starts to laugh and I am laughing as I get my bike to pull out onto the Hwy. The rain becomes harder making me hunker down behind the windshield laughing out loud all the way down into Silverthorn 25 miles away to stop. There we had a bite to eat drying off and warming up. A fairly nice ride thru Eisenhower tunnel and the Continental Divide into Denver. Next door to our motel is a bowling alley and we go over to look after settling in our rooms. We walk in looking like a Biker gang all dressed in leather and boots. I don't think this is something you see every day, a bunch of Bikers going bowling. We get some shoe's and our lane is at the very end of the alley away from everyone. In my mind my lady won because she looked the best bending over throwing the ball. J.T. just thongs baby. Back to the motel and up the next morning, are you excited, yeah baby I am very excited and we will be in Sturgis by night fall. Out and on I-25 headed for Cheyenne WY.

and there is a lot of road strait thru a lot of nothing. In a sense it has its own beauty and reminds me of our national song, amber waves of gain. The open roads are very nice for awhile as we pass bikes coming and going by the 100's. Stopping to do the 50/50 and look to see some wild elk right there beside us on Hwy 85 in Wyoming. As you know the animals are special to me and seeing them is a dream in it self. After 250 miles of amber waves of gain and enough of ambers and looking to see something else. It is now mid day and you can feel the heat. We are getting water when we can to stay fresh. My ladies Intruder has a small gas tank on it about 2 gallons and we have been riding with this in mind. The problem that exist in Wyoming is there are no gas station. So if go to Sturgis be aware of the gas thing from all directions. Just before Hawk Springs a dark clouds comes over us and we are drenched with rain at first. The rain turns to hail coming down out of the sky hitting us as we ride. They are not big enough to warrant stopping and I see no danger. I can see blue sky all around us except for this one dark cloud setting in one spot and we are under it. They are small hail balls about the sizes of peas and one flies over my sunglasses hitting me in the eye. It blinded me for a minute as my eye started watering. It is hurting as if someone poked me in the eye. For some reason I find humor in this and I start laughing the whole time about ten minutes as we hunker down again to ride out the storm. I am remembering all those great storms of the past. They mean so much to me and my lady tells me when we stop to get gas she was doing the same. I looked down at my arms because they were itching for some reason. There are red marks up and down my arms where the hail balls had hit them. I was not wearing my jacket or anything other than my vest and gloves. My windshield is small and is designed to cut then wind off me a little. My lady always wears a sweater or something and also they have big windshields. They were not hit as much as I was and were fine. At Riverview WY. looking for gas and we are surrounded by bikes there. I see no river and there is a bar for Bikers and that is it. My lady goes on reserve still 30 miles away from New Castel WY. This is where we will turn to go into South Dakota on Hwy 16. She has 25 miles to empty. Being my first trip up there I did not know that the cities along this route don't even have stop signs let alone a gas station. The Ghost, Jim's Standard and the wide glide have 5 gallon gas tanks and never really a problem. She knows what to do from her past experience during the 4-corners rally. Believe or not one mile outside of New Castel she is done and pulls of to the side of the road. Jim and his friend seemed concerned about all this. I say ok my love I will be right back leaving all of them there on the side of the road. I am pretty smart really about these things and knew that it would be close when it came to the gas thing. Putting a couple plastic juice bottles in my saddle bag at our last stop. Off I went and five minutes later I was back at there side with gas in the juice bottles and down into the city to fill up. We are only 10 miles down the road on Hwy 16 to South Dakota and the Black Hills National forest now 5 PM Thursday. It has always been a life long goal of mine to see the Black Hills Forest, Mt Rushmore and Crazy Horse Monument. This is more important to me than seeing Sturgis at this time. The bikes are 1000's as we ride thru the forest and you can see where the fires have taken the toll because of the drought. The Black Hills forest looked so good to me because of the miles and miles of amber waves of gain that we had just done. The roads in western South Dakota are the finest roads you will ever ride on. They are well maintain and lots of curves and wonders to see along the way. We stop still doing the 50/50 and Jim's friend in a car trip in the past with his family had seen Mt Rushmore in the night. They have a nice show about the history of Mt. Rushmore and then light the side of the mountain up playing our National Anthem every night. Now 7 Pm and Rapid City is a hour away. I think this is a must do in my mind and a once in a lifetime thing to see Mt. Rushmore at night. As we are riding along I see the sign Mt. Rushmore exit and pull up the road aways to stop and say we must do this. Everyone agrees paying $32.00 to park our bikes. We could have walk a ways and parked for free. Jim thinks in a small way the money will help keep the places looking nice for years to come. The parking pass is for a full year which will be the next time I am there at Sturgis 2003, 100 years of Harley and it will have just expired. I don't care who you are, even if you don't like the outdoors or you don't care anything about history. You really should go and see this night show at Mt. Rushmore. It is a very moving experience. Crazy Horse Monument is a little more than a scratch in the rocks at this time and I think that at the rate they are going it will take 50 years before it is finished. After the show we headed out the back way to Rapid City thru a little town called Keystone. It is all lite up and full of bikes lined everywhere. What a beautiful site to see for a Biker although the place reeks of money and smells like Aspen CO.. Down into the city and the motel. As we get there Jim says something about his friend snores a little and we all are to share a room that night. Jim's friend says yeah it can get loud sometimes. I am looking at Jim feeling there is no place to hide and giving him the eye of wonder. I have the same feeling I had in Arizona that day in Camp Verde when Jim said O' yeah there is no house and there is no water cooler either. I don't have any camping gear or any chance of getting a motel room. Rapid city has been book up for a year now and prices are $250.00 a night for a room out in the shed. I am some what concerned because I am a lite sleeper as you know and think that everyone else will be fine with a little noise, especially Jim being a heavy sleeper. A herd of buffaloes could come thru the room and he would wake up the next morning and wonder where the mess came from. My lady is not a heavy sleeper but sleeps just fine most of the time. Lights out with anticipation of what is to come. Jim is on the floor in a sleeping bag and out like a light I am sure. My lady and I are in a queen bed. Jim's friend is in the other bed. 10 minutes and a sound that is beyond imagination. At first you think this is a joke and it can not be real he is just playing around. It is so loud that it is rattling the head board of my bed. This sound is so penetrating that you cant even hear the Harley's revving there engines outside the door. My lady wakes up and looks at me as I start to laugh and she starts laughing as well. I have never heard anything like this before coming out of a mans mouth. It is a two way snore, long in and even longer out. With two pillows on my head and my lady doing the same, all the pillows can do is vibrate with this noise from hell. There is no escape, no where to hide, nothing to do but wait till morning. I thought about asking him to sleep in the bath tube with the door shut and the vent on high but it is his room and I have no rights as to how things should go. Jim in the past had slept thru a helicopter landing on top of our tents. He had even slept thru trains running thru our room but this was more than he could sleep thru and

it kept him awake for a little while as well. I don't understand how someone could sleep thru these things but he does. Bear meat comes to mind
camping in the forest. The real problem was we had one more night to
do and all day to think about it. Up the next morning Friday after no
sleep and over to the convention center there in Rapid City. While we are
there we see the new bikes, 2003 line of Harley's. They are very nice and I
love the silver colors with black, Mmmm. Out in the parking lot we see a
pro dirt bike jumping group of three guys call the Menace. They fly 20
feet up in the air and 70 feet out doing the greatest tricks you have every
seen. They are on there way from or to the X-Games on ESPN. I ride dirt
bikes and I love to fly but these guys make me look like a baby bird falling out of the nest hitting the ground trying to learn how to fly. Later a
friend looking at the Harley web page on the internet about Sturgis, sees
a picture of me and my lady in the background as the Menace jump and
do tricks. August 9th the 8th picture standing at the fence. Jim and his
friend are there near by but are really interested in looking at the new
bike line. We separate here as I want to go riding in the Black Hills and
see Mt. Rushmore along with Crazy Horse once again. Jim and his friend
went off to see the Harley House there in Rapid City and then on to
Sturgis for the day. Riding back to Mt. Rushmore we see a accident that
just happen. It seems a guy and his lady packing on a bike were to hot
into a corner and off the road they went. Every kind of cop in five states
are there, it looked like to me have showed up to see the show. They are
haled off by the ambulance and reminds me of the day I took my ride in
the back of an ambulance. I do not wish to take a ride again with them.
Please be careful it is very easy to make mistakes out there on the roads.
This is the only thing I saw the whole time I was there in South Dakota
that was bad. A beautiful day, no wind, clean fresh air and Mt. Rushmore
looking as it does in the pictures you see in the brochure. My lady and I
are a lot like kids in our hearts and we stop at Bedrock City to see Fred,
Barney, Wilma, Dino and all the rest of the people in the town of Bedrock. We took a ride with Fred and Barney on the bedrock train and saw
the sights. Funny thing was we were not the only Bikers there and a real
good time. A very nice ride in the Black Hills and over to Crazy Horse
Monument and back to the motel where we spend some great quality

time in the hot tub alone kissing and playing around. Around 6 PM we get dressed and head for Sturgis which is a short trip 20 miles away. The bikes have been every where the whole day by the 1000's. I miss camping and seeing all the great people along the way. I feel like a yuppie of some kind being in a motel. Along the way to Sturgis we see so many wonderful camping places and hope to be there next year for the 2003 rally. Riding into Sturgis feels like a pilgrimage fulfilled and next year plan to spend the whole time there in the city. Parking and walking around seeing all the great people having fun and as far as I know not much trouble there at all. While my lady and I are walking around downtown seeing all the bikes and great stuff. This fairly nice looking girl comes by wearing a thong bathing suit and chaps and that is it. I think it looks great and my lady tells me if I wish to sleep with her anymore I better stop looking and not take any pictures. So I did and no pictures were taken. "Well what would you have done". We got some Sturgis 2002 pins for our bikes and headed back to the motel and into the hot tub again. Decided to try to get some sleep before Jim and his friend came back that night around 12 midnight. 10 minutes after there were back and lights out and the sound from hell. Nothing works, my ear plugs, pillows, tissues crammed in my ears and another long night without sleep til morning. Packing the bikes and heading back is always hard for me. I wish someone would pay me to ride out there on the roads all the time never having to think about ending my trips. Always on all my trips I love to ride and spend just as much time going there as heading back and don't believe in hurrying either way. Riding thru the Black Hills taking a different way down the back roads on Hwy 89. Seeing some very nice rolling hills on a prefect Hwy in my eyes. The nice thing about South Dakota are the roads. There are the best I have ever ridden on, well maintain with very few bad spots to look out for. Utah roads are close to being equal to those in South Dakota. We are riding thru the Buffalo National Grasslands with vision of millions of buffaloes roaming free in these fields before they were all

My Lady in the grass lands on the border of Wyoming and South Dakota.

killed out to help thin the population of Indians. We get gas in Lusk, Wyoming and stop in Torrington for a burger at a very nice drive in place, the heat is there with us. Heading for Cheyenne on Hwy 85 and I have miss calculated again on the gas in the Intruder. 30 miles outside the city she goes on reserve. A long uneasy ride waiting for her to run out of gas and just making it to I-25 where she pulls off to the side 2 miles from the gas station. A point here please, never stop on the side of a Hwy, always try to get off the road even if you have to push your bike. The problem is when someone driving a car or truck sees you. They have a tendency to head right for you because they are looking right at you and in a since focusing on you. This is a fact, just ask a cop and please take this advise to heart and stay safe. I still have the bottles in my saddle bags for gas from before. Jim and his friend stay with her and 5 minutes later I am back with gas and down into the city to fill up in Cheyenne 2 miles away. Toady I carry a 3/8 " 5' foot long siphoning hose in my saddle bag and suggest that you do the same. You never know when it might come in handy. Along the way I see people on bikes out of gas and a few come to me asking if I have any to spare, I am sorry I do not and this is where I think about the hose. One guy I saw had his bike towed on the back of a tow truck into a gas station as we were filling up. You must be aware of the gas thing when you are in Wyoming. Being conservative I have made 275 miles on a tank of gas on the Ghost with a half a gallon to spare. The Intruder like the old Sportsters have a small gas tank and 100 miles is about it. After filling up and talking to a 70 yr. old man about bikes and how he wants to learn to ride. I tell him what he should do about learning how to ride. I suggest that he take a riding corse at a reputable place like Harley. Saying see you later and heading south on I-25 into Denver Saturday night to our motel relaxing with a long hot shower with my lady. I feel somewhat bad for Jim and how he will deal with the noise from hell that night. I know him and he will probably sleep thru it. He tells me later that it really only bothered him that one night, "how can this be". Jim's friend has been home sick since we left and always on the cell phone like E.T. "Phone Home". He is up very early Sunday and leaves us with a note saying thanks and I will see you later I am headed home. I can understand being home sick. I have been there myself. I do believe when you ride as a group you stay as a group looking out for one another even if they don't need looking out for. There are always exceptions. Something comes to mind here. Some people like to have random trips where they just go and what ever happens is fine. For me I like to plan a trip with the people I am to be riding with and know what I am going to see and do. I like to know where I am going to be each night. In this way you don't end up at home saying damn man I did not get to see this or do that. This also cuts down on the confusions and arguments that may happen along the way. Of course you should be flexible but stick to the plan and as always there will be side trips to think about and do. I have rode with lots of people over the years and see the problems occur on the roads with other Biker groups. Riding in the wind should be a joy for you to remember and not a bad moment in time. Makes for a very un easy ride which goes against why I am out there. Which brings up another point, take some time to talk to those you ride with about the trip. I find it really works. Packing our bikes we take a nice easy ride thru the Rocky Mountains over Eisenhower tunnel always stopping to take in some views along the way. I speak of Cripple Creek 2002 in two weeks and wonder if Jim and my lady will go with me. Going over Vail pass with blue skies and a nice wind at our backs all the way home. I loved this trip it was a dream fulfilled. The funny thing was my lady started her minstrel period the day we left on this trip and never complained. Something here for you guys to think about. There might be a reason why the ladies are a little offish some days. When we rolled into the yard of my house Sunday evening she was off the bike and started fixing dinner, washing cloths and getting ready for Monday. I was like, damn girl as I try to hide not wanting her to know how beat down I was. I still helped with all that she is doing and playing with her while we did things. In Jim's words she is amazing to go thru all that and never saying anything negative at all the whole time. It was a great trip and I cant wait to go back. Yes 100 years of Harley and all the great rally's that will happen this year 2003. O' my now what will I do, yeppers I am headed for Cripple Creek and the Veterans rally 2002. Are you going. I hope so.

Cripple Creek 2002 Veterans Rally

Cripple Creek in my mind is one of the most important rally's you can go to. It is all about our Veterans and as always even if you are not a Biker you should go at least once. Jim is working in the log house construction business somewhere near Steamboat Springs CO.. He is help building a $ 1.5 million summer house for someone. I don't understand. He is spending weeks at a time there rather than travel back in forth to home in G.J.. Because of this he will miss the Cripple Creek rally. My lady after doing Sturgis two weekends before wants me to go without her. I am not to happy about this but I do understand finding a baby setter is always hard. I think she has had enough of riding and knows we will be going to the 4-corners Iron Horse rally 2002 the next weekend. Although it seems that the Iron Horse Rally may not happen due to some problems between the committee and the Indians. So there is a question rather there will be a 4-Corners Rally this year 2002. I really want to go to Cripple Creek and she thinks I should go even if I had told her I would not leave her there alone again. So this becomes the plan I will go to Cripple Creek camp out Saturday night and a round trip of 600 miles. Getting up early August 24th and heading out Saturday morning. I am telling her to stay in bed so she does not have to see me ride off but there are still a few tears in my eyes. Once again a lite rain that fail in the night and a little cool at 7 AM. It is a good 5 hours over the mountains to Cripple Creek. I have never done Independence Pass out of Aspen Co. on a bike and decide that is the route I will take. I-70

175

thru DeBeque Canyon and fairly cold with moisture in the air but still clean and fresh. Believe or not fall begins in the high mountain the middle of August here and the temperatures can be near freezing at night. At Glenwood Springs taking Hwy 82 headed east up and over Independence Pass. Aspen has a beauty of its own with quant houses of old history and lots of money makes it all just right. People come from all over the world to ski and play in the wonderful mountains there all year round. Better take lots of plastic because they don't except your good looks in Aspen. A steady climb up and out of Aspen down a narrow road to the top of Independence Pass close to 12,000 feet elevation. Along the way you see a old ghost town from the 1800's near the top. Looking at this town in a lush forest deep in the high mountains. I think it must have been a hard way to be. Those people were as different from us as we are to the Eskimoes in Alaska. The winters must have been brutal, long and cold. This pass is short but equal to Red Mt., Lizard Head and Wolf Creek Pass in beauty. The road is narrow all the way up and down giving you a sense of danger knowing that one mistake and it is a long way to the bottom. Down into the valley on the other side still headed east picking up Hwy 24 south along the highest pikes you can see at one time. Hwy 24 runs along the Continental Divide which is where the waters part in the continent. One side goes to the Atlantic ocean and the other to the Pacific ocean. The Arkansas river heads for the Atlantic and the Colorado river heads for the Pacific. On this Hwy there are 14 mountain pikes of over 14,000 feet that you ride along on Hwy 24 thru Leadville to Salida. I will turn at Johnsons Village staying on Hwy 24 to Cripple Creek. A must do ride people. Passing by the herd of buffalo and the picture that I did not get last year riding with the Hog group 2001. He is standing close to the road, big, proud, magnificent and I take his picture. I feel as though I had made up for a mistake I had made the year before. You can never go back and somehow in my heart I know that the picture the year before was much more than the one I took. So guess what, I am going back again to Cripple Creek 2003 and maybe this time I will get the picture that I lost. Once again passing the old gas station at Glentivar where the old man had been so mean to me about the paper towels in the first Dream. The place still looking like a trash dump. Maybe it is just me but every trip I take means so much to me. They are the breath that I take into my lungs keeping me feeling alive. Always fresh and clean. The noises that I hear along the way are soft and sweet sounding like music to the ears. These trips are the only things I can truly see and the feelings that wake me in the night. I sometimes wake up thinking and waiting on the next ride to the most wonderful places on earth. Sometimes as I ride down another wonderfully road, tears come to my eyes because I know there are so many of you that can see what I see. You can not know what I know or feel what I feel and that is why I am writing this book. I hope in my heart that you are able to see and feel and know some of the things that mean so much to me. Anyway turning and up Hwy. 1 out of Florissant to Cripple Creek. I have been pushing it a little to get there because of the parade of Veterans that happens at 12 noon Saturday. I have missed it again now 12:30. I missed it last year 2001 trying to get back to my lady and fix our relationship to avail. The parade consist of 1000's of Vets and Bikers that ride into town from Woodland Park about 20 miles away. This is a parade of Heros in my mind. I get there to see the last of them pull in. The streets are lined 4 bikes deep down main street on both sides over a mile long. They are lined up on every side street as well. The towns people block off the whole city to cars and trucks for the rally and all you can see is bikes everywhere. It may be in my eyes only, this is more awesome than Sturgis. The city of old history and views of the Mountains that surround you along with the roads that are exceptional near by. I think this is what separates this rally from the rest. Parking the Ghost and walking around the town. There are every kind of Veteran you can imagine that there is from WW1, WWII, Korean, Vietnam, Gulf war and everyone in between filling the streets. Some speak of there days in the war, others speak of those who have giving so much so that we may be free. Most talk of the days on the roads that mean so much to all of us. Walking thru the people seeing all of the great things there and I hear the wopp wopp of a helicopter. Looking up as it flies over us very low and circling to land under neath a massive American Flag that was hung all the way across main street. This was very heart warming for me and a awe-inspiring site to see. There are people putting on shows, bag pipes and a western gun fight downtown. Vendors and shops in the

Cripple Creek Veterans Rally 2002. A city full of Hero's and there bikes.

street everywhere that are full of black leather and chrome. The one thing I know about Bikers for sure, they love to spend money when it comes to there bikes and stuff related to them. Most of all they love to have fun while doing it. Riding up and down main street a few times and off to Victor a small city of old history and where we turn down Phantom Pass in the first Dream in the snow on the Yamaha 650 twin. Now looking for a place to camp riding back towards Florissant and seeing a great little valley off to the side where a lot of the Bikers are camped. Pulled in and everyone saying hello how's your trip. Great man, asking the guy how much to throw my tent on the ground. He says how much do you have. I said I am just a poor guy who loves to ride. He said is $4.00 to much. I said no man that would be just fine and off I went to put up my tent. The people at this camp ground Los Burros have gone all out for us in every way. They have a outdoor grill and tables set up for eating on. A mini bar for those who like to drink. Good old rock n roll playing on a nice out door stereo. Showers and towels if you need them. $4.00 and I remember Bryce Canyon where they had none of these things and wanted $50.00 for a poor Biker to lay his tent on the ground. Back into Cripple Creek talking and walking with some of the most caring people on earth. The buildings are old and for the most part the same as they where when they where built. The best thing is they have not let modern civilization move in and looks the same as the day I first rode into Cripple Creek 25 years ago. 9:00 PM and back to the tent where I speak to some nice people who are camping as well. A nice dinner cook by the owners of the place and off to tent to get some sleep thinking of my lady always. About midnight a long loud crash of destruction. Looking out of the tent to see, someone had drove there truck thru the mini bar, tables and the stereo laying it all to waste. I was thinking that the Bikers will get blamed for this and next year they will not be as open to us. The funny thing is the owners friend had come by to see them and forgot to set the parking brake. So as he walked away from his truck he watched it roll thru everything and the destruction that followed. That must have been a bad feeling standing there and nothing can be done but watch. Up with the sun peeking thru the tree as to say good morning and packing to see a prefect day to be on the road in the wind. Heading out the back way down a paved road Hwy 11 near Guffy to Hwy 50 the main road east and west. A nice peaceful ride in the back roads of the high country coming out by Canon City and the Royal Gorge, Buckskins Joe's which is east. Turning west on Hwy 50 to Salina the whole time I am doing the 50/50. Monarch Pass again from the first Dream, equal to all that I have done. Wide open forest of everything that you mind and body can feel and see. Riding by Blue Mesa Lake still empty of water from the drought. Remembering the trip we made to 4-Corners Iron Horse last year 2001 with Jim and my lady and all the rides I have done on this road all the way back to Montrose. As I am riding I wonder if Jim and my lady will be going with me this year to 4-corners. When I get home excited to see my lady, she chews me out for not calling Saturday night. I don't have a cell phone, I don't really want to be struck to a phone acting like E.T. She was always on my mind and I had told her this. I am upset by this a great deal and think is there no pleasing her. She says go and then chews me out for doing it. DANG MAN. You surely know by now what is on my mind, we have a winner, next weekend is the 4-Corners Rally which turns out that it may not exist or does it exist.

4-Corners Iron Horse 2002

Sometime in June I hear that there is a dilemma going on about the 4-Corners Rally. It seems that the Indians want a lot more money and it is about triple the amount for us to use the Fair grounds there at Ignacio Co this year. The committee is working on the rally in some kind of negotiation with the Indians and they all give up, saying there will be no Ignacio rally this year. Jumpen Jimmny what the hell is wrong with you people, I think in my mind. This rally has been going on for 20 years and now some money hungry group of leaches want to end it. Sorry about that. Problems occur every day in every city and people do stupid things in cars and on bikes every where. People cerate problems all the time whether they are at rally's or not. It makes no since to blame the Bikers for what a few people do in the rest of the world. From what I have seen as I travel, there is very little trouble at all the bike rally's I have been to. I will not go into this stuff about people out of control just yet but you know this violence is more than I can understand. Not sure if I every will. Durango, Co. close to Ignacio is thinking about picking up the rally and tells the world they are not sure about doing this. I call down to Durango long distance to the Chamber of Commerce in late June talking to one the head people there. I tell her that Bikers are decent people and don't mind spending money on things they love to do. Durango would be foolish to pass up this rally. Continuing our conversation I tell her that they should pick this rally up and make a yearly thing, caring on the tradition of Iron Horse. I said you have a nice big fair ground and lots of wide open spaces to make this rally as big as any in the U.S.. Along with all the hotels and motels there every one would be happy Bikers and the people of Durango. Then I mention the money that all Bikers bring with them including me a poor guy who loves to ride and having fun is what we do best. She agrees and says she will bring up my points at the next meeting, thank you after a 20 minute conversation. By July they are saying because all there motels being booked a year in advance and motel cancellation coming in by the 100's. Along with the drought that has taken a lot of tourists out there city and now they are telling the Bikers please come we will do the best we can. I decide that we must go but you know that at a drop of a hat I ride. Unfortunately Jim is still involved in log home building in Steamboat Springs and he will not be going. This does not set well with me, it is a lam summer house for someone who does not care except about themselfs. I know I can hear you, money makes the world go round but I don't want to talk about that right know. My lady and I talk about the trip and she wants to go. Things are not as they were between us, I guess you might have seen this coming. I know I did and I feel this will be our last trip together. There are a lot of problems and other factors that I will not talk about in this book but if you want to know ask me and I will tell you what is wrong between us. I assure you it is not me. To me Trust is the corner stone to all relationships and is very important in my relationships. I am still trying to fix the problem but see no hope. We talk about the trip and decide on a two night two day trip leaving Friday evening 5 PM and camp near Ridgeway that night. Friday comes and we are a little late taking care of her two boys and the baby setter but still very excited. Slapping her on the shoulder and saying are you excited, damn man, I am excited, are you excited and off we go now 6PM.. Headed on Hwy 50 east and thru Montrose, taking Hwy 550 south which will carry us thru to Ridgeway. South of Montrose we stop at a very nice camp site. We had deciding that dark was coming earlier this time of year and that a lot of deer where moving around this time of the evening close to this Hwy now a little after 7PM. I know this area very well and safety is always a main concern to me. There is a small lake close by and we go to see it holding hands and as always messing around with her. Going back into Montrose and eating at Long John Silvers. Funny name for a fast food place and good food with nice people there as well.We ride over to Indian Museum about 2 miles south of Montrose. Chief Ouray's wife is buried there along with some others from the past. There are 6 or 7 T-pees set up around the grassy fields that surround the museum building. Great stories can be found here. Across the Hwy. is the Hanging Tree service station and rumor has it that some men have seen the Hanging Tree form a swaying position. Reminds me of a west Texas café and the ropes hanging on the wall that day in the rain outside Ft. Worth in the first Dream. A very nice night with her and got some sleep as well. Waking up with her is always a pleaser because she is a morning person. You could feel the warmth of the sun sneaking thru the trees the next morning. It is another prefect day riding down Hwy 550 seeing 20 or 30 bikes on the road with us. Some are on there way to 4-Corners and other are just riding the great roads between Montrose and any direction you go, north, east, south or west. You know there is always one place you can count on for a decent breakfast, that would be Denny's. It may not be the best food in the world but it is clean and non expensive. You also get a fairly decent amount of food to eat and it is pretty good to the taste. I always look for these places and trust that I will get something good to eat no matter what time of day it is and that is what we did Saturday morning. Back out and down the road we went riding into Ridgeway taking a right on Hwy 62 over to Placerville. Then Hwy 145 which goes right by Telluride CO.. We stop in Telluride because my lady has never been there and I wanted her to see the place. We pull up and the annual Telluride Film Festival is taking place on the downtown streets there. I felt like we just lucked into this and see some great people were there. One of them is Darrell Hana from the movie Splash and another man that directed a major movie that I am not sure about and his name is Michael Moore. We stayed there 10 or 15 minutes seeing people from all over the world walking around and back to the bikes headed up the hill towards Lizard Head Pass and Rico a spot in the road that is all. Somehow this is a famous city because of the views you get as you travel there. Rightly so. I know you have heard this before but Damn, you got to do this ride. The forest are lush, green and the smell of fresh pine fills your body along with the road that is close to prefect. Riding across Lizard Head Pass near the top of the mountains that surround you. There are wide open fields of lush grass and flowers, clear clean standing water that turn into little creeks headed in the same direction as we are, down. Stopping at the place where Jim and I had stop on the way to Arizona, Stoner Creeks café. Where we are treated as if we are family and somehow I think if you stop there they will treat you the same. Fantastic food, nice people and some great conversation with my lady and the family that owns the place. The father tells me there is a cattle drive coming up the road and to watch out for our self's as we ride off saying I will see you next year. M-I-C will C you later K-E-Y Y because we like you M-O-U-S-E. Very excited and we are always doing the 50/50 riding down into Dolores taking Hwy 184 over to Hwy 160 and into Durango. When ever I am on the road I always talk to people because I wish to hear there stories of the day and the wind that blows for them. Because I was a member of the Hog club and there photographer for a little while. I also took the pictures of the Toys Run 2001 and other things as well. Along with the Moses accident people know me and I know them. I say hello to all that I know and some shake my hand while some of the ladies hug me. My lady thinks I chit chat to much with everyone. She gets very jealous and angry at me when I talk to another lady that I knew form the road or a rally or the Hogs. There really is nothing else to it. This kinda puts a crimp on what I like to do best, ride and talk to people from all over the world. This happens a lot when we travel together and puts me between a rock and hard spot on the road. I do the best I can to please her and my way of seeing the world. Now in Durango around 4 PM. we find a nice camp ground on the east side just outside the city. I notice that there are bikes around but not as many as I thought there would be. On the trip over we saw few bikes but we also took the long way to get there. This is not the main route to Durango form G.J. which is over Red Mountain Pass thru Silverton CO. On Hwy 550. There is a guy who comes in the shop Paul and tells me his grand father was one of the first engineers that built the rode over Red Mt. Pass to Silverton. He showed me some great pictures from then and his grand father in a horse drawn wagon taking supplies and equipment building the road. We plan to take Hwy 550 back to G.J. on Sunday making a big loop out of this trip. Tent is up and a shower playing and having fun with my lady all the time. We head into town where there is a sea of bikes going to and from Ignacio. Some are up and down Hwy 550 to Silverton which is full of majestic mountain peaks and forest that are un equaled in the world. Downtown main street Durango is lined with bikes and people talking and riding up and down the streets. Everyone seems to be having a real good time. There is no gauntlet, very few vendors and most of the Bikers are hanging out there on the main streets downtown Durango. There are a lot of police, sherif's and Hwy Patrol hanging around the streets and riding around in cars. One of the city policeman I notice had on some of those lead filled knuckle gloves for beating someone to death with and looking for an excuse to use them. Others carrying large lead filled night sticks as to say do something and I will beat you to death. Most were very nice, helpful and trying to let people have fun. I believe in controlled chaos. This is where you have fun but never step across the line obeying the law right to the edge of breaking it. Makes life fun. Unfortunately a few people don't understand this and cause problems for all of us. I would like it if we tried not to provoke the police and that the police try not to provoke the Bikers or anyone as far as that goes. Everybody has heard this before I am sure, "Can't We All Just Get Along". Haha. Anyway we hang for awhile and grab a bite to eat and ride over to Ignacio passing 100's of bikes coming and going. At Ignacio there are armed guards at the gates of the fair grounds.

The city is empty except for a few us that have ridden over to catch a memoire of the year before. Most of the Bikers are at the casinos's just up the road from there. Heading back to the tent for the night I feel a sadness because someone was able to take this rally from us. We should not let this happen again. It has been a terrific ride over Lizard Head Pass and look forward to the ride back across Red Mountain Pass and as always it don't get much better than that. Sunrise and a new day dawning Sunday morning and the Hardly Angels are in town and will preform around 10 AM.. There are a few vendors there in the parking lot where the Hardly Angels will do there demonstration of riding skills. My lady and I talk to Pam which is one of the main organizers of the Hardly Angels from the beginning and she is working on bringing 4-Corners back to life next year. She is telling us that she is working hard to see this

The Ghost , George and Sturgis 2002. Enough said.

rally continues and wants it to ether be there in Durango or Farmington New Mexico which is fine with me. These ladies are terrific bike riders and do one hell of a show. Funny thing is one of the lead ladies is riding the Ghost exactly like mine. I thought this was so cool. She actually bumped the back of another bike during the show but they managed to keep there bikes up right which shows a lot skill on there part. The Hardly Angels have a un-schedule parade planned for downtown after the show and invite all to participate in it. We head back to watch so I can take some pictures. They come in from the back side surprising me and I did not get the picture I wanted. The police no about this non permit parade and line up a gauntlet to see that all obey the law and start to write tickets to those who step across there line. We jump in at the back of the parade with our bikes and ride with them down main street Durango. Now it is time to start home and turn onto Hwy 550 headed back and it is 12 noon Sunday. Very nice day and the ride is even better across the mountains to Silverton as usually, of course you know this is a must do ride and then home. I know in my heart that my life with my lady is over and wait for the end to come. Three weeks later she is gone again and it is for the best. We tried to work it out. I tried so very hard to help her understand what it takes to keep things going but she has other plans and in my mind I think it is best if she makes her plans come true for herself. I don't blame anyone for being who they want to be and would not have it any other way. There is that one word that means so much to me, FREEDOM, I really do believe in the word, it is not just for me but for everyone and I will fight to the death for it. It is now September 20th the house is quite and the problem is I miss her. I think if it was just her and things might have been different between us, maybe not. If you don't know by now I loved her very much, more than I have every loved anyone before. You know how when you find a baby bird with its wing broken and it cant fly. You spend all that time healing it and teaching it to fly again. Growing very fawn of it and always having it near by you but you know in your heart when the baby birds heals, you must let the baby bird go even if it breaks your heart. Fly away my baby bird, be free and live the life that you are destine for. Life is so short and you should try to be happy. You should do what you love to do best and that is the way it should be. For me I am waiting on spring and 100 years of Harley. This is going to be a very exciting year for Bikers. Not just Harley riders but all riders who love in the wind on the road. My first major rally will be The Laughlin River Run 2003. Then the next Dream, The Light House Run Hwy 1 California. I am also looking forward to Yellowstone, Cripple Creek, State Rally, 4-corners no matter where it is held, the Toys Run 2003 and of course Sturgis 2003. Are you excited, man I am excited, are you excited, I am so very excited. I love you my lady but you know what I must do, I ride in the wind because that is what keeps me alive.

Parade of Presents Toys Run 2002

The rain starts to fall late September and in my mind it is to late and to early to do any good. The damage to the forest, rivers, lakes and animals has already taken its toll. As I ride I see dry lakes, none flowing rivers, forest burned down and animals being killed looking for food and water. The rain is to late to help the forest and to early to be snow for the mountains. Most of the water flows away down the rivers to the ocean useless. Have you every heard of the Ocean being to low of water and needing some, I have not. After riding with Jim and doing some short trip here and there thru the months of October and November. Jim and I rode up and over the Grand Mesa seeing the fall colors and another ride thru Gateway to Naturita which is a terrific ride. Then over to Blue Mesa lake with no water in it from the drought still. If you don't know by now I kinda like to ride. This is when I started to write my book. It is very difficult because I am not a accomplished speller or write very well. Jim is going to the December Hog meeting December 2nd and suggest that I attend the meeting next Tuesday 7PM.. I decide that I should go, walking in about 50 people there with everyone that knows me saying hello and where have you been. Telling them I have been on the road seeing and doing so many wonderful things. At the meeting they talked about the 2002 Toys Run and how it will be handled this year. I had been a member of the Western Slope Hogs for one year and one year later after of being on the road 15,000 miles now checking on them. I am seeing some of the people who mean so much to me are still there. Some make me feel as through I never left. There are a lot of new faces as I look around setting down. During the meeting they do this thing where they ask new members who they are and what they ride with everyone saying hello. This meeting is always very stiff and that is ok. Lots of stuff for them to talk about and lets go home type thing. The director of the meeting ask for new members to stand up, say who they are and what they are riding. I raise my hand to say my name is Engulbert Humberdink and I ride a Honda 50. Most everyone laughs and the director has a negative thing to say as always which is understandable. Some of the best ladies in the world are there. I wanted to mention a few, Joanie, Nancy, Linda, Kathy, Sharon, Kate, Colleen and Marty. No words can tell you how special these ladies are but lets try. Great, wonderful, terrific, awesome, fun, caring, marvelous, beautiful, sweet, lovable, honorable, strong, hearts, fantastic, phenomenal, to mention a few. They mean so much to me. They have been involved with the Toys Run for many years. Taking there time to think about others and know what the true meaning of Christmas is. Sharon is a 2nd grade school teacher and loves to ride as much as any Biker should. She rides a nice Harley Low Rider with a skill level that is as good as anyone's and I am Hot For Teacher (Van Halen), Kate is a beginner with the heart of a Biker who loves to have fun and very special to me, Nancy is Moses's wife and the dearest one to me with wind in her blood as deep as any, she makes me smile always. Joanie loves to ride as much as anyone and the biggest heart of a Biker seeing her makes me feel good every time. She is like a big sister telling me to behave when I get rowdy and always has a kind word for everyone when they need one. Colleen a beginner as well but now on her way to being a Biker and the sweetest caring person you can meet, Kathy sees that we are all taken care of, helping anyone who needs help. She is fun and loves us all. She does not have her own bike but packs behind Curtis her husband one hell of a decent man. He has a lot of honor that flows in his blood. Marty is like a little sweet bee, always bussing around taking care of things. She is a very caring and a kind woman. Marty rides behind Bob and has for many 1000's of miles. Bob has the knowledge of the roads and you can always count on him to tell you what you need to know. Bob and Marty love the roads and the wind as much as I do. There are lots of others that are special people to me and that are involved in the Toys Run. I bet there are 100's of people just like these in your cities and I would love to meet them. Jim and I had rode our bikes over that night to the Hog meeting and afterwards went for a little ride. Stopping at a dinner for some coffee and a little conversation about the book and the next dream, the Light House Run. This will be a major trip for us and will take some planning to see that every thing works out the way we want it to. The ride home that night was cold 30* or so and although I was a little frozen, I always enjoy a ride. Yes, even riding a short distance always brings a little joy to my heart no matter how far or cold it is. The day before the Toys Run as always I dress up the Ghost to look like Christmas and find riding spots for the bears that are gifts. This is my small part of this exceptional day. December 7th the day that will life in infamous and WWII. I meet Jim early Saturday morning as he is one of the parking lot Guards there at the Harley house as he was last year. We are some of the first people there 9 AM.and want to go see Kathy at the dinner for some breakfast. Out in the parking the bikes are showing up, trickling in a few at a time. By 11 AM 800 bikes fill all the spaces there at the Harley shop and down the street one quarter of a mile. All kinds of people from every walk of live, every kind of bike on the planet setting there together. Santa shows up on his orange Harley with a side car. If you promise not to tell anyone it is Eddy again and you know he his my hero. He rides thru the crowd saying Merry Christmas as proud as Santa every has, stopping his bike near little children there in the parking lot saying hey, your name is and asking how old they are. The children would say my name is Cindy, he would say O' yeah I remember you, you are 10 years old, Cindy saying no Santa I am 11 years old, he would say, your right that was last year when you where 10 yrs old, have you been good this year. Then handing out a few present to some of the delightful kids there in the parking lot. The HI's, hello's, how you doing, great seeing you is every where as I walk thru the Hero's of this year. The amazing thing to me, there I am standing in the middle a few Biker Gangs, the guy with a sweat shirt, jeans and a used helmet riding a old Honda 350, next to him is the guy wearing a $5000.00 set of leathers and a totally chrome platted bike. The ladies are there some packing others riding, some with $1000.00 outfits on, others with there work coats on. All with one purpose on this day. To see that some less fortunate families and children have more than they did this Christmas season before we were aloud to be apart of there life's. Jim who is as sincere about this as anyone I have every met. In my mind these 900 Bikers are some of the real hero's in our city and I know that in your city there 1000's more Biker hero's all across the United States. The city of G.J. has once again kept this Parade down to a little more than a peep show riding down 7th street with very little public to see and that's ok with me because in my mind this is about the kids. But I also think that when great people do something worth while, someone should care. I know that there 250 kids and 100 parents that do waiting for us at the Eagles Lodge.As always the parade of presents and the bikes are over-whelming in my eyes. It is a wonderful sight to see them riding across the 5th street bridge to the Eagles. When Jim and I got to the Eagles I told him that I wanted to show him something. They have a long hall way as you walk in. There are pictures of the important people on the walls from many years past. We came to the end of this hall way and I pointed to a picture of a young athlete standing there with his awards in the background. There is a signature at the bottom saying thanks J.T. Thomas. The Eagles had helped me help my son go to some sports camps with donation to help with the sports fee's. They helped my son along his way to being who he wanted to be, an athlete. I am a member today. Up the stairs and walking into the room full of smiling face. The first babies and small kids I see, my bears now have a new home and I love them all. Everyone is excited, some of the Bikers where there last year along with some of the families for whom we came to see. Santa sets in his chair with a Ho Ho Ho Merry Christmas, his voice ringing thru out the room. He is listening to the children's wish list of things they want and a nice instant picture for them as well. Eddy is a Biker, hard, tough, roughed and has his own way about him but to those kids and to me he is Saint Nicklaus. The best. My problem with this whole thing is it is over in a flash. Some of the kids walk around holding there presents in there arms tightly with more than joy in there hearts. Most show there appreciation and we talk to say thanks for letting us, the Bikers be a part of your life. This means so much to me and everyone I am sure. The kids take there presents and leave going home with more than just gifts. They know that there are hopes in the world because of a few Bikers who care about them more than themselfs. The Bikers head downstairs to a party with a live band playing Rock n Roll music and some chili provided by Wendy's restaurant. You know Dave Thomas who died not to long ago, no relation to me but still a sad day. Everyone talks of the days and the days to come on the road in the wind at this party. It is a very nice day outside near 50* mostly blue sky and Jim and I decide to go for a ride across the National Monument about 7000 feet elevation. The Monument is a close and a magnificent ride any time of year here near G.J.. Riding up onto the end of the longest plateau in the world, Uncompahger Plateau. There is a little snow on the road in the shady spots so we had to be carful. I try to use the hand signals I mentioned early to tell Jim what is in front of me. Thinking as we cross high point there and heading down the snow will be gone. Feeling free of all that is wrong in the world that I live in is what riding does for me. The rock formation are unique along this rode I am riding along enjoying the views. Then looking up to see that I am riding to hot into a corner with snow and ice all over the road. I am trying to hand signal Jim about it. I try to straiten the corner out so I will not go down. Sliding and balancing the bike into the other lane where I am lucky there is not a car coming at me in the lane. It could have been bad but all the time we were up there we had seen very little or no traffic on the road. I was not to worried about it because I was paying attention. This is the problem with riding in the winter you never know if there is a shady spot of ice here in town on the streets and hwy's. Just be carful please. Coming down off the monument heading into Furita there is a tunnel. A Hwyway Patrolman is parked in the road at the tunnel. At first I think there is ice in the tunnel and someone has had a accident. He walks up to me and Jim and I say what's up, he says well I am looking for a couple of bike riders. I said Oh' man its not me, no way, he says really, I said hey man you got to be kidding, your not really looking for Bikers, he said yeah, they are filming a T.V. commercial and will be finished in a minute, smiles at us and walks off laughing and I am laughing as well. Jim the whole time looking paranoid and needs to get home so he can take his son to the Parade of Lights which is a annual thing every year here in G.J. now 4 PM.. The cold is starting to penetrate my body as we head back. The Parade of Lights Starts at 5 PM. What a great day to be on the road in the wind and I really hate that it has to come to end. Unfortunately that is the last ride of the year for me until March 2003. Yeah I will ride here and there but nothing long. I will always be out there in the wind. So now what do I do, I plan for the trips that I will do in the year of the Harley, 100 years of biking a celebration of people being in the wind no matter what kind of bike you ride. A world that means so much to me. I will be planning the Laughlin River Run in April along with the Light House Run in May 2003. Are you excited, damn man I am excited, are you excited. December 22nd 2002 the shortest day of the year and feeling like a wild animal in a cage trying to get free and back out there in the wild where I belong because that is what I do best.

A Biker called Jim

To say Jim is a Biker is a little more than a understatement. He has as much Passion for Riding In The Wind and on the roads as I do. Biking flows thru his blood more than anyone I have ever met. He has a never ending cycle of hopes and dreams of being in the wind. Jim is far more than a Biker with a heart the size of Alaska. He is the kinda guy you can count on when you are down and out and I have been down in out a few times. He is always there when you need someone to say something good about something that matters to you. He will be there with a smile and a story that makes you feel good. I am fortunate that he calls me his friend and I think the world of him. I don't use the word friend loosely and I have only had a few that I would put that name on. Friends truly do care about one another and when things get really bad you know they will be standing there beside you. Jim would be one of them. Jim has two real life's that he lives in. His family is one and they are his world and mean a great deal to him. He takes care of his family and loves his wife and kids very much. He tries to spend as much time with them always but they have nothing to do with his second life, Riding In The Wind. To me Jim is a real Biker. He fights a world full of people telling him what he does on the roads in the wind is wrong and he should give it up. He cant do this. Jim could not give up riding and neither could I. It is embedded in our souls, hearts, minds and bodies. It is what keeps us alive and makes dealing with the daily routines worth it. Unlike me he grew up in a sheltered world called Ohio. Comes from a nice family of love and caring. Even today they all live in different parts of the U.S. but they are never apart. He speaks warmly of the days where his brothers and him rode on the back of there uncles bikes and played around them all the time. His dad had two jobs to keep his family with things they needed to be happy and for them to succeed in life. His biking life started before mine did as a kid 12 years old with his family having the wind in there blood. Jim went to the same schools in a district, played football and graduated with Honors in high school. He was accepted into collage on a football scholarship and graduated with an Accounting Degree in Ohio. If you looked at him you would say no way, he can not be an accountant. I know I don't see this when I look at him either. Jim and I are so different coming from opposites sides of the railroad tracks. It is funny how we see things the same way and so different at the same time. Always arriving at our goals from opposite direction and ending up in the same place. The bond that holds us together is Riding In The Wind. He will step up and fight for his love of the roads and your dreams as well that mean so much to you because that is the kind of person he is. He believes in the roads and damn you to hell if you try to burn them down. He believes in America, moms apple pie and Harley Davidson. He stands on "H" as a proud man taking care of a legacy called biking. He served in your military with honors and did his part. Now all he ask is to be able to do what he loves best in life, ride his bike. I refer to his bike as the Lady because she is not to fancy with a classical look that says lets ride. She is a real class act. She does not want to show off. She does not need all the fancy decoration. All she wants to do is take Jim Riding In The Wind because she knows that is what he loves best. She means so much to him. His eyes light up at the sight of her always saying, you know she is not to fancy and I would not trade her for any other bike made. He told me that sometimes he will go out into his garage, take the cover off her and just set on her remembering the days on the roads in the wind. You know what, I bet some of you do this too. I know I do and funny thing is some of my biking buds tell me the same story. If you don't have a real love for your bike then you will never know what Riding In The Wind really means. Jim knows, I know and I bet there are 1000's of you that know too. Do any of you have someone you feel when it starts to get rough out there on the roads. There is that one person you can count on always riding there beside you. That would be

Jim no questions ask. If you were cold he would give his jacket. If you were getting wet and cold he would give his rain suit and his jacket. If you were tired he would stop and let you rest and never hesitating about doing this. He never thinks about himself first. Always has a smile for those who need one. In my mind he stands with a few that are breed apart. He is what a Biker should be and what biking is all about. I tell you what, if you ever see Jim walk up to him and say hello. I promise you he will treat you like you have been his friend all along because in his mind and mine, all of you out there on the roads are our bothers and sisters. He loves all there is that comes along with being a Biker as well. He has a Passion for his bike that flies thru air, the roads that take him on his journey, being in the wind, the people along the way Bikers and non-bikers, the beauty and wonders of the roads, mother nature showing him her best and treating him to her worst. He loves being a part of something world wide that lives in the hearts of millions. Traveling with him is easy, he understands how important it is for me to take pictures and loves doing this as well. Sometimes he tells me you need to shoot that picture this direction or this way. "H" sent me a sticker in the mail the other day. I don't have any H-D stuff all over me or my house or walls or my cars. When you walk into my house you see adventures of Riding in the Wind. Knowing Jim as I do. He loves "H" and has stuff everywhere except in his house where his wife has no use for "H". He told her that he was helping with my book and she said why would anyone want to read a book about Riding in the Wind. If Jim could his house would be like a museum of "H". Anyway I put this sticker on my front door to see if Jim would notice. It is a small sticker 3x4". He comes up to the door and says, that has never been there before, the first time he walks up to the house. He does not know that I put it up there for him. Anyway I am setting here during lunch Tuesday and a knock at the door. There stands a woman 25yrs.old or so. She says I am selling vacuum shampooers would you like a demonstration. Then she sees the sticker on the door and says what's up with the sticker and the Yamaha setting in the front yard. I was like Ouch!! Man that hurt. I said that is my work bike and my real bike is in the garage would you like to see it. She said yes and ok I understand now. Your Harley is for riding and the Yamaha is for the burden of ever day routines. By job I think she has got it. My H is for Riding in the Wind. Jim's H is for the same thing and even after a long journey he still sees the roads as he did when he started. I see a never ending story for him on the roads Riding In the Wind. During the whole time I was writing this book he would tell me, keep going you are doing just fine. If it were not for his encouragements I would not have been able to finish this book. So when I say Jim is a Biker and it is a little more than a understatement. I truly do believe this.

Riding In The Wind

Wind, I can feel it coming thru me in the air tonight as I set here. I remember aw so well and how could I ever forget the first day the wind hit me in the face. The wind surrounds me like a blanket of love with the aroma of freedom passing thru my soul. Ever so sweetly it takes me down the road helping me along my journeys. It tells me of the day when proud men walked the earth. Shows me what it has created thru out time for me to enjoy. Whispers sweetly in my ears telling me all I need to know. Brings me the music and sounds that it has blown in the past. Riding in the wind is all I can feel now. I had been a Biker all my life and never knew it.You know how when you stand at the top of a beautiful mountain, the sun warming your body and you are looking off into a long and deep valley with a river flowing thru it. There are tall green trees, fields of colored flowers that smell like heaven and then you see a Bald Eagle fly by with a gust of wind that tops the mountain. You can feel the wind blowing right into your heart and thru your soul. Well, that is how the wind feels to me when I am on the road. Yes I know, it beats me down, makes me cold, drys me out, burns me up, makes me do silly things as I go down the Hwy. It even puts me in danger sometimes or maybe it is telling me to be carful because it loves me as much as I love it. Wind is nothing more than air molecules floating around us all the time or is it. The wind is a gift from the trees and plants that exist in our forest and oceans. The wind is as old as time itself and with its help so am I. At the same time the wind is all that keeps us a life and brings us hope that we might be able to take another Journey on the roads. The wind does not care who you are, how much you have or where have been or does it. It blows thru us all every day seeing who you really are on the inside and what you have become. For me all the wind wants to know is where I am going on my next trip. Funny thing about the wind and me, I hate the wind that blows on me standing in a door way at work. When I am walking down the street to the store or somewhere. When I am waiting in a line to get into the movies or at a gas station. It is blowing on me all the time for no reason, telling me nothing, showing me nothing, taking me nowhere and always reminding me of the days. Always telling me where I belong and the stories on the road riding with it around me. Riding in the wind on a motorcycle is as close to flying as you can get. Yes I know parachuting is flying as well but you only go down and it is very fast and a short time. I would have to say that Hang Gliding would be closer than riding a motorcycle but once you land you cant get back up in the air and you have to find away to pack the glide back up the mountain. On a bike the roads are endless taking you always somewhere with out ever coming to a stop. As you fly along with only inches of your bike touching the ground, in some cases you are almost light as a feather on the road. As I travel the wind becomes my friend taking me home to the most beautiful places on earth where I feel one and at peace. I believe in the old Indian ways. Sometimes as I ride the sound of my engine balances with the wind blowing thru my soul reminding me of Indian drums beating out a rhythm of peace and pride around a camp fire form days past. Jim also feels this in his heart as well and the way. The Indians and I are one with mother nature. We consider it to be our equal and we exist with it on its level. It is to easy to destroy things and to hard to move along with mother nature for those who don't understand. Eventually the wind will stop making wonderful things for us to see if we don't start taking care of what it has created for us now. Coming out Cisco Ut. on the old Hwy 6. The wind at my back, putting me in a vacuum of silent motion and sound. I felt like it picked me up and was caring me along on its back like bird in flight. Topping a small hill about 50 mph, where there is a bridge at the bottom form years past. There set the biggest fricken Bald Eagle I have ever seen. He is standing there in my lane in the middle of the bridge. He looked to be 4 foot tall standing there eye to eye with him. He jumps up opening his wings to fly, all I could see was this massive wing span of 10 feet blacking out the sky. He is looking me dead in the eyes and I could hear him say lets fly along together for awhile. I did not sense fear form him of any kind. He turned heading in my direction as I slowed the bike a little. He just flew there along side me in the other lane for a mile. He is always looking me in the eye and me doing the same to him. He then said I will see you later and flies away from the road. He is always looking back over his shoulder until we were out of sight and I am doing the same. To me the Eagle stands for the very word that means so much to me Freedom. This is why I ride in the wind. These moments in time are all that matter. In the end this is all you will have when you meet your maker and he will ask you what have you done. I think you should have some answers. Jim loves the wind as much as I do. One day I tell him that the Raven watches over us. I tell him that the Raven is my guide on the road and shows me the way. I said I feel the Raven protects me and him as we ride always looking out for us. At first he just laughed at me as a friend would. I know he would never do anything to hurt me. As I ride I will look over and there by my side will be a Raven. They seem to fly right there beside me looking me in the eye as to say we are here, be safe. It is a matter of split seconds really that separate us in time. Why does a Raven choice that very second to fly along the Hwy so often. Why does he decide to land and watch me doing things when there are so many others around. Why does he appear out of nowhere at the strangest times. Why does he set and wait for me to wake up in the morning. At first Jim did not believe and after me showing him time after time and every where we go, he stopped laughing and began to wonder if there is something to my madness. I think where it all came together for Jim was on the Grand Canyon trip. I pointed them out to him constantly as we rode. A Raven sets in the top of a tree watching us un pack the bikes setting up the tents and still they are always watching. We were standing on the rim of the Grand Canyon admiring all that it had to offer. He looked up and pointed out into the canyon at a bird telling me, well you may have the Raven but I have the Golden Eagle as my guide laughing at me in a nice way. The bird seemed to turn and head right for us as he said this. Flying right up to the edge of the canyon where we were standing was this giant Raven looking us in the eye. He then turned away to finish what he was doing. Jim looked at me and all I did was smile at him. I do not take there trust in me lightly and don't consider myself to be special. I do like to think someone is watching over me. There must be for me to have gotten this far. The funny thing about the Raven, my lady use to be a dancer and she was known as the Raven long before I met her. Thru out history birds have been the massagers to so many. I have a big bay door window that I look out everyday at work seeing my Dreams and Dreams to come. There is a large tree 40 feet tall next door in a lot. December 24th 2002 just before I leave early on Christmas eve. There are 12 Ravens setting in it along with 100's of others types of birds and all looking down on me. The day before there was a Perigon Falcon setting in it as a giant stork fly by the tree. The next day for some reason 15 Ravens stood outside my bay door window looking for something and I had never seen them do this before. How many of you really see this day in and day out. That same day as I stood there looking out the window a Raven the size of a Eagle flies right at the window in front of me and then strait up just before he hits the window. He is looking me in the eye the whole time. Weeks before one day I was standing in front of the window and a pigeon landed there in front of me 6 feet away. A flash of feathers, then a Perigon Falcon standing there on top of the pigeon looking me in the eye until someone moved and off he went with his meal. I was in the mountains a few years back, always looking to see what ever I can. A pair of Bald Eagles fly over looking me eye to eye and began to mate. The female flies along with her talons hanging down. The male comes up from the bottom and flips upside down grabbing her talons with his and he is hanging upside down and they begin to mate this way still flying along. I see so many wonderful animals as I travel in the wind. All are special to me. The phonographs of the Perigon Falcon that day in Montrose, yellow belled marmots, woodchucks, porcupines, squirrels, chipmunks, lizards, deer and elk, birds of all kinds and so many more. They help keep my memories of how fortunate I am to life in such a beautiful world that is surrounded by so much destruction. One more thing as I am setting here writing this story right now. I have MTV on in the background. I hear a song about riding the ghost, there is a new Rock N Roll group out called the Raventones and there song is called Riding the Ghost. I am not sure I understand. There is one thing that I notice riding in the wind when I am a by myself. People look at me differently, you know like I might be up to something bad. I wonder if they think that I am some kind of loner and want to be left alone. Maybe they think there might be something wrong with me and I am wanting to start some trouble. This bothers me a little. Most of time after I say hello how are you doing, they open up and all is well. It might be just me thinking this way and I will need to look in to this and try to fix it. It also seems when I was with a pack of Bikers, people were still a little offish and intimidated but also warmed up a little after me saying hello how ya doing. It seems different when Jim and I are out there on the roads, everyone is so very nice to us. Form the little kids to there grand parents and everyone in between. Always talking to us and we love to hear there stories. I guess you cant blame them for being cautious. There has been some unruly Bikers in the past along with the violence that our world has created. I wonder who is in more endanger me are them. Camping out there riding in the wind can be some of the best experience you will ever have. I meet people with so many different views about what they see in there world. Most are as happy to talk to me as I am to talk to them. What I love the best is to hear of there days riding in the wind and the machine that took them there. So often I hear people say, I rode til I had children, my answer "get another bike". I rode til I hurt my leg and I cant lift it up, "get a lower center of gravity bike". I cant afford one, "get a cheaper bike". It is to dangerous, "drive more carefully and get a bike". You know if you have some kind of an excuse why you cant ride a bike in the wind I will come up with a answer why you can, try me. Don't even think about it, you cant see, "find someone who can and get a bike". Come on try me. Well there maybe one, I am dead lying in a box in the ground, humm, "have someone dig you up who has a bike and get a bigger side car for the box". I guess if I did not have any money I would sell everything I had to get a bike and I don't care what kind it is. Another thing that I see out there on the roads is most all Bikers will show you respect as you travel with a hand sign. It seems the non Harley riders are the friendliest people on the roads and the Harley riders are not, Humm why is that. Is it possible

The Raven always there watching me Riding in the Wind.

the non Harley riders love to ride more than the Harley riders. I don't think so. Are the Harley riders egos bigger than those of the non Harley riders. Maybe. Is that the way it has always been in the past and should be today. I don't think so. I guess people are different and that is a good thing. For me I don't care what kind of bike you ride, you all matter to me. I wish there were more American bikes to choice from that are affordable but that is not the case. I am not a big fan of the Jap bikes but if I had to, no problem. Riding in the wind is more important than riding a particular kind of bike. Riding in the wind is more important than egos. Riding in the wind is more important than money. Riding in the wind is all that matters to a real Biker. B.B. King once said Lucille is all I need making sweet music to my ears. His guitar is named Lucille and he has a real passion for his music and you can see it in his eyes when he plays. All you need is a bike to be in the wind and that is where my Passion lies. In my mind riding in the wind is a Passion that cant be replaced with excuses why you can not be in the wind. If you have not figured it out yet the only thing that you can use as an excuse for not riding in the wind on a bike is a real fear of riding one. If you truly fear riding a motorcycle you will make a mistake that might cost you your life or someone else's that you love near you. A real fear of bikes can not be overcome I am sad to say. I do know with real Passion you can crawl out of the darkness and into the wind again. The reason I know this is because I have done it. Riding is not for everyone which is a good thing and those of us who do should not take it lightly. It is a gift that has been handed down to us to carry on with dignity and honor. We get to see some of the most wonderful places on earth that the wind has laid before us. Are you excited, Man I am excited. Can you feel it, can you touch it, can you hear it. I can, it is calling me to come Riding in the Wind. I can hear the wind telling me I have so much to show you.

I am waiting...............

On The Road

Roads are nothing more than rocks, sand, tar and cement laid flat in a strait line or curvy way going in some direction. Roads are so simple, all you have to do is walk out your door and there they are heading to any place you want to go. Most are governed by laws and regulation that are different in some states but all are near the same. Some roads are better than others, flat, smooth and interesting to the eye with nice winding curves that give you a real feeling of Freedom. Other roads are long and strait with imperfection along the way to beat you down and in the end always taking you to somewhere wonderful. Without roads there would be no wind for me to ride in. I have logged close to 250,000 miles riding in the wind. Most of it has been on the back roads of our beautiful country west of the Mississippi River. I never get tired of being out there on the roads. It does not bother me seeing the same roads all the time because it is never the same. If you take in consideration the change that the 4-seasons bring along and with all the emotion that you have. You always bring a different emotion with you every time you go out. Each time the people are the same but not really, even those you have seen before are different. Each tree, river and animal has grown or died in the process of time out there on the roads. The fields of flowers along the roads always seem to change as they fight for there lives as well. Sometimes there beauty is beyond description as you fly thru there fragrances with a relaxing smell. Always riding, I turn another corner on the road to see the most phenomenal sights you can imagine. Often I nearly fall off my bike with a true feeling of appreciation and aw that I was able to choice this road that day and time to go down.

The first hour on the road is the best and I feel as though I could ride forever. I also know at the end of a 500 mile day I will be tired and wanting off the bike for awhile. Getting to the destination for that day is only a part of my journey. It is all that lies between the roads that means so much to me. The roads in Utah are well maintained and have so much to offer. There rest areas and outhouse are the best I have ever had the privilege to relieve myself in. Utah seems to make sure that there are enough clean rest area to make your trip a nice one. Utah has some of the nicest people that take care of there roads. I am not talking about Hwy workers but the people you meet stopping for gas, food and lodging. There is only one place there between Green River and Salina where there is no gas or food for 100 miles. But along this stretch of Hwy on 1-70 there are plenty of nice rest areas to help you out. They are always nice, clean and well taken care of. Utah reminds me of ancient times and you can see it in the valleys and deserts on the walls of the hills that are everywhere. The wind has created so much beauty there. I call them time lines. The roads thru the mountains there are nice as well. Traveling in the valleys and over the mountain passes are beautiful but no where near what there are in Colorado. The roads in Colorado are not as well maintain as in Utah. I think that it might be because there are so many more here. The rest areas and outhouses in comparison to Utah are not as clean and don't seem to be as conveniently located. But when it comes to the roads and riding in the wind Utah cant compare itself with the roads that run thru Colorado's majestic mountains and valleys. You can take one road and continue for days on end riding over and thru some of the most marvelous looking forest, lakes and rivers that are in our country. The nice thing about Colorado, the wind has blown time lines here as well. From the Great Sand Dunes in the southeast, Dinosaurs Nat. park in the northwest, Mesa Verde Indians in the southwest, Garden of the Gods in the east and a must do ride along the Arkansas river towards Pueblo CO. on Hwy 50 east from Salida. In the northeast corner with Pawnee Grasslands and a lot of amber waves of gain and that is about it. In my mind every Hwy here in Colorado is as good as it gets and a must do ride for all. Unlike Utah which is old world, Colorado is new world with forest that are young in time but mountains that as old as anything in Utah.

Wyoming on the other hand in the southeast corner is as bad as it gets. The roads are rough, long and miles and miles of amber waves of gain. They are not very well marked and not having any gas station or rest areas that are convenient. I have not been to the western side of Wyoming and I will have to get back with you on this in 2003. I know that Yellow Stone park and the Tetons are there and I cant wait to see them. When I set here I realize there are so many roads I have not seen and I wonder if I will have enough time to ride them all. Man I hope so. I love the roads they are like home to me. I have spent my whole life traveling the roads as much as I can out there. As a kid riding my one and only bicycle everywhere and as much as I could seeing and going anywhere that was possible. Thinking back in time it was a short time having a bicycle and the day it was destroyed by my dad in the driveway of my home. After that I walked miles on end always looking to see what was just around the corner or over the next hill. When I look back on my life I realize that traveling has been a major part of every thing I did. At first I would walk or run, then later ride a motorcycle or a drive car. Always seeing the most beautiful things our world has to offer. Even after that day in 79' that took my biking life away for awhile. I still traveled as much as I could on the roads that mean so much to me. Having a family meant that I would be able to show them all the wonderful places that I know and find other dreams as well but it would have to be in a car. The beauty of the world stays the same once you step out of the car but on a bike the beauty is always around you in plain site. Always hearing, smelling, feeling and seeing things as they are and this is what keeps me on the roads. It is in my blood day in and day out and all I can see are the roads and where they might take me. The roads show me so much and one of my favorite things that makes me laugh are the signs along the way. The sign in Arizona as we head towards Kingman and the Laughlin River Run. I am being beat down by a cross wind 50 mph, the worst they have had in years. I see a sign that says Don't Drink and Drive and I am thinking, "hell man I cant even keep the bike on the ground let alone try to drink something". Always seeing on the roads are the signs that say Buckle Up It's The Law, "Damn man I am not even wearing a belt on my pants, I hope they don't find out". A very interesting sign in Denver, Keep

Accidents Of The Freeway, "I guess they want you to limit your accidents to the side streets. Man, I bet you really get into trouble if you have accident on the freeway". I am in a canyon outside Torrey Ut., the wind is hitting me 40 mph in the face and a sign that says Gusty Winds May Occur, "Yeah the bike is being pushed to a stop and me thinking does the sign mean that is going to get worse". I always look up in the sky to see those Watch Out For Falling Rocks, "you know this would really hurt if you were to be hit by a 5 ton rock falling out of the sky". Stay Off Media. "What the hell is a Media. I don't think I would want to be on top of it if they have to put up a sign telling me so". Exit 27, No Access Back To The Freeway. "Is that crazy or what, why would I get off there if I cant get back on". Watch Out For Trucks Turning On The Road, "damn strait I am going to be watching out for trucks turning on the road and at the same time how could miss something as big as building floating down the Hwy". Sign says Live Stock On The Hwy. "What the hell are they doing on the Hwy. There is no grass or water and at the same it makes a little since to me, maybe they just want to get a closer look at the bikes as they go by". There is a sign here in the mountains with a silhouette of a deer standing up on its back legs in a jumping motion, saying Watch Out For Deer but I have never seen one do this before, usually they walk out in front you and stand there looking at you wondering what kind of bike your on, they are saying, "is that one those new V-Rod' s". Rest Area Ahead 1 Mile No Services, "I did not know they had Services at some of the rest areas". 8 % Grade Hill, "where the hell is my calculator, just how much is that and 8% of what". This is a scary one to me, Run Away Truck Ramp, "how safe do you feel now and what are going to do if one of them is running away at you". You are in the middle of nowhere 50 miles away from anything on a flat road with no traffic with a sign saying Indian Reservation Slow to 50 mph. 5 miles later a sign saying end of Reservation and 65 mph. "You got to be kidding". A sign with car and wavy lines on it saying Slippery When Wet, "Da if you don't know that you really should not be driving". Another strange one, in the middle of the summer just before you get to a bridge and a sign saying Ice May Be On Bridge, "funny thing is I always look to see but there never is". This is always confusing to me, Next Exit Left To Go Right, "What!?!, in my mind in some cities if you take the wrong exit you might end up in Nebraska and damn man that ant funny". You have seen those signs on the back of trucks and delivery vans saying How Is My Driving call 1-800. I want one that says How Is My Driving call 1-880 like I give a rats ass. You are riding along there and in front you a Semi truck with a sign saying Hazardous Waste Material Please Stay back 200 feet, "Jumpin Jimmmny they are driving on the roads with stuff that is that dangers". Sign says Caution Dangers Curves Ahead, "Well!! alright go like a bat out of hell". Sign says Tunnel Ahead, "Yeah baby honk your horn and rev you engines all the way thru". This one is to weird, Watch For Children At Play, "someone needs to tell there parents that streets are not for kids to play in and there are very large object out there coming from all direction and will turn you into a pancake". This one is a little upsetting, Noise Laws Stickily Enforced, "well that about keeps most of the Harley's out of there cities". Pedestrians Have Right Away, "wouldn't you just like to run over one them just one time, you know the guy who slows down in the walk way as he is crossing, just trying to irritate you. Ah come on you know you would". You gotta love this. I was talking to a friend, Gary who sold me Passion. He just started riding and bought an older Road King. He said I did not realizes how incentive the motion detectors are at red lights to you guys on motorcycles. I laughed at him and said yeah I know. You are setting at a red light in the middle of nowhere, your bike is not heavy enough to trigger the sensor and the sign says No Right Turn On Red, do you set there. No way turn right but look first for the man he is out there and would love to give you a ticket. One more thing about those red lights, you pull up wanting to go left and your bike has not triggered the light and you set there waiting for someone in a car to help. Me I just take a right on red, then u-turn and I am on my way the direction I wanted to go. Here is what you should do if the light does not trigger. Most are compression sensors so if you stomp your foot on the ground sometimes this will trigger it. The problem is when people see you doing this they will wonder what is wrong with you. My very very favorite sign, Rest Rooms Exit 1 mile. Here is a funny thought, you spend a lot of your life trying to find a place to go to the bathroom. You know what a bad feeling is on the road, when you go by a cop and he has his radar gun pointed right at you. How about traffic jams, man they take up so much time and you could be out there riding. Although it does give you a chance to talk to those you are riding with about the trip you are on. One day in the spring of 2002 I took my lady up on the National Monument here in G.J.. You climb out of the valley 5000 feet to 7000 feet and some very nice views of the city down below. I pulled off to the side of the road on Passion, my Sportster parking it in some gravel that was hard packed. It looked far enough off the road and safe from traffic. Took my lady by the hand and walked up a hill to show her one of my favorite views. 5 minutes and back to the bike we went. Coming out of the woods I see Passion is laying on the ground. Of course I freak out running to pick the bike up. Looking Passion over to see if there is any damage. There was a tiny scratch on the saddle bag and the foot peg, other than that nothing. I was very lucky she landed just right with no damage. Walking around the bike still looking in amazement. I see a Park Ranger headed at me from one direction and another Ranger from the other direction. They surround me with there trucks and both get out saying is anyone hurt. Huh!, I said, he said someone report a accident and we have called for ambulance. Huh!, I said my bike fell over that is all. He said have you been drinking. Huh!!, I said my bike fell over that is it. Then he is asking my girlfriend if she was hurt. Huh!!!, saying again, ah! my bike fell over. Then he ask me if the bike was stolen. Huh!!!!, I said are you kidding my bike fell over. I am starting to get pissed off now and my lady is telling me to calm down. Mean while there are people stopping on the Hwy to see what kind of criminal they have got surrounded there on the road. He said are you sure you have not been drinking, Jumpen Jimmnny man!!, I don't drink, there was no accident, the bike is mine and all that happen here is my bike fell over while we went for a walk to look at some views of the valley below. Then he tells me he will need to call in and see if this bike has been stolen and to see if I have any warrants out for me. Huh!!!!!, what, my bike just fell over in the gravel are you kidding. He said I need to see your driver's licence, registration and proof of insurance and off he went. 10 minutes later he tells me, you have no warrants, the bike is yours, you have not been drinking and I see no evidence of an accident. I said yeah I know, my bike fell over in the gravel and that is the first thing I told you in the beginning. Getting on the bike and off we went back down to the valley shaking my head all the way down. Yeah I can hear some of you saying well they were doing there jobs and looking out for you. Bulls Setting in a bathroom somewhere making a stinky. As a American citizen I should be able to drive up a road and have my bike fall over without someone accusing me of being a criminal and trying to find a way to put me in jail. But that is just me. I guess I see things differently. Think about what would happen if two bikes were to fall over at the same time, they might call out the National Guard and declare martial law. I guess it upsets me to think that I cant ride my bike on the roads without someone trying to ruin things for me. Most of us out there, the Bikers on the roads are decent people and love them because they are our lives, hopes and dreams in a world full of Bulls Setting on toilets. I find that Bikers in general are more caring than what I call the non bikers or straits. One day in August 2001 on Passion my Sportster. I was heading out thru downtown G.J. on 4th street which is a one way street riding south. It was early and I was headed for the Olathe Sweet Corn festival. There is car in the right lane three car lengths a head of me. I was in the left lane and doing the speed limit. As always I am watching. All of the sudden the car slows and pulls right in front me sideways across the street taking a left turn out of the right lane. I locked the rear tire up and then the front with them squealing. With the bike sliding and using body English to the point of being sideways with the car and still heading for it. Time slows down and all is in slow motion and it is taking me forever to come to a stop. It could not have been more then 40 feet between us form the beginning. My tires are squealing as I watch the car coming at me. I managed to turn the bike so the rear tire was facing forwards. The guy looks and panics stopping the car. Sliding right up against the car pinning my leg between the car and Passion. My exhaust pipe dug a whole in his rear door. I am setting there looking this guy in the eye with my handle bar thru his window 8 inches away. Blood, death and destruction where my first thoughts. He started screaming over and over, O' my god are you alright. I set there looked down and I was not hurt. There was a little tiny scratch on the exhaust pipe and that was all. My nerves were a little damaged as well. The pipes were used and I had put them on with the baffles drilled out and were not prefect to begin with. I said Man, you might have killed some else, you are lucky it was me riding today at this time. He said I am visiting here and my mother is in the hospital. He said, I was not thinking right. I said, you need to be more carful and pay attention to what you are doing. We all make mistakes even as Bikers, please be careful and I went my way. It only takes one mistake so please be careful my brothers and sisters. No matter where I go on the roads I know I can always expect to see a friendly face and usually they are riding a motorcycle. Even in the big cities I find so many friendly faces and some that I can talk to about on the roads. The problem with the cities is the traffic.You can easily be run down in the madness they call bumper to bumper. Everyone is in such a hurry to go nowhere. Usually it is to the next stop light or stop sign or traffic jam. The exhaust fumes are the worst as there are so many cars and trucks around you. Have you ever been behind a diesel truck dually bumper to bumper trying to get out of the mess your in. It smells bad and you cant see around it but that is not as bad as trying to see around a semi-truck in heavy traffic. This is why I try to stay out of the big cities. To me there is very little beauty there to see except maybe the zoos, museums, botanic gardens and some other stuff. I am not sure that it is worth the danger you are in when you are riding in the big cities. Curious question, is there anyone who really likes riding in the big cities. Maybe so. For me it is fresh air, wide open spaces, trees and beautiful water that draws me to the roads. Riding in the wind and on the roads is cool mornings, animals waking up to say hello. Sunrise peeking thru the trees and over the mountains with rays of warmth feeding everything it touches with life and love. The sun can warm you on a cold day out there on the roads and at a different time in a different place the sun can beat you down to nothing. Being on the road is not easy and is not for every one. You have to have a real love and a real Passion for the two lane black top we call home. There is so much to deal with, you are riding along the roads with things that out weight you 100 times over. The weather always changing hot to cold, wet to dry and then it snows or hails on you. The roads can change one state to the next as you cross the line, good to bad or bad to good. Even when you cross another county line, this county may take care of there roads or not. Look for this out there you will see it. Today Law Officers are more tolerant of us if we stay with in the lines. In there minds the roads are there roads and we are just using them. To me they are my roads and the Law Officers are there to keep them safe for me. I do feel that the laws are there to help me and at the same time should not be used to beat me down when I am out there on the concert pads doing what I do best and that is Riding In The Wind. For a true Biker, as I see it, the roads are all we have. All we need to feel alive. Riding to rallies like Sturgis gives me a hope that someday we can have peace. If half a million different kinds of Bikers with ego's can get along for 5 days packed in a small city the size of Sturgis. My question would be? What the hell is wrong with the rest of you in the world??. For the most part rallies are fun with lots of interesting people who have on thing in common, we love Bikes and being Bikers. Yes I know, there are always a few who cant see it. If they could see the roads as I do the madness would stop. At the Cripple Creek rally there is a bond that goes beyond a certain kind of individualism. It is a love for what we stand for, Freedom. We know the price so many have payed to keep it. Rallies are important in my mind, we must show the world that we know who we are and what we stand for, Freedom. I guess it is no surprise some of my favorite roads are here in Colorado. The mountain roads here are without end and continue thru out the whole state north,east,south or west. I could never get tired of them. Utah has to be right up there with its roads of wide open spaces of time and colors beyond imagination. Arizona has the heat and a silent beauty about it and long roads leading to places of wonder. Oklahoma is wide open spaces, dry with a lot history along there roads for you to be apart of. Arkansas with its roads of lush forest and clear clean rivers are more than worth seeing. Wyoming with its rough roads always taking you for a long ride to wondrous places. South Dakota has the Black Hills and the Bad Lands along there roads which are the best for you to enjoy and of course Sturgis. In my mind New Mexico has all the best of the states I have mention with roads of time, history, mountains, rivers, lakes and beauty that is equal or above any in the world. If it were not for all the people in Texas and the seer size of it. This state is a wonderland of roads that can take you to anything you wish to see. From the ocean in the Gulf of Mexico to the forest in the east and wide open deserts in the west and south. There are great mountains that run along its border in the west. Yes, I can hear you say what about my state. Well give me some time and I will let you know. I have just begun to ride the roads with the wind. Even now I cant wait to see my tires rolling down the roads even if it is only for a short ride tomorrow, that would be fine with me. But what I really want to do is see me going on long trips to places I have never been before. There are so many. I am late and I have so much to do, so little time, the rabbit said to Alice standing there in wonderland. This is how I feel about our country. It is 100 years of Harley, a celebration of all kinds of Bikers. For me I ride on the roads so I can feel alive and because that is what I do best. Roads are simple things or are they.

A Bikers View

A view is the way someone sees things that are in and around there world. Everyone has a view about everything they know and see.You have a view about all that you are and everyone you have ever met. Your views will always be different from all others because there is no one like you in the world. I know most of you will not agree with my views of things and what I have to say about them and that is ok. In my mind, don't you think this is the way it should be. We must see things differently because that is how we find out which is the right view for you. If you cant listen to someone else's views without getting mad then how will you ever learn. You must be able to give and take views without a closed mind. Your heart has a view of its own making you see things with kindness and love. When you turn around your heart shows you the sadness that come along your way riding your roads. I was setting at a red light on the Ghost today January 5th my birthday and I realized something. I am not a Harley rider. I don't stand on "H". I am a Biker that is all. If I could not afford a Harley I would be riding a Triumph or BMW. If I could not afford a Triumph or a BMW I would be riding a Yamaha or anything I could get my hands on. It is not the bike that makes a Biker. It is a Passion for Riding In The Wind out there on the roads. Don't get me wrong I love the Ghost and what Harley stands for today. Riding a Harley to me is like riding on an American Flag. It stands alone for the very word that means so much to me, Freedom. I was talking to Charlie who brings the uniforms to the shop about what I do and telling him about some of the book I was writing. He stops me and says, "man is that all you do ride a motorcycle". I said, yes that's what I do. He said damn man, talk about Freedom. That is corrected Charlie. He said Freedom to me, having a big family is setting down on Sunday and be able to watch a football game. I did not know what to say to him. Each of us sees Freedom in different ways I guess. I love Riding In The Wind more than I love riding a Harley and at the same time there is very little difference that separates them. Knowing all that I know about the world today I could never go back to riding a Jap bike. The soul of our economy depends on our loyalty to our country and those who work here to make a living. The people that live here in our country today have a Passion for bikes and Bikers young or old. Motorcycles which are nothing more then pieces of metal, plastic and rubber put together in a certain way so that you can ride on it like a horse. Most have some kind of personality that separates them from the rest. Maybe some have feelings and care about there riders. All are forged from a history of dedication to one thing, Riding in the Wind. If you go back to 1920's and watch the films of yesteryear. You see the joy in the faces of those who really rode bikes. You can tell it really meant something to them. Motorcycles in the beginning where for riding and having fun on in the wind. They were not for looking at. In my mind if you are riding a motorcycle for the show you are not a Biker. "O' look at me people". If you are trying to prove something to someone else you are not a Biker. If you are trying to make a statement or make a point to show that you are a Biker you are not a Biker. Jim thinks that there are all kinds of levels when it comes to saying what a Biker is. He said you have to have a real love for bikes. A biking way about you and Passion for riding on the roads. You really don't have to dress up and look the part. You don't need to go to rallies and you don't need to ride in groups. He said the rider on the used Suzuki is just as much a Biker if not more than the guy who is on a $40,000 Harley motorcycle. It a Passion that makes a Biker and all that come along with it. You know what, Jim knows. Amber does not have a Harley and rides her own bike. She works at the Harley house in the parts department. Amber loves what she calls Open Air on the roads. A nice way to put it. Catching some open air is what a Biker is in her mind. To her it is a real Freedom that she enjoy's and it does not matter if you are one or 20 you are still a Biker. She said, you must have a real Passion for riding on the road to be called a Biker. It is not the show that makes a Biker. Damn Amber knows too. Bob, Marty's husband and the new director of the Western Slope Hogs said riding in the wind is all that matters. Not the bike, not the time, not the place or how many miles you have logged or even where you have been or where you are going. It is the Passion for riding that makes a Biker. Bob knows. I know this kid DJ 19 years old. He rode with his mom and dad to Sturgis almost every year since he was 7 years old. He has an old Pan that he loves to ride and work on. He has a motorcycle and car fabricating shop not quite like the famous Jesse James. I was talking to him and he said a Biker is someone who is a biking way. He does not carry a credit card to get his motorcycle oil changed. They don't carry a cell phone to call the shop to come get there bike to get the oil changed either. He said, a Biker can feel and hear his bike and know when something is wrong and what to do about it. A Biker does not let someone else take care of his bike, he does it himself. He said a Biker has a true love for all that comes along with being a biking way. By Jobe I think DJ knows too. Do you have a biking way. Have you figured it out yet. Some people watch the movies and think James Dean, Marlon Brando and Elvis Presley where Bikers. In all reality they where a little more than actors that road bikes in the movies. Yes I know they owned a few bikes but were mostly for show. Riding in the Wind was in there hearts a little but not apart of there soul and never a real Passion. You might say Michael Parks was a TV. show actor playing in a TV. series Then Came Bronson. You would be right, he really did not ride in the wind. Dennis Hopper was not a Biker as well but helped build the biking empire as it stands today along with the rest and wearing the name Biker would be a stretch. I do think the roads flow in Peter Fonda's blood and Riding In The Wind is deep in his soul. Out of all our for fathers the one that stands above the rest has to be Evel Knievel. There is no doubt that he has the right to wear the name Biker. As I talk to people in the wind along the roads, Bikers and non-bikers. They seem to have so many different ideas as to what a Biker is. I still struggle with this question my self even today. What is a Biker?. Joseph who does not ride and also spent 4 years in the Marine Corp told me, Bikers are guys who wear vest and call each other brothers. He said they hang out and party most of the time. Riding in Wind on the roads had nothing to do with being a Biker. A lady dancer at a nightclub told me, Bikers are people who love to have fun and party and take rides in between, she is a non rider. Another guy a non rider told me that all the real Bikers died out in the 70's and lived in the 50's and 60's like Elvis, Marlon and James Dean. He said, that we are nothing but a bunch of recreational hobby riders today. That kinda hurt feelings. Cheryl a non rider who helps with the books at work said, a Biker is someone who takes trips on bikes all the time and that is what they do with there lives. She said that she never had opinion about Bikers til she met me. She also said that we where all a bunch of Hooligans smiling at me. Some people say, I don't know I guess they are people who ride motorcycles. Others say, well James Dean and Elvis Presley and Marlon Brando were the original Bikers, Huh!!, excuse me. Shirley the accountant were I work, said she had a real opinion on what Bikers were and it was not to good. She said because of me in her mind I had redefined what a Biker is and maybe we are the good guys. Morgan who is a non and owns the shop that I work at, said, a Biker is someone who lives a biking life and that is were there Passion lies. This is as close as you can get. I said what about me, he said, you are defiantly a hobby rider laughing at me as a friend would. He then said you have more Passion for riding then any buddy I have every met. Morgan is young in years but has the intelligent level of someone much older. He takes care of me and keeps me out of trouble. He sees that I get to ride and do my trips because he knows that is what keeps me alive. He accept the fact that my Passion about riding is no different from his passion for making his shop the best in our city. He keeps my daily routines interesting so I don't go crazy being locked up here in the city. He knows always when I look out the window what I am seeing, Riding In The Wind is all that I am. I can not begin to tell you about him, that would take a whole other book and it would be very short and not very interesting. OK, here is his story. He comes from Nebraska. He rode a dirt bike as a kid and never rode a street bike. They have some very good football teams there in Nebraska and it is pretty close to Sturgis. There is a whole lot of amber waves of gain from one corner to the next there in Nebraska, end of story thank you very much. When I told Morgan that I was going to try to write a book about my biking life, he said well that want take to long. I said yeah and besides that why would anyone want to read my book. Morgan said there are a lot of people who have a passion for reading books and it is know different from your Passion for riding in the wind He has a son Tyler which is almost 3 years old, comes in the shop everyday with his mother Cheryl I spoke of earlier and they are a kick to see. I always say, Hey Man What's Up when Tyler walks in. He always says loudly, Hey Man pointing up, there is whole in the ceiling. He loves motorcycles but it is not because of me. One day I road by them and they are walking down the street honking my horn at them, Tyler yells out "Hey Man" as I rode by. Cheryl, Tyler's mother helps keep the books in order at the shop and she is one heck of a good cook which is more important in my eyes than keeping books, Ummm chocolate cake, cookies and all kinds of yummy stuff. One day in front me in October 2002, Morgan tells Cheryl that I am writing a book and it will take me about a hour to finish it. We laughed and she said really I am a English major. "O' My now I am going to get it". I had started the end of September writing my book with 20 pages finished at this point. I was very hesitant to ask her to read some of it because I knew she might tear me apart. I am a long ways from being a English major. So I am standing there looking needed I am sure and she says, would you like for me to read it. The idea of someone reading my book was very exciting and scary at the same time. No one had seen any of the book and only heard about it. I gave a copy to her of what I had done and told her to be kind that I was doing the best I could. She said ok and I will underline anything I see wrong as I read it. Cheryl does not care any thing about bikes or Bikers or being on the road. I figured she might read one page and put a big F on it and give it back to me. She is very honest and I knew I could count on her to tell me the truth. I was very nervous the next time Cheryl came in. When she handed me my book, there were a lot of little black marks all over it. I looked at her and said, it was that bad huh. She said no, it was very good. I looked at her and said, "Are You Sure". She said yes, I read the whole thing and there are parts in the book that are very good and worth reading. Then she said I really liked it. This did not make any sense to me. How could she have liked it. As I wrote in the book I would get frustrated and want to give up the idea of this book. These few words out of Cheryl's mouth is what kept me going all those long days and nights struggling to write. Her words were an inspiration to me. I would tell myself that she said, "It is very good and I liked it". I don't read so well and I don't spell so well either. I can not type nor do I understand what grammar is. Day after day I was ready to give up writing and then I would remember what she said, it was very good and I liked it. I am very fortunate that Cheryl and Morgan have been apart of my life. Even today I want to ask Cheryl, "Are You Sure". My point is, you may not realize how sometimes a small thing can be what propels people into doing something great. I don't consider this book to be a great story but what if it motivates someone else to do something great. To me Cheryl has helped put something in motion here that will never end and I thank you. I need to thank two other people here and they are both Mark's. One of them works for a oil company and takes care of some of things we need at the shop. He hears me talking to the other Mark about the book and says, you know I would like to read some of it. I said are you sure, he said I really would. I did not know what to expect the next time he came in. He said man that was a kick in the pants I love it. It was like a blast form the past and I loved the stories. I hope some of you see this too. He also helped me thru those long nights writing and I thank you Mark. My other Mark works with me there. He rides a old Yamaha 750. When you look at him on his bike you think he is a wanta bee biker. He is not. He is not like me but he does love to ride. I am not sure he could ware the name Biker but maybe so. All this time he has encouraged me to continue with this book and I thank you Mark. All these people above have been great to me. There is nothing great about riding a motorcycle. There are no medals to be awarded for Riding In The Wind. You can only be recognized as someone who has a Passion for riding and then be called a Biker by your piers. You can be known as a kind, gentle and caring person for those you have helped along your roads. The people on your roads will decide who you are and what kind of person you will be known as. The people on the roads are not always kind hearted and caring people you would like them to be but don't let this stop you from finding those who are and the best people in the world when you are Riding in the Wind. The one thing that has not changed over the years is the Bikers who rode Harley's in the 50's, 60's and 70's were very loyal to Harley as they are today. Before that in 30's and 40's they were just people who rode bikes for fun and it was something new to see. Some rode them because they were economical, easy to handle and most of all cheap transportation. I think back then people had a lot more to worry about then Riding in the Wind. Trying to survive WWI, then the depression. Strait thru WWII and then right into the Korean war. By this time it was 1955 and everyone was trying to rebuild there lives. Woman were stepping out of there homes and into the work force and the men did not know what do about it. I believe the recreational generation was born at this time. That would be me and most of you. Families were buying nice cars to travel in. Most cars were for there wives and mothers to drive there families around in. Boats were the boom and it seemed everyone had one. TV was born and you were bombarded with commercials of what and when and where and who you are constantly. Smoking was something everyone did and if you didn't people though why. They were inoculating me with drugs at school to protect me form viruses and diseases all the time. I hated this. When I think back laying on the floor under my desk at school is not going to protect me from the atom bomb in the early 60's. Black people got there rights and it was a struggle for all. Vietnam steps up and kicks us all right the teeth. I was so tired of all the craziness. I felt like a punched out boxer. Senseless violence's started on our streets and cities and were a common site. Horner and Pride had nothing to do with this violence. People were starting to be mean just to be mean. All I wanted to know is why. I still don't understand. My family got a new car in the early 60's and we travel a few place close to home. Down to the Alamo in San Antonio, over to Galveston on the beaches of the Gulf Of Mexico, out to the lake with our boat a lot. Driving up the interstate to my grandma's. All this time alcohol was playing a part of my life and I was along for the ride. By 1965 all that was left for me to do was trying to survive. The best thing that happen to me in those days was our trip to California back in 67'. We loaded all we had in a u-haul trailer and headed out from Dallas TX. towards San Francisco. We stopped at Carlsbad Caverns, Santa Fe and Flagstaff, New Mexico. Into the deserts of Arizona seeing the Painted Desert and the Petrified Forest along with Meteor Crater and the Grand Canyon. These were some of the last things we saw as money got short and we drove strait thru to San Francisco. While there some friends and I hitch hike all over the area around San Francisco and across the bay to Oakland. Down the coast to Santa Cruz and Vera Cruz catching a little surfing when we could find a surf board. Driving into the city with my family and seeing Alcatraz and Fisherman's Wharf downtown San Francisco. All this time I was thinking about a girl that I had to leave behind without choice back in Dallas. We had been together for three years in grade school and jr. high. She was my first true love. Her name was Susan. One year later no one was happy there and back to Dallas we went. Same apartment, same school. All that I had left behind no longer existed. My girlfriend had a new boyfriend with a damn car. I was back on the streets trying to deal with guns, knifes, alcohol and also trying to stay in school. But wait there is more. Drugs were being introduced to us and we did know any better. The younger people were not happy and started seeing things for the way they were and wanted changes. Jimi Hendrix, Cream, The Doors, The Who and so many more spoke of freeing your mind and that is what we did. The generation cap was born. It became violent and sides were drawn that exist even today. By 1970 I did not know who was telling the truth any more. I had been lied to by everyone from the Pope, to the President, my mother and father, the TV, my teachers and it seemed people were patting you on the back saying it will alright the whole time they are trying to take advantage of you. In early 1971 I found motorcycle riding. Motorcycles don't lie or try to hurt you. They don't make you feel guilty or try to take advantage of you. I did not understand this at the time. Bikes just felt right to me. Thru the years I have hung on to this one feeling. It just feels right. So many times someone has tried to take this feeling away from me and each time I fight back so I might be Riding In The Wind once again. When I think about it, it is a good thing that people are not like me or see Riding In The Wind as I do. If they were I would have no place to go because they would all be there. Can you imagine trying to go to Sturgis with 6 million people there. Man what a nightmare. I think some people belong behind desk buried in there jobs, "not me", in front of TV's thinking soap operas mean something, playing Nintendo's, hanging out in bars, digging holes in there yards growing flowers, "this is not me", building cars to race and look at, "this is close to being in the wind but not really", painting pictures on the sides of the roads, "very nice", walking and shopping for things I don't need, listening to someone tell them how to think and feel, "I don't think so". I think this is fine for you if this is what you want but don't tell me what I do is wrong because I am not interested in what you do or think it is necessary. It does matter to me that you have a Passion for something and I wish you well. All I ask is that you do the same for me and my bothers and sisters. Wish us well a simple thing. I think life is measured by what you do for others and not what you do for yourself. It is not selfish to have a real Passion. It is selfish to keep someone else from having a Passion. Mine lies on the roads Riding In The Wind. There are a lot of Veterans on the roads and I am proud to ride with the hero's of yesterday, today and tomorrow. Please don't get mad at me but I wanted to say something here about Hero's. Hero's don't get paid to be Hero's. Hero's are people who risk there personal life to help others and sometimes they give up there lives in the process. Does this sound familiar, "Let's Roll", a voice rings out as a jet liner crashes into the ground, 911. Hero's don't get paid to save lives. There have been millions of hero's over the years that have never gotten recognition. If you would sometime? Look out across the world and say thanks to the Hero's that have made a difference in our world and you don't even know who they are. You should know they are out there always and most never ask for anything. We don't need anymore hero's. There is enough to go around and somehow they keep showing up everyday. As you were growing up you saw some Hero's along your way. Each of us have seen the world as it was in the city you were raised in. It does make a difference how you see things. If you were in a small city, it was nice and everyone knew everyone. In the big city you had to be careful, you can die there and no one cares. If you were poor, you saw poor people and the struggle. If you were middle class you saw it that way. If you were rich, things were laid before you as gifts. I was raise in Dallas lower middle class. No one ever gave me anything. My first job was shining shoes in a barber shop at 8 years old. I had to work for minimal wage most of my life and buy all that I have with all the blood and sweat that I am over the years. No one gave me a car or made it easy for me to get one. Your views change form one side of the railroad tracks to other. Christmas Eve I am leaving work at 12 noon for the day. There is a bum, drunk and leaning against the shop building wall facing a main street. He unzips his pants and starts to pee on the wall right there in front of the world. I stood there for a second and thought, how sad, all he has to do on Christmas Eve is be drunk and piss on a wall in public. Of course this is highly against the law. I went ahead and got on my bike and went home. Hoping someday his life might change. I am still lower middle class today and I have never forgotten the roads that have put me where I am right now. I do not blame anyone for anything that has happened to me. Everything that I am is because of everything that has happen to me and I don't want be anyone else. I wish I had more patience and understanding and maybe in time I will learn these things. I was born in the USA in a little city called Oak Cliff, Texas. In time Dallas grew up around it turning Oak Cliff into a ghetto and a very dangerous place to live. I moved 27 times by the age of 16 years old. Went to 13 different schools in the three states, some of the schools I went back to twice. I graduated the ninth grade with very little honors. Out of those 13 schools three were high schools and I struggle with the tenth grade for two years until there was nothing left. In 1971 I gave up and move out into the world. Each of us have made so many mistakes thru time and ever day I say I am sorry to all that I may have wronged over the years. Today my lady is gone and I am alone. I have hopes of finding the one who knows that I am the one and once again to be able to call her My Lady. I am a fortunate person to be able to write this story about something that I means so much to me. Riding In The Wind. Like me, Harley Davidson has struggle to become what it is today. The marketing strategies that AMF taught Harley Davidson in the 70's has taken them far. They have built a mastic around there bikes that is hard to resist. For me throw all that out the window. It is the last American motorcycle company to survive the wars of time. It could have easily been the old Indian motorcycle that survived and made affordable. I would be a proud man to ride and own one of these Indian motorcycles.

There history is as great as Harley's. I think the government contracts are what kept Harley going thru the lean years up til 1960. AMF stepped up in 1969 and Harley sales took off. But it was not til 1990 when Harley finally got into the main stream of the population. This was there goal from the beginning. In 1985 Harley manufactured 30,000 motorcycles I believe, don't know how many of them they sold or had left over from the year before. In 1990 they made 60,000. By 1995 over 100,000 bikes made. In the year 2000' a unbelievable number, over 200,000 manufactured bikes. Who knows how many for 2003. Some say over 250,000 bikes and a celebration of 100 years of Harley. Today I think 50% of the people who ride street bikes in the US. are on Harley's and half of them are Veterans of some kind. I was talking to a old man yesterday about 85 years old, he has a Purple Heart form WWII. He said he was standing in the trenches in the Philippines fighting the Japs. He told me there was one shot fired that day as I looked at his hand with three finger's missing. He said he felt something hit his rifle and then a sharp pain as he fell to the ground. The bullet had hit his hand taking the three fingers and then bounced off his rifle going thru his ribs. Then thru his left lung and out his back. He said, as I laid there on the ground I saw my Sargent laying there beside me and the bullet had lodged itself in his foot. Can you imagine how you would feel. One Shot Fired All day. I ask him about motorcycles back then, he said they were mostly for show and only a few around. I ask him about Bikers today, he said I think they are some pretty good people. Bikers are pretty good people. I hear this a lot from all kinds of people young and old. Has anyone figured out what a Bikers is yet. I now know. Mike who does not care about motorcycles at all. Is one of the guys at the shop were I work. He said, a Biker is a seasoned rider with years of experience on the roads and that is what they do in there life. Now I know I am going to make some of you mad here but if you ride in a sidecar you are not a Biker. No, that is why they call it a sidecar and not a side bike. One thing I know for sure about being a Biker is you have to ride on a bike to be called a Biker. You might call yourself a sidecarer and that is about it. You cant stand next to a motorcycle or have it in your garage to look at and say you're a Biker. You have to actually set on it, "well ok", you have to start it and go down the road, "wait a minute", maybe you should take a trip to the store, "well not quite yet", maybe you should take a trip down a Hwy somewhere and back and then maybe you can call yourself a Biker but I don't think so. This is going to make a lot of you mad but If you are less than 1000 miles form Sturgis and you trailer your bike there, you are not a Biker, you are a Trailerer. In my mind you need to stop somewhere on the road and unload your bike and ride the rest of the way for at least 500 miles to Sturgis. "I could be wrong about this". Some of you woman will love this. Cars and Woman are for looking at and other Woman and Bikes are for riding. "Ooo! Did I say that". Please don't yell at me. I love you Ladies out there on the roads in the wind. All of you. Most of you have a great attitude and know how to have fun and understand that we are just guys and that is all. I love everything about you ladies. The way you look, smell, walk, talk and most of all how you feel to the touch. Without you ladies the wind would not be the same and you are all very important to us guys. Ladies please always take care of yourself and know where you are at all times. But if you get a chance give us guys a smile and a little shake. It really does make our day Riding In The Wind. If one us gets out of line, just say Hey!, you can Look but don't Touch and everything will be alright. You Ladies have know idea how much we enjoy seeing you out there on the roads having fun. While I am making some of you mad let me say this to smooth things over. I believe as long as you are having fun it dose not matter what you do or how you get there riding in the wind is all there is. Bikers today are the good guys out there on the roads.Well think about it, we travel all over the country telling people stories of great things. Giving people hopes and dreams and helping anyone who really needs help along the way. Some of us making sense in a world gone crazy. We are misunderstood by most and most of us are decent people who happen to love riding motorcycles. We take care of our people and the roads we ride. When it comes to the best people in the world the Toy Runs that take place all over our country is were you will find them. This is where you can see Bikers really show who they are and they are the best people in the world. The holidays bring out the best in some people and it always brings out the best in Bikers. Christmas to me is nothing more than the birthday of the greatest man that once walked the earth. I try to base my life on how he might see things. The day after Christmas I gave Jim a present saying, be very careful not to spill it. He opens it and inside is a shot glass and on it are the Eagle Wings of 100 years of Harley. He looked at me as to say I don't understand. I said it is full to the top of hopes and dreams of the days to come Riding In The Wind and you should take care of them. He said I will. You know what I believe he will. We went for ride the other day around the valley here the first of January. The sun was out and a little cold 30*. We stopped at a red light and I said to him, "damn man I love riding". He said, "yeah I know so do I". How many of you really love to ride. How many of you have a Passion that burns in your heart for riding. How many of you open your eyes everyday and all you can see are the roads. Do you wake up in the morning wondering what a nice day it might be in the wind. Are there any of you who say hello to your bike as you walk by on your way to work. How often do you stop and look out the window thinking man this is a day to be in the wind. When another bike goes by do stop to see what kind of bike it might be or do you think man I would like to be going where ever he is going. How many of you look at map and wonder how that road might feel in the wind. When you see a picture does it remind you of a place where you have been or want to go on the roads. You hear the sound of a Harley go by and your heart starts to beat faster and all you want to do is get on your bike and go for a ride. Someone says something to you and it reminds of a conversation you had somewhere else on the roads. You smell some food and you think of that special place that you found Riding In The Wind in a small city out there on the roads. Do you try to find a reason to ride your bike. Oh! Did you drop your hat, lets go for a ride. How many of you are thinking what are you talking about. I am talking about what I think a Bikers is. Passion is what a Biker is. Passion for wanting to be a Biker. A Passion for all that comes along with being a Biker. A Biker does not need to attend club meetings to discuss club policies. He really does not need a group of people to ride with. He does not need anyone's approval of what he is wearing or what kind of bike he is riding. A Biker does not need anyone telling him how cool it is to ride. He does not need to read a magazine to show him what riding is all about. A Biker does not need to go to Laughlin, Daytona, Sturgis or any other bike rally for someone to say he is a Biker. He does not need to ride across the country and back so everyone thinks, man what a Biker. What he does need is lots of Bikers who are his bothers and sisters that Ride In The Wind and know what Passion is. These Bikers see the wind with there eyes of Passion for the roads. He needs all those great people along the way to talk to and to enjoy there stories of there days on the road. But mostly he needs a long road heading to somewhere nice and a motorcycle to take him there. Passion is what makes a Biker. Passion for all that comes along with being a Biker. A Biker is a Biker that is all there is to it. It is not a choice for him to make, he just is. Whether or not you think I am a Biker is how you see me and that would be your view. In my mind I have a real Passion for all that I have done and seen on a bike in so many years past. I think I have paid my dues and have the right to wear the name Biker but only because there is a word for what I do. I guess I have to put a name to it because everyone else does. Everyone tries to label it as if it needs to be labeled. I am not sure that it needs a name. I am not sure that you need to explain what it is. At the same time what else would you call it. The word is "Biker" and I am proud to wear the name. This brings me to the end of this story and the beginning of the next one. It is called, "Riding In The Wind 100 Years Of Harley A Bikers Celebration On The Roads. If my book has inspired any of you to ride my job is done. Please be careful, be safe because I do care and I will see you out there on the roads Riding In The Wind.

Your friend J.T. Thomas.

"Biker": definition: J.T. Thomas: "Passion is the word"

About the Author

I am a simple man with simple needs who loves riding a motorcycle in the wind. That is not to much to ask is it. My book is about everyone not just me.

0-595-26933-8